Ray Whitrod was born in Adelaide in 1915. He matriculated from high school during the Depression. While cycling around South Australian Riverlands in a vain attempt to find work as a fruit-picker he learnt of a scheme to recruit teenagers as police cadets. Thus began a police career — interrupted by war service and a stint with ASIO — that led to his appointments as the Commissioner of the Commonwealth, Papua New Guinea, and subsequently as the Commissioner of Queensland Police Force. After seven hard years trying to eliminate malpractice in the Queensland force, Ray Whitrod was forcibly presented by the Bjelke-Petersen government with a deputy commissioner, whom he knew to be deeply corrupt. Whitrod resigned in protest in 1976.

Ray Whitrod was active in the establishment of the South Australian Victims of Crime Service. He had a lifelong involvement with Scouting and was awarded many honours, including appointment as Companion Order of Australia and a doctorate from the Australian National University. But once, when asked on ABC Radio what he personally regarded as his finest achievement, he replied, "Marrying Mavis." He died in 2003.

RAY WHITROD

BEFORE I SLEEP

MY LIFE FIGHTING CRIME AND CORRUPTION

UQP

First published 2001 by University of Queensland Press
PO Box 6042, St Lucia, Queensland 4067 Australia
This edition published 2015

www.uqp.com.au
uqp@uqp.uq.edu.au

Cover design by Luke Causby
Printed in Australia by McPherson's Printing Group

Queensland Government Arts Queensland

Sponsored by the Queensland Office of Arts and Cultural Development.

National Library of Australia cataloguing-in-publication data is available at http://catalogue.nla.gov.au

ISBN 978 0 7022 5340 9 (pbk)
ISBN 978 0 7022 5470 3 (pdf)
ISBN 978 0 7022 5471 0 (ePub)
ISBN 978 0 7022 5472 7 (kindle)

University of Queensland Press uses papers that are natural, renewable and recyclable products made from wood grown in sustainable forests. The logging and manufacturing processes conform to the environmental regulations of the country of origin.

For Mavis

But I have promises to keep,
and miles to go before I sleep.

Robert Frost,
'Stopping in the Woods
on a Snowy Evening'

Contents

Introduction

When I was a boy I lived in a little faux-colonial suburban house in a Brisbane suburb called The Gap, a handful of kilometres west of the CBD. The Gap itself was quite literally the narrow S-bend between Mount Coot-tha and the Taylor Range, in the folds of which the suburb nestled.

I had a happily mundane childhood except for a few things. One was this — in the street parallel to mine, Barkala Street, there lived an important man. I know he was important because he had a driver who picked him up in a big, fancy American automobile each weekday morning and presumably dropped him home again in the evening. I saw the car and the attendant driver many times, but never the important man.

Four decades later, while researching my true crime books on Queensland police corruption, I would put two and two together and understand that the man was none other than Francis (Frank) Erich Bischof, Queensland commissioner of police from 1958 to 1969. I would further learn that Bischof — supposedly one of the finest detectives the state had ever produced — was the primary architect of institutionalised police corruption known as The Joke, that would, decades later, infect virtually every arm of government in Queensland and inflict damage upon the lives of hundreds, if not thousands, of honest police officers and their families.

At the end of Bischof's near 11-year tenure as commissioner, he was soon replaced by Raymond (Ray) Wells Whitrod. It was Country Party minister for police Allan Maxwell (Max) Hodges who convinced Whitrod to relinquish his post as commissioner of police in Papua New Guinea, and try his hand at cleaning up the Queensland police force. He took the chair in early 1970.

Even before landing in Brisbane to be interviewed by members of the Queensland Cabinet, Whitrod had heard whispers of a group known as The Rat Pack — this was a triumvirate of officers, Terence (Terry) Murray Lewis, Anthony (Tony) Murphy and Glendon (Glen) Patrick Hallahan — who had supposedly acted as Bischof's bagmen and dogsbodies.

The story of Whitrod's attempts to reform the Queensland police force has been told and discussed in many forums over the years. He believed in educating his troops in a force that, when he took over, had three members who had matriculated beyond grade 10. He believed in the need for more women in the force, rightly arguing that the many benefits of this included the hopeful dilution of a special brand of Queensland misogyny that wracked the police service. And he believed in promotion by merit, not seniority.

What can never be discussed enough is the lead-up to and manner of Whitrod's resignation. It should be studied as a pure example of abuse of political power, as a case of political assassination, designed and executed by corrupt police. In 1976, after Whitrod had endured almost seven years of genuine threats and childish pranks from members of the force supporting The Joke — truckloads of gravel dumped on his driveway in St Lucia, ambulance officers turning up in the early hours of the morning given false reports that the commissioner had suffered a heart attack — two watershed events occurred.

The first was a student street protest march in Brisbane when a young woman, Rosemary Severin, was beaten with a police baton. The moment was captured by television news cameras. Whitrod promptly ordered an investigation into the violence. His Premier, Joh Bjelke-Petersen, interceded and stopped it.

Then police, looking for drugs, raided a hippie commune in Far North Queensland at a place called Cedar Bay. They shot up the place and assaulted residents. Whitrod ordered another inquiry. Bjelke-Petersen said no. Whitrod went ahead with the inquiry and as a result Hodges was sacked as Police Minister and given a new portfolio. Around the same time Whitrod also lost to retirement his trusted deputy, Norm Gulbransen. It left the Commissioner completely exposed in an unfavourable political climate.

When obscure Inspector 3rd class Terry Lewis of Charleville was vaulted over more than 100 officers into the position of Whitrod's assistant commissioner, Whitrod fought. He had put forward the names of three competent officers for the assistant commissioner's position, and was ignored. He had known for years Lewis was one of Bischof's bagmen, and Lewis' appointment would see his attempts to clean up corruption come to nought.

Whitrod argued with his new Minister, Tom Newbery, and demanded to see the Premier. Newbery told him Cabinet was solid on the choice of Lewis. Whitrod demanded to speak to Premier Joh Bjelke-Petersen and was rebuffed. Smart enough to see the situation as hopeless, Whitrod tendered his resignation and Lewis quickly replaced him as commissioner.

The loss of Whitrod from the helm of the Queensland police force was a tragedy on many levels and had profound ramifications that are still being felt in Queensland today. It took Lewis seven years to rid the force of Whitrod's trusted team, and it was done at great cost. Careers were crushed. Families were destroyed. Lives were literally lost. Dozens of police were either ejected from or turned their back on the profession. Their places were filled with Lewis appointments, and the cycle of corruption jump-started all over again with catastrophic results. The force was instantly politicised. Within a handful of years, the government, the public service, the judiciary and the police force were thoroughly compromised. The Joke soon flourished in a second incarnation, interrupted as it had been by Whitrod's tenure.

Today, the mention of Whitrod's name in Queensland is synonymous with fairness and honesty. In 1983, having returned to his home town of Adelaide, Whitrod started training for marathons. He shed a lot of weight and in photographs was almost unrecognisable as the man who had tried to rid a police force of endemic corruption.

He never forgot those dangerous years in Brisbane. He had struck head-on a system that would not be exposed and dismantled until more than a decade after his resignation as commissioner, courtesy of the Fitzgerald Inquiry into police corruption from 1987 to 1989. Whitrod had tried to tell the world of its existence through his actions. It wasn't enough.

Yet, despite being vindicated by history, he never crowed his achievements and equally didn't express bitterness over this unfortunate period in his life.

There is an anecdote about Whitrod that says a lot about him. As a young boy living in Adelaide, he once "jumped the fence" at a local Australian Rules football match and left without paying the gate fee. The guilt gnawed at him so profoundly he returned the following week and settled his account.

It never happened again.

When Ray Whitrod ultimately went to sleep, it was as a man of unimpeachable honesty and integrity.

Matthew Condon

1

Where I come in

(1915–1925)

IN the early years of the last century, the smell from Burfords factory in Sturt Street, Adelaide, was so strong that tenants in the surrounding cottages were charged lower than normal rents. My grandmother, Clara Haylock, and her two unmarried daughters took advantage of this economy, renting a three-roomed cottage in nearby Russell Street. Burfords produced long yellow sticks of soap from the fat of boiled down animal carcasses. In those days, few people were able to afford the more expensive toilet soaps, even for personal washing, and I remember that, for many years, my mother shaved pieces of bar soap into the outside copper in which we boiled our weekly clothes wash. Burfords eventually burnt down in one of Adelaide's more spectacular fires — one that rivalled even the conflagration that destroyed Charles Moore's in Victoria Square.

I was born in my grandmother's cottage on 16 April 1915. The Russell Street address is also shown on my birth certificate as my mother's place of residence. I doubt that my parents normally lived with Clara Haylock and her two other daughters. My mother, Alice Olive, had probably moved back to her mother's house for the confinement. Clara was an experienced midwife, so I was probably delivered by my own grandmother. Clara had learnt the midwife's art on the lonely cattle stations around Birdsville in far west Queensland. Indeed, the demands of midwifery so shaped my mother's early years that it is worth starting this story not in the Adelaide of my birth, but in my mother's native Birdsville.

When they arrived in Birdsville in September 1890, Clara and William Haylock had been married for ten years and already had a family of five boys, although four of these were from Clara's previous marriage to a Mr Finlay. The Haylocks had travelled from Tibooburra, in central New South Wales, with a view to taking up a land grant at Charleville in Queensland. However, by the time the family reached Birdsville, Clara was about to give birth to Alice. On her ninety-sixth birthday, Alice told a reporter from the *Adelaide Advertiser*, "A doctor in the town talked my father into staying for a few days, because my mother was quite pregnant. It's a good job they did, because it was a difficult birth and I don't think I would have made it without the doctor."

The enforced stay in Birdsville cost William Haylock his grant of land in Charleville. In those colonial days, Birdsville was a major staging post on the droving route from north Queensland to the rail head at Marree. It boasted a police station, three pubs and a customs house. There has been little change in the surrounding country from that day to this. The flatness is broken by sand dunes that run in long, jumbled lines to the north west. Between the sandhills are broad flats on which cattle can find enough pasture to keep themselves alive, although the casual visitor may often doubt that this could possibly be true. The watercourses are usually dry; when they are not, they are in flood. In times of flood, the Diamantina can be many miles wide. Clara and her family stayed in Birdsville for fourteen years. With the meagre resources available to him, William set himself up as a carrier along the Track. When Alice was eight, William's team of twenty horses was stolen, and while he was tracking them on foot he perished — perhaps he drowned in the endless Diamantina which was then in flood. (My brother Frank's version of this story is that William simply got fed up and left. At this distance it is impossible to tell what really happened — William's body was never found.) Clara battled on, working as a midwife, attending to the needs of pregnant women on station homesteads.

To be present at a birth, Clara had to arrive at the station well before the baby was due, and she would not leave until both the baby and mother were doing well. As a result, she was often absent from her own home for weeks at a time. These days it is almost impossible to imagine leaving a nine- or ten-year-old girl on her own to run a household which consists of herself and four younger children. Yet outback life at the turn of the century was like this and Alice, my mother, routinely became the acting head of the household. She also had the responsibility of providing the town with its supply of fresh goats' milk. This required not only daily milkings, but also driving the herd of twenty goats to and from the town common every day because of the danger of dingo attacks at night. Her elder brother and her four older stepbrothers were by now working as station hands elsewhere and were not in touch with the family — perhaps because they were illiterate, perhaps due to lack of interest, or perhaps because of distance.

Years later, when my mother used to tell me stories about her life in Birdsville as she was tucking me into bed, she would recall how, if any of the children got sick while she was in charge, she would go across to the police station to seek advice. She well remembered the kindness of the sergeant who would take down a big book on home remedies, and the two of them — the big, old policeman and the little girl unable to read — would work out how best to use the limited medication available: castor oil, Bates' Salve, bread poultices, and the like. On other occasions there would be rowdy, drunken brawls at the nearest pub, which was only a short distance from their home. Alice would try to comfort the other children while she waited for the sergeant to restore order. Sounds magnify at night in the desert, and these violent encounters and bad language must have been terrifying to a small girl.

My mother would often tell me how she would look across the intervening paddock at night and see a light in the police residence — something which helped calm her anxieties. She described how she would take her sisters and brother out to the sandhills to play with Aboriginal children, or walk down to the Chinaman's garden by the lagoon to buy fresh vegetables.

My mother would describe to me the terrible drought which lasted from 1898 to 1904. Water holes became claypans; cattle died in their thousands; the Diamantina and Cooper's Creek were totally dry. Supplies in Birdsville fell so low that people were reduced to living on weevilly biscuits because the usual carriers could not get up the Birdsville Track from Marree. My mother recalled how the townspeople would listen at night for the sound of camel bells. Years after the event, she would speak with emotion about the feeling of relief that washed over her when that distant tinkle of bells heralded the arrival of the Afghan camel drivers and their essential supplies.

Alice was very conscious that she could not read, so when a little one-teacher school opened when she was ten she was delighted. On her ninety-sixth birthday, she told the *Advertiser*: "It was lonely for us kids, but when the Birdsville school opened in 1900 our whole life changed. We had a school picnic once and I remember staying awake all night, I was so excited."

My mother always referred to her teacher as "strict Mr Duggan", and he may well have been the source of her fierce desire to obtain the best possible education for her own children. Alice, however, was only able to attend school for two years because when she was twelve her mother, Clara, found a job for her working in the store at Mulka. Gladys, the next oldest girl, aged ten, then took over as surrogate mother during Clara's absences and assumed responsibility for the goats.

Mulka Store, just beyond the Natterannie Sandhills in the centre of the sand country, is a lonely spot halfway between Marree and Birdsville. The store has since crumbled, but it was an important calling-in place for all the hardy souls who then used the Track. Few in numbers, these travellers must have been the store's main customers. Tom Kruse, who for many years carted mail up and down the Track, once said of the Mulka Store: "You'd see it there in the distance, its iron roof shimmering in the sun. It was a very welcome sight." Sometimes wandering Aborigines would call and curiously inspect the stock. The store managers, a husband and wife, also ran a small cattle herd and were often absent. So, at the age of twelve Alice would spend days by herself, seeing nobody and nothing but the empty Strzelecki Desert. She found a set of Charles Dickens books in a crate in one of the sheds and she read and reread them all over the next two years.

My mother and I flew to Birdsville in 1974 when I was the Queensland police commissioner. We called at some of the nearby stations and some of the people we met remembered Alice and her brothers and sisters from the old days. At Birdsville, I was accepted as I had been nowhere else in Queensland. I was treated as part of the family, I had come home. In Brisbane and the rest of Queensland, I was always regarded as "mexican" — someone from south of the border.

When Alice was fourteen, Clara Haylock moved her family to Adelaide so the younger children were able to attend state schools. William, the elder boy, aged sixteen, had already taken a station hand's job, so he stayed in Queensland. Alice found herself a job as a waitress at West's Coffee Palace, a cheap hotel in Hindley Street. There were a number of so-called coffee palaces in Adelaide in those days. They had earned their name because coffee and tea were all they served — no liquor — but they provided inexpensive accommodation in the centre of the city and were attractive to station hands and other working folk from out of town. Many of the station hands from along the Birdsville Track would have made their way to Adelaide and a bed in a place like West's, as it was easier to go south rather than east to the Queensland coast for holidays. Years later, when I was a young constable in the South Australian Police Force, I often had to call at West's Coffee Palace to inquire whether anybody on the "wanted" list was staying there. I never told the proprietor that my mother had once worked in his establishment as a waitress.

After the Coffee Palace, Alice found another job with better hours — as a chocolate dipper at the confectionery factory of A.A. Walton in lower Grote Street. A photograph taken at the time shows her to be an attractive young lady of about twenty with dark hair, bright eyes, a tidy figure, regular features and a pleasant smile.

It was while she was working at Waltons that Alice met my father. He had been christened Walter, but was generally known as "Tim" (from Tiger Tim because he was the smallest by far of his brothers.) At the time, he must have just finished his five-year apprenticeship as a confectioner and was working in the "starch" room at Waltons making boiled sweets and "jubes".

My father's father, Raamiah, an unmarried shoemaker, had migrated from Norfolk in England, in 1871 when he was thirty-two years old. The Whitrod family were long-time residents of the Fen country, having recorded births and marriages there since 1550. They had been mainly country folk, farm labourers, small farmers, yeomen. Village shoemakers were made obsolete by the large output of footwear from city factories that had sprung up during the Industrial Revolution. The shoemakers seem to have dispersed — at least from the small villages in southern England — and at least one, my grandfather, migrated to that far-away land, Australia. Perhaps he was able to do so because he was single.

His emigration may also have had something to do with George Fife Angas's campaign to recruit free settlers for South Australia from amongst the Protestant religious fellowships in England. In Adelaide, Raamiah became a committed lay preacher in a Methodist circuit at Thebarton. But he first settled at Mt Barker, which was then a thriving town presenting itself as a possible rival capital city to Adelaide. He probably worked as a shoemaker/repairer. Two years after he arrived in Mt Barker, Raamiah — then aged thirty-four — married Elizabeth James, a girl of sixteen.

For the next twenty years, the couple lived at Mt Barker, producing nine children at two-yearly intervals, before moving to Thebarton in west Adelaide. Perhaps the move was the result of Raamiah's ill-health. He died not many years later. I do not know how his much younger widow and her younger children survived. All of Raamiah's sons secured stable employment, only one following his father's trade of shoemaker. The others became a driver of horse trams, a driver of brewery wagons, a railway guard, a boilermaker, a jeweller and a confectioner (my father).

My father, then aged twenty-four years, and mother, aged twenty-two, were married in a Methodist church in Morphett Street in the

City on 4 December 1912. It is likely that this would have been, for both of them, their first serious relationship. Their first child, Sidney, was born a year later, and I appeared two years afterwards. Sid died some time during the First World War from diphtheria and I survived as their only son until Frank was born in 1923. There were no other children.

My earliest memories are of our home at 1 Murrays Lane, in the West End of the City of Adelaide. I must have been about four years old. I can dimly remember walking with my father and mother to King William Street to join an enormous crowd celebrating Armistice Day 1919. We stayed for a while and then, on the way back, my father carried me on his shoulders.

Murrays Lane is a short dead-end street off Gouger Street near the West Parklands. Number 1 was at the start of a series of terraced, three-roomed cottages. A similar terrace occupied the other side of the lane. I spent my first six years there quite happily. In our house, my parents had the front room. I had the middle room which had a skylight. The small kitchen had a wood stove, and there was an outside copper for boiling the Monday weekly wash. The small backyard was bounded on two sides by the narrow lane which in earlier years had allowed the passage of the night cart. This had been the sole method of sanitation when the houses were built. All the privies were, of course, at the bottom of their respective yards. They were equipped with ten inch squares of old newspaper on a wire loop. I first discovered paper toilet rolls when I was about sixteen. I cannot recall anyone in Murrays Lane having the newspapers delivered, but everyone saved them, both for lavatory use, and for swapping at Turners, the local butchers, for a pound of sausages. The butcher used them to wrap the purchase which had been first wrapped in a small sheet of more expensive greaseproof paper.

There were no shrubs or trees to make our backyard green, and the topsoil was hard brown clay. The only tap was outside the kitchen door near the dividing fence. This fence, like the others in the lane, was only five feet high. Any pair of neighbours using their taps could freely exchange gossip. Our neighbours were Mr and Mrs Bill

Boushall and their three children, Millie, Winnie and Fred, who had migrated from England a few years earlier.

During the First World War and the years of the Depression — 1919–39 — confectionery firms had a difficult time for money was scarce and unemployment high. Lollies were not one of life's essentials, and my father had long periods of work at half-time. This meant that the family had to exist on half-wages, which in practice meant a weekly income of thirty shillings. My mother took in washing and ironing whenever it was available, and I remember how tired she became on occasions from scrubbing floors. On Mondays, the rentman would appear at our front door, and so would another collector, Mr Gooch. Mr Gooch called to collect the weekly payment of two shillings for the hire-purchase of our Singer sewing machine. We always had the latest model. It was the only item of any value in our little three-roomed house. I used to wonder why we could afford it until I worked out that when our doctor's bill became too pressing, my mother would trade in her current machine for the latest model. For this she would incur a much higher debt but would also receive a small cash refund. The refund would be used to pay the bill. This trade-in transaction was the only access to extra cash that my mother had. Mr Gooch called for years and years and I got to know him well. He was a kindly man who was just as much caught up in the system as we were.

I can remember how all of the front doorsteps in Murrays Lane were polished, and how "the fronts", which included the adjoining strips of the street, were swept each morning. The curtains in the front windows (in our house, they were only the ones we had) were always immaculate. The wives may have been poor but they kept their homes spotless and if they could afford linoleum it was polished to a high sheen. I never saw flowers in vases to brighten the dull interiors while I lived in Murrays Lane, nor were there any creepers disguising the bleakness of the exteriors. No vines, trellises or fruit trees grew in the small backyards — indeed, there were no garden plants of any kind. Perhaps nothing was planted because this would have indicated an outlook of permanency. Gauging by those living nearby, everyone saw their stay in the lane as temporary — it was a place to live until they could afford a better address.

My mother and Maude (Mrs Boushall) became firm friends and remained so for the rest of their lives. They were about the same age, and from comments I overheard, I gathered that Mrs Boushall deeply missed her English family of six sisters and parents. The Boushalls never returned for a visit to London, and the only news they had was an occasional letter which Maude would share with my mother over the fence. Bill Boushall was a dark, good-looking man with something of a temper. He too missed London, especially the evening pub life. In Adelaide he was denied this by the six o'clock closing custom. He kept his little family and wife well controlled and I suspect he thought that I was a spoilt only child. In this he was right. I never got smacked, even when it was well deserved. My punishment was to be sent to my room, and since this was almost empty, it was very boring. Once, feeling that this banishment had been particularly unjust, I took my revenge. In our house there was one large box containing the family's valuables — the wedding certificate, birth certificates and some large photos of my father's football team. I pushed a nail through the eyes of the footballers. My father took the vandalism philosophically and didn't punish me.

Maude Boushall was a lovely lady with a rosy complexion, most attractive in appearance. She liked me. I was nearly a year older than her Fred, whom I played and chattered with. Our house had a front verandah, which finished just a foot or so from the front fence, and in this space Fred and I talked about the things that interest small boys. I remember him telling me that girls were not like us. They had only a slit between their legs. I asked him how he knew this and he said that he had peeked during the family bath night on Saturdays. At the time I was only mildly interested in this bit of biology. It didn't make any sense to me. We soon passed on to something far more pressing. Just what had happened to my guinea pig which had vanished from its small cage in our backyard? Fred and I considered the possibilities from the joint store of our four-year-olds' knowledge. (I later suspected that my father had returned the guinea pig to its donor at work because my mother might have protested against the animal being kept so closely confined.) Pets were unknown in Murrays Lane, despite the many recent arrivals from animal-loving England. Pet food cost money and nobody had any money to spare — even for a canary.

Across the narrow street lived Mr and Mrs Jackson, another English couple, with their adopted daughter, Edna. Everyone knew them as Mr and Mrs Jackson — I later discovered this to be a standard English working-class monicker. Mr Jackson had been at Mons where he had been gassed. This qualified him for a full pension. Mrs Jackson was an eternal optimist and she became a lifelong friend of my mother's. The Jacksons' adopted daughter was older than I was and we didn't talk much to each other. Mrs Jackson became an ardent ALP worker and was soon well known in Adelaide.

Next to the Jacksons were Mr George and Mrs May Hardy, a childless Australian couple. They were new arrivals in Murrays Lane, having come from the coppertown of The Burra. George worked at the Mile End goods yard as a railway cleaner and set off on his cycle each weekday morning in black coat, black shirt and black trousers. His cycle was the only one in the street of twelve families. He was proud of that bicycle and kept it spotlessly cleaned and polished. He would carry a large black wooden box slung across his shoulders by a strap. In it was his "crib" — food for his meal break. If I remember rightly, the box was for sitting on while he ate.

Occasionally, I was invited to go inside the Hardy home. Their front room was indeed a "front room" maintained for visitors. It had a sofa and a highly polished sideboard, from the cupboards of which Mrs Hardy would produce a large tin marked with a "Signal" brand, filled with Griffiths Bros tea. And for me there would be a small Griffiths Bros chocolate. I think the sofa and the sideboard were legacies of the Hardys' Burra background. As far as I knew, nobody else had a "front room" in our lane (Griffiths Bros have long left their Hindmarsh Square offices.)

George Hardy was the first to introduce me to Stephen Potter's concept of oneupmanship, although of course I did not then recognise it as a social strategy. It seemed to me that Mr Hardy always managed to encounter my father on his way home from work on a Thursday evening. By Thursday, my father would have run out of smokes despite his intention to ration his supply until Friday night. My father was addicted to cigarettes, which he had smoked since his youth. Out of his weekly wage my mother would allow him a ration of one two ounce tin of Capstan Navy fine cut, together with two packets of Rizlah papers. These were bought when my parents shopped on paynights at the market. My father would then happily fashion his first smoke by attaching one Rizlah paper to his lower lip, leaving both hands free to rub the tobacco into something resembling a tailor-made. He would try to make the tin last a whole week but he never succeeded, and by Thursday would always be a little grumpy.

When George Hardy met him in the street, George would produce a well-filled tobacco pouch and necessary papers with a grand flourish, and invite my father to have some. My father would always hesitate and then give way, knowing that he could not return the favour. Whereupon George would produce a small silvery cylinder, put in a paper, then tobacco, close it, revolve it a few times and then, with another flourish, produce an almost perfect tailor-made, which he would smoke with gusto.

My father was an unselfish man with a slight speech impediment. He was a little timid, being the last and smallest of a family of burlier brothers. But he had managed to get himself into the finals of the Bay Sheffield footrace without the advantages of a shrewd trainer, and he had been awarded a medal by the South Adelaide Football Club for his play. With him, his wife always came first, then his family, and last himself.

In my career I have only met a few men like my father: quiet, unselfish people, competent enough at their jobs, unaggressive, very neighbourly, law-abiding and accepting of their lot in life. But I have come across a number of George Hardys. One of the worst was a deputy commissioner of my own choosing, a man I appointed in the 1960s who had many fine qualities, but who lacked loyalty. Whenever I went on my annual four weeks' leave, he would use the opportunity to introduce departmental changes. These were ones that I had not approved when he had recommended them earlier in the year. On my return I then had to somehow retrieve the situation, which was not always possible. You can't very well rescind someone's promotion because you wouldn't have approved it yourself. Perhaps my early exposure to George Hardy's social game-playing had made me ultra-sensitive to these sorts of tactics. But whatever the reason, to this day I remember my deputy's antics with considerable annoyance.

Apart from my mother, who "took in" washing and ironing, none of the wives in Murrays Lane had jobs to go to. So they had time to exchange news and personal information when out cleaning the front of their houses. Since we lived at the start of the lane, we always had a good idea of the comings and goings. Our door was always unlocked — it might deter a potential visitor if it was locked — and often ajar. I played out in the front, taking in the activities in the lane.

I still remember being fascinated by the weekly visit of the corporation dray. I would sit on our doorstep and watch its progression down our lane from Gouger Street. In front would come two middle-aged men, sweeping the dirt and especially horse manure into small heaps. Slowly walking behind and alongside the horse would come the driver, who shovelled the heaps into the dray. The horse, a great half draught, with jingling brightly polished brasses and harness, needed no instruction. He would stop at each heap, wait and then patiently plod on to the next. I liked those horses. I saw that the same thing happened with the horses of the baker's cart, and the milkie's. Hot, windy or cold, these gentle animals were an essential part of the procedure, but as far as I could tell they never got a chance to roam free. Some were released into the Parklands on Saturday afternoons and Sundays, but only because it helped with their conditioning. They were truly slaves to their human masters.

I vividly remember the dreadful summer of 1921–22 when some demented soul obtained perverted satisfaction on Sunday nights in the west Parklands not far from our house by tethering one of the grazing horses to a tree and then cutting its throat. This horrible, gory story was repeated Sunday after Sunday. As far as I know, the offender was never caught. It was a matter of concern to the residents of Murrays Lane with their unlocked front doors, and especially to us children. We talked about it endlessly and I could visualise the scene in the Parklands: the evening twilight, the large, friendly horse walking confidently up to its killer's outstretched hand, expecting a small titbit but finding a halter around its neck. Then being led to a nearby tree, a cut-throat razor slicing its throat. The poor animal left to die in a growing pool of red blood.

Some years later I was expected to join in the singing of church hymns which promised salvation by being washed in The Blood. I could see in my mind's eye a bath filled with tepid blood in which I was supposed to wash myself! Perhaps somewhere in my unconscious there were memories of those murdered horses. Anyway, the idea revolted me. At first I was appalled at the enthusiasm with which my fellow Baptists sang the words. Then I excused them on the grounds that they had been brainwashed by their spiritual leaders. It has become increasingly clear to me over years of worshipping in various churches that emotion is given precedence over reason. I have never heard a single sermon on "how to think". I have often asked pastors not to choose hymns with inappropriate words, but their response has always been: "But people enjoy singing those wonderful old tunes." The underlying message, it seemed to me, was an appeal not to rock the boat: "Members are comfortable with these hymns." But those who were most vocal about the therapeutic benefits of immersion in blood were clearly those who had never attended a fatal road collision, or attempted to lift a dying mate from a damaged aircraft. For some reason, I used to place them in the category of "shoddy-dropper" — those fast-talking salesmen who tried to sell their inferior woollen suit-lengths door to door by saying: "Don't worry about feeling the thickness — look at the width." The shoddy-droppers were a common sight around Murrays Lane; they normally wore a seaman's cap and jacket and carried their suit-lengths in a dirty brown paper parcel. Their claim was that they had just jumped ship and had intended to have a civilian suit made, but were short of cash; the suit-length could be yours for half the normal price.

But, to return to the horses, I think my early difficulty with the Christian dogma — that God made animals subservient to men — began with my observations of those large, gentle beasts. At the time, I was unaware that for centuries Christians had had no moral difficulty applying the same dogma to black people. As I grew older, I also wondered about the prevailing view that it was necessary to "break a horse's spirit" in order to get the animal to accept its "slave's role". (I noted recently that the Queen's horse trainer demonstrated to a surprised audience that this procedure was unnecessary.) For a similar reason, I also have had misgivings about the fervent evangelists who require potential converts "to be broken in spirit" before becoming acceptable to God.

None of my primitive theological musings would have interested the people of Murrays Lane. As far as I could tell, no one visited a church on Sunday, nor did any clergy or mission ladies call on anybody. Yet I suspect that everyone would have told a census collector that they were Anglicans. Priests, politicians and police were never seen in Murrays Lane. Nor were there any ethnic families in our street at that time. Everyone was either Australian or English and little distinction was made between the two. Nobody belonged to any of the friendly societies such as the Oddfellows, the Druids or even the Rechabites — all English-bred organisations which might have provided help with finance and medical expenses. I picked up from overheard conversations that a few people in our street did know some lucky folk in these bodies, but Freemasonry and Rotary were terms I didn't hear until very much later.

Medical help came first from home remedies and, if these failed, the district nurse might call. Occasionally there would be a visit to the outpatients department at the Royal Adelaide Hospital. And, as a last resort, there was the family doctor. Ours was a Dr Wells, whom my mother held in such high regard that my second name is Wells. His accounts always took time to pay — even with recourse to trading in the sewing machine — but he never complained. I cannot recall a death in my years in Murrays Lane, but there were always illnesses, especially children's complaints. And often people had stomach disorders.

Sanitation was not well understood. Although the manure was regularly removed from our street, the Parklands were close by and the grazing cows and horses provided ample food for flies. No one I knew washed their hands before a meal. The flies were a nuisance, but none of the houses was fitted with flyscreens at the windows or doors. Coils of sticky paper were hung up inside and these caught some of the airborne pests. The absence of screens helped on hot nights, when my father would carry our two mattresses into the passage and we would sleep with both front and back doors open to catch the slightest breeze. We had nothing to attract burglars. Disorderly conduct was rare: nobody was drunk; there were no indications or mention of spouse or child abuse. I never heard any bad language. I can't remember seeing a policeman until I was about eight, and then he was directing traffic at an intersection.

The butcher did not deliver to Murrays Lane, but every week the rabbit-oh's small truck brought cleaned but unskinned rabbits which cost threepence each. The licensed marine store collector called for empty bottles and "any old iron". Each morning the milkman delivered half a pint to the doorstep, and the postman delivered twice daily and on Saturday mornings. But sometimes the postie did not walk down our lane because he had no mail for any of the twelve families. If a letter did arrive, it was usually from a government or corporation department. Few, if any, of us kept weekly or monthly accounts, paying by cash daily for our milk and bread, the money under the front doormat. Everyone knew of this practice. The money was never stolen and the amounts were never queried by the tradesfolk.

Life in Murrays Lane was quiet. Musical instruments were not heard (radios had not yet arrived) unless the Salvation Army Band from Whitmore Square was playing outside our nearest licensed premises, the Angel Inn, a short distance away in Gouger Street. Sometimes we heard the Boys Brigade's bugle band marching along West Terrace from its headquarters in Light Square. On windless nights, we could hear the GPO clock in its tower half a mile away chime the quarter hours and we could count the hour strikes. It was especially quiet at night in winter. As soon as the kitchen stove fire had died down, we all went to bed because of the cold.

My bed was only covered by two ex-army blankets and often my mother would make a hot water bottle for me from the kettle on the stove. The bottle was an empty Woodrofe's lemonade container with a reusable stopper. If the hot water was poured into it too quickly the glass would shatter. This was disaster. At any time we only had the one bottle as they were returnable for a penny each. We rarely drank Woodrofe's or Hall's products because of the cost, and finding a discarded empty was exciting. Even at Sunday School picnics, bottled drinks were a luxury and I can't recall ever being given one.

Gouger Street was an interesting place for small boys and it provided almost all the necessities of life. On the next corner to us was the Angel Inn, which was really just a small bar. Then there was Turners abattoirs on the corner of Lowe Street. I can remember small flocks of sheep being driven along Gouger Street to the abattoirs where they were met by a scapegoat. The goat was well trained and would lead the sheep into the abbatoirs where they were all killed — except for the goat who lived to lead the next small flock to their doom. There was also a corner store near us that was run by my future wife's grandmother and her family. The store sold small boxes of chalk and I would sometimes buy one for a penny. When I was about seven, I was served there by Mavis's auntie. Further down Gouger Street was a Chinese laundry that starched collars — which all men wore on formal occasions in those days. I remember that the place had a distinct smell, of starch and steam. The Gouger Street markets were not as extensive as they are now and the stallholders were mainly English and Australian. On Friday nights there would be Cheapjack Stalls. These were temporary stands in front of an array of prizes. The stall holder held a bundle of tickets in his hands and for threepence you could select a ticket. If your ticket carried the right number, you won a doll or similar prize.

On a few occasions in the summer while it was still light, I can remember two of my mother's sisters playing cards — euchre — with my parents in our kitchen. But we never possessed a full pack; it was always a couple of cards short. I would mislay cards while playing with them after kindergarten on a rainy afternoon. But in those days the main form of entertainment was simply talk, perhaps over a cup of tea. Richer folk than us might have had a piano, in which case the talking would sometimes turn to singing. We had no radio and no morning paper. I would have gone to the cinema about twice a year.

As twilight came, the gaslighter would arrive on his bicycle and with a long pole light the sole lamp in the street. Luckily this was right opposite our front room and provided enough light for my parents to go to bed. We did have one kerosene lamp and I went to bed with a candle. There was no clock in the house. Walton's whistle blew at 7.15 each morning and my father made it to work by 7.30. It blew again at 5.00 p.m. to announce knock-off. After midday on Saturdays, we estimated the time. My father eventually inherited his parents' family clock, and this simplified getting off to kindergarten on time.

Soon after my birth, my mother had put my name down on the cradle roll of the Lavis Free Kindergarten in the next street, Wright Street. It was run by the West End Baptist Mission. From age four until I turned six, each weekday morning my mother walked me to the kindergarten and then escorted me home in the early afternoon. I enjoyed my time there and maybe it is the reason why I have stayed a Baptist. There were some other kindergartens in the West End but these all charged fees, something my mother could not afford. My preschool years at the kindergarten helped me to learn to read, but there were no books at home to look at, except the rent and the time-payment books. Mrs Hardy occasionally had a women's magazine, *Violet*, which her husband had rescued during his train cleaning duties. It was never offered to me to glance at, presumably because it was considered not suitable for young boys' eyes. I did note that it had advertisements for corsets and underwear! Nobody ever mentioned a public library and I don't think my parents even visited one during their lifetime. Perhaps because of this lack of access to literature, I somehow developed a strong urge to read — to read anything. No doubt this reading helped with my general education but later, when it came to boys' weekly periodicals, it became an obsession.

I sometimes heard through the common wall of our adjoining houses Bill Boushall "rousing" loudly on his children but they never mentioned being hit, nor did I ever see on them any signs of evidence. Such harmony came partially from the fact that neighbours never borrowed money from each other (nobody had a surplus except perhaps the Hardys) but they — and we — did occasionally ask for the loan of a cup of sugar. We had sugar with our breakfast, which was always bread and hot milk. I have forgotten our midday meal, probably because on weekdays I ate at the Lavis Free Kindergarten. The weekday evening meal, which was placed on the table punctually at 5.30 each day, was stew, or minced meat, or sausages and mash which we ate with slices of bread. But for lunch on Saturdays, without fail, we had the weekend "roast" of a leg of lamb, and because the oven was hot, my mother would always bake a delicious apple sponge. Then we would have the lamb in cold slices for Sunday's main meal with hot mashed potatoes. Except for weekends, I always left the table still hungry for more food. But there was always the daily spoonful of codliver oil to prevent colds.

My mother, no doubt because of early childhood responsibilities, was a capable cook and handy with the sewing machine, so that my short pants were always home made. My father, however, was not a handyman and I have followed in his footsteps. It should be said, however, that a large amount of my father's incapacity stemmed from an absence of tools. For example, each evening he chopped up the next day's supply of wood for the stove or copper. This was a hard chore; the axe was always blunt — we could not afford a sharpener. And because it cost too much to oil the handle, it quickly splintered. When we had saved enough, father would buy a new handle but without the necessary tools, fitting this into a socket already occupied by the broken handle was not easy.

After the Boushalls had moved to better accommodation at West Croydon, our family spent Christmas week with them for a number of years. It was a cheap holiday. I enjoyed playing with Fred again, mostly trying to kick an old football around. When we finished we would go inside and Fred would ask his mother for a "piece" for us both. A "piece" was a thick slice of white bread, which his mother would spread with Nestles condensed milk. Our stay overloaded the three-bedroom house but nobody seemed to mind, especially the Whitrods, for this stay gave us an opportunity to have a decent hot bath. The Boushalls' new house had a chip heater. In Murrays Lane, the residents boiled hot water in the outside copper and carried it by hand bucket to a large tub in the lean-to extension at the back. Other domestic facilities were equally primitive.

I remember meeting my father's mother when I was about six. She was living with her youngest daughter, Alice Dixon, and my father and mother visited her. She must have been about seventy and, to my young eyes, a very old lady. She died when I was fifteen years old. My father and mother would take me to visit her on a Sunday afternoon, about three times a year. The Dixons lived at Kilburn which was quite a walk, perhaps 2 miles [3 kilometres], from the Enfield tram terminus. My uncle, Lionel, was a slaughterman at the nearby abattoirs, and in regular employment. He shot quail in the nearby stubble fields and kept a trotter in a stable in his backyard. On our visits, we always had to inspect the mare before we were offered cups of tea. Lionel's horse never won a race. The drivers of the trotting rigs were notorious for deciding beforehand who would win. They never decided in Lionel's favour — but he probably never realised how artificial his run of bad luck was. The Dixons did not return our visits.

My brother Frank was born late in 1923, by then I was eight and in second grade at the nearby Convent School. My mother had decided that the Sturt Street state school was too rough and that I would get a better education at the Catholic school. This cost her sixpence a week. The traditional Catholic–Protestant rivalry was alive on the streets, and on the way to the Convent the Sturt Street kids would chant "Catholic frogs jump like dogs, in and out the water". There were two other non-Catholic students at the Convent. We were excused from mass and would sit out in the yard reading books. The Sisters were tolerant of our heretic status and never tried to convert us.

Soon after my brother's birth, my parents moved out of Murrays Lane. I don't know why. Perhaps the earlier departure of the Jacksons to a War Service Home at Ovingham, then the Boushalls to a Tram Trust home at West Croydon, and then the Hardys to somewhere I have forgotten, may have influenced them. It was 1923 and it turned out to be a bad year for our family accommodation-wise. We moved first to Wellington Square in North Adelaide, but the house was full of white ants.

From there we went for a short stay with my grandmother, now living at Torrensville. I remember Clara as a small, wizened old lady who had begun to suffer from dementia in her seventies. She was often difficult to get on with and I think my mother had a hard time trying to prevent Clara's more determined eccentricities, especially her habit of wandering away from home. But one thing I do remember with fondness is that Clara never forgot how to prepare potted meat in the old Birdsville style. This involved boiling down a shin of beef for some time — days perhaps — and then placing a plate with a rock on top of it on the cooling mass. A basic necessity in her day when meat prepared in this way would last without refrigeration far longer than fresh meat. We had it often in Torrensville and I found it delicious. We then moved to Ovingham to mind the Jacksons' home while they went back to England for a few months. From there we moved into rooms on the Parade at Norwood, and then finally to 318 Halifax Street in the city. So that year, for short periods, I attended new schools at North Adelaide, Cowandilla and Norwood. I should have moved from the Norwood school to a city school, but my mother thought I had already been moved too much, so I stayed on at Norwood. I was still in Grade 2.

At Norwood we had a King and Queen money-raising campaign. I was elected King by the class. We were given cards in which little holes were punched for every threepence collected. I didn't bother to take mine home, we had no spare threepences. The Queen's mother let me know in clear language that my family had let the class down because my mother had not joined in any of the activities. I had not really known what was expected of us, and had not told my mother. I was eight years of age. It took a long time for me to get over the feeling of inferiority which stemmed from that dressing down.

For some reason, my mother never gave me a cut lunch. I received sixpence to pay my tram fares to and from Norwood Public School and later Adelaide High School and this left fourpence for lunch. I only travelled one way by tram, which meant that I would have fivepence each day with which to buy boys' comics. I did this for all of my school days, going without any lunch on most days when I could not persuade another lad to trade a sandwich for one of my comics. After school I walked each afternoon from Norwood to Halifax Street, a distance of four miles. I preferred to walk and have comics to read, rather than to ride — comic-less — on the tram. I have always tended to over-eat, but even the desire for food took second place to books and comics. The comics were all English and full of stories about English boarding schools. Billy Bunter appeared quite regularly. It seems odd now, but in those days I never felt that the culture they depicted was alien or strange. Australia then was an extension of England — we shared a language and a sense of humour. For many of the people I knew when I was growing up, England wasn't called England, it was simply Home.

When I was about twelve and selling newspapers at weekends on Hutt Street corners, I found it easy to smuggle out novels from my employer's lending library. I must have taken half a dozen, mainly Zane Grey's and Edward S. Ellis's cowboy yarns. That was not my only shopstealing — I also stole tins of sardines from the Adelaide Co-op.

When I was nineteen, I went back to both these places and compensated the surprised managers. I explained that I would be expected within a couple of years to arrest people who stole items from shops. I could not do this with a clear conscience unless they accepted my apology. We parted friends.

My mother persisted with her dream of giving me a good education. This included an ability to play a musical instrument. I went down by tram every Saturday morning to a private tutor in Lockleys for a half-hour session of violin instruction costing one shilling. I did this for five years, though I did little practice. It was difficult to practise without access to a piano. I hated the small violin my mother had somehow obtained, no doubt at great family sacrifice. As soon as I could, I revolted. I must have greatly disappointed my mother, but she never nagged at me.

In many ways, the move to Halifax Street was a success. The house was a nicer three rooms, but still with no electricity. We still had no ice-box or even a Coolgardie safe. (I wasn't to live in a house with an ice box until I was married in 1938.) The Halifax Street house was set back about 12 feet (4 metres) from the footpath and in this space grew a few neglected shrubs. There was a concrete bath in a bathroom outside, but this still had to be filled from the copper so usually I had a bath in a large tub in the kitchen. There was no shower in the bathroom, and only one kerosene lamp. There was a grapevine around the back door which each summer produced bunches of sweet, white grapes, but the vine was covered in mildew and we couldn't use the grapes. There was a fig tree which struggled to produce some tasty figs each year but which received no encouragement from us. We were also able to keep a few fowls, but rats were a nuisance. My parents must simply have accepted the rats as an inevitable part of city life, for they took no measures to get rid of them. Big Uncle Fred, who lived nearby in a substantial two-storeyed stone house and kept a large collection of prize-winning pouter pigeons, made his cages ratproof by cementing the floors, but then his wife owned the premises. Fred was probably a bit of a disappointment to his wife. He was a big man and worked as a train guard. He would often arrive in Glenelg on the last train of the day and then cycle back to the city in the middle of the night. He enjoyed his life but never fulfilled his wife's expectations of social success.

For me, however, the big advance was living almost opposite the Baptist Mission. This had a large Sunday School of neighbourhood children. Our youth leader at the Mission was a well-known young West Torrens cricketer and YMCA member, a Mr Gar Gooden, a fine gymnast and at the time a bachelor. He also taught me rudimentary chess. I attended the Sunday afternoon school and found myself with six local lads of my age — ten — all from families of a similar socio-economic class. I won my first prize for a short Bible essay and this helped to establish me with my peers. That was important for, during the next five years, I spent much time at the Mission. It ran a boys' gym, a basketball team, a cricket team, took some of us to the beach on hot nights and had a Christian Endeavour Society — all of which I belonged to. The Mission also had electricity. On nights when our house was dark and there would be little to do at home but go to bed, the bright lights of the Mission were irresistible. I was seldom home before eleven and managed to do very little homework. This didn't matter very much while I was still at primary school, but by the time I got to high school my academic progress had slowed.

2

Finding the future

(1925–1934)

IN 1926 a classmate at Norwood walked the eight miles to and from my place in order to persuade my mother to let me join the Boy Scouts. My mother was so impressed by this feat of endurance that she said I could join despite the cost of the uniform. I soon found myself in the company of fellow enthusiasts in a very good troop at the Adelaide YMCA. I read *Scouting for Boys* by Baden-Powell and was enthralled. Our scout leader was a young surveyor aged about twenty-three, with a good imagination and a flair for enthusing young lads with a spirit of adventure, both in outdoor activities and in intellectual pursuits. And so, for the next four years, I went without fail to the regular Friday night meeting at the YMCA in Grenfell Street. I was smartly turned out in the costly uniform that my mother had scraped for and later washed and ironed every week. We had a fierce annual inter-patrol competition that ensured that punctuality, teamwork and personal achievement were rewarded. Several times a year, our patrol of about six boys organised weekend camps. We always went to the Sturt Creek Reserve in the hills just outside Adelaide. On Saturday afternoons we would take the train to Blackwood Station and then, laden down with our gear — which included a heavy canvas cottage tent, walk the one and a half miles to the Reserve.

By the time we had erected the tent it would be time to light a fire and start cooking the evening meal. We always cooked stew. We did so because one of the requirements of the Scout's Second Class badge was the ability to cook this particular meal. Sausages would not do. This was a pity because we could easily have grilled sausages to perfection in half an hour. As it was, the long, slow simmer that is necessary for a good stew was always cut short by our growing hunger and the meal was eaten half-cooked. Once or twice it rained in the night and we thought how splendid it was to be dry and snug inside a tent while the rest of the world soaked. On Sunday morning we struck camp and walked back to the station with all our gear. Little else was achieved on these camps, but the simple experience of being on our own and fending for ourselves — if only overnight — made it all worthwhile.

Once a year, at Christmas, the whole troop went off to an exciting new campsite for ten long days. One year we went to Long Island in the Murray, another to Silver Lake at Mylor and once we went to Tailem Bend just upstream from Lake Alexandrina. Our leader had a flair for introducing city kids to the delights of the country. In my teenage eyes he was a model bloke: clean-cut, active, enthusiastic and ambitious. He was a surveyor by trade. After I left the scouts, I lost track of him, but years later I met one of my fellow scouts and asked after him. It was extraordinarily disappointing to learn that he had married and settled down in a country surveying practice where he had grown fat and taken to a life playing bowls. There was no reason why he shouldn't have done just this, but it is always disconcerting to learn that the heroes of our youth are merely human.

Unconsciously I must have internalised the moral code that Baden Powell had succinctly summarised in his Ten Scout Laws, for they have provided me with clear ethical guidelines ever since: trustworthiness, loyalty, helpfulness, brotherliness, courtesy, kindness to animals, obedience to a superior, cheerfulness, thriftiness, and purity. (This last used to give me trouble until I defined "purity" in a more mature manner.) I remember being greatly impressed by an account of the way in which an American visitor to London in 1912 had been helped by an English scout who had refused a tip, saying that he had undertaken to do a daily good turn. When the businessman returned to the United States, he formed the first American branch of the scouting organisation. I have tried to keep that simple undertaking to do a daily good turn myself. Many years later, my belief in the practical ideals of scouting was reinforced when one of my senior Commonwealth Police officers, whom I had recruited from the New South Wales Police Force, sneeringly referred to one of his former colleagues, Superintendent Ford, as "just a boy scout". Bruce Ford had gained accelerated promotion in a force where seniority was almost the sole criterion of preferment by an act of "extreme bravery". Happening upon two bank robbers fleeing from the scene of their crime, he had tackled them both and managed a double arrest. Ford was brave and honest; he was not a man to take bribes. It was this latter trait that my cynical officer regarded as typical boy scout behaviour. My own assessment of the officer was immediately modified. I also wondered if my own commitment to honesty was not well enough known in my own force for him to have ventured that comment. But I was pleased that the scouts tenet had been recognised by hard-bitten police. Subsequently my own officer's three sons became members of my scout group in Canberra.

To return to Halifax Street, our neighbours were a Mrs Ryan who took in a male lodger from time to time and, on the other side, a dear old pensioner, Mrs Bennett. My mother's two sisters and their boyfriends or husbands visited us slightly more often than they had when we were in the Murrays Lane cottage, but my father's many brothers and sisters still never came to our house and we very rarely went to theirs. Some we never visited. I was unaware of any rift in relationships — it just seemed that no visits were made.

I was allowed a lot of freedom. With hindsight, I suppose that's how the younger Haylock children behaved in Birdsville under my mother's supervision. I was at home very little. I formed a mateship with another young boy who lived nearby and who went to the Mission, Jack Chesson, and another, Alan Lovell. Alan Lovell was an expert at making wire prongs for shanghais. To these we fixed rubber bands and then cut out the tongues from old shoes to make a pouch to hold the BB shot or small stones. We hunted birds in the east

Parklands. This was before I had made the Scouts' promise to be "kind to animals".

In the evenings there was usually something on at the Mission and I went there with my mother's approval. Friday evenings were reserved for the scout troop. I never developed a habit of doing homework. I disliked schooling, both primary and secondary — partly because I couldn't see much advantage in it, and partly, I suspect, because of an administrative move at Norwood School. After I had been in Grade 5 for a term, four of us were moved into Grade 6 on the grounds that we were bright enough to cope with that year's standard. But I think the real reason was to balance out class sizes. These were, in any case, quite large by modern day numbers: forty children in a class was common. I did catch up scholastically with the rest of the grade 6 pupils eventually, but there was an unexpected bad outcome. The Grade 6 boys spent Friday mornings at a distant carpentry school learning woodwork. We four arrived in second term, but the carpentry instructor — he was a tradesman rather than a trained teacher — made no effort to provide any elementary instruction for us. I felt unwelcome. We were three projects behind the rest of the class and I, for one, had never held a plane or saw in my hands before. I hadn't the slightest idea how to sharpen a chisel. I tried hard at woodwork but just made a mess. Nobody came to my rescue. Teachers and principals were not as approachable then as they are now; it didn't occur to me to ask them for help. I became so fed up and miserable that one Friday morning I stayed away. Since the roll was never called, my absence was not noted, so for the rest of that year and the next I wagged it from woodwork lessons. I would spend Friday morning walking the lanes of Kensington in the hope of finding an empty bottle or two that I could return for the penny or halfpenny deposit. I never received a proficiency certificate for my woodwork, but I didn't care.

Joining the Mission brought me into contact with local lads of my age and participating in the various activities gave me some experience of teamwork. One of these lads, Keith Davies, lived nearby with his parents, and four brothers, in an attached cottage similar to ours. Keith was our enthusiastic wicket keeper when we played scratch games of cricket in the Parklands. I visited the Davies' home on a few occasions after school to borrow a bike spanner. Each time I found Keith and his three younger brothers studiously doing their homework under the eagle eye of their mother. The Davies boys all succeeded in adult life in varying professions. In later years I have regretted that in those days I was not similarly organised in relation to homework. Relying on a good memory and some intuition I was able to do reasonably well at primary school without any homework. I topped my Grade 7 class at Norwood Primary with a qualifying examination result of 610 but there were two Grade 7's and another lad topped the school with 630. This gave him a small scholarship when he went on to high school.

At Adelaide High School, I similarly coasted along and managed to pass each year, but with increasingly less success. I still did little homework. I had no goal in mind: I was just passing time. I could not have been an attractive pupil. I wore a heavy serge suit that had belonged to my mother's brother, Bill. He had developed stomach ulcers on the stations around Birdsville and had retreated to Clara's house in Adelaide to die. He left no will and few possessions apart from his suit. Bill had been taller and thinner than I was, so his suit fitted me very poorly. Most of the other boys had better fitting school blazers and, of course, the girls in our mixed class were neatly attired. After my Intermediate year, I was one of the younger and obviously poorer members of the Matriculation class. The afternoon classes were especially tedious for I was usually hungry, not having had any lunch. But this feeling may have had a psychosomatic element, for after school I found energy enough to go to football practice without fail. On Friday afternoons in winter I played soccer for the school team, on Saturdays football for the school, and on Sunday morning I went down to Victoria Park and kicked a football around with some mates. In summer I was captain of the school athletics team and most Saturdays ran the mile and the half mile in competition with other secondary schools.

I was in my Intermediate year at Adelaide High School before I fully grasped that there were two types of beings on this planet: one male and the other female. I suppose I might have been a slow learner in this regard, but I didn't fully realise the extent of the difference until I began mixing with the girls at Sunday School and became conscious of the girls in my Intermediate year classes. There were some much older lads doing Intermediate and these boys talked a lot about girls and sex.

All through my life I have been uneasy in the presence of women. Perhaps this is the result of being an only child for eight years and then only gaining a brother. I noticed that Alan Lovell and Jack Chesson, my two mates, seemed more at ease with the girls at the Sunday School. Alan Lovell had three older sisters — very attractive ladies who were Sunday School teachers and whom I much admired. And Jack Chesson had a younger sister by twelve months. She was a bit of a pain in the neck, always wanting to join in whatever activities Jack and I were planning. We had to almost forcibly exclude her from our outings. But I realised that both my companions were better able to talk to and understand girls than I was. I noticed that girls were able to stare meaningfully into each other's eyes and smile, without saying a word. Often there was an indirect, almost ambiguous, note to their sentences that I couldn't grasp. They seemed to be more interested in talking about people than about things. Jack and Alan and I talked about sport and events in the outside world. The girls seemed to be more interested — whenever I listened to them — about what each other was doing. Some of this talk seemed a bit spiteful, some of it seemed mere personal gossip, and it didn't interest me at all. Recent studies of the brain show how different males and females are from one another — that male and female brains are "wired" differently. This affects both outlook and behaviour; there are real differences between the sexes.

I used to walk home from school in my Intermediate year and on the way I sometimes encountered a girl called Rosie who was in my Sunday School class. She was also engaged in a Commercial Intermediate year and so we had similar teachers who taught us similar subjects. On the way home we would stop and talk about our school work. Rosie always seemed to be much ahead of me in grasping what the teachers were saying. She was about a year older than me, a recent arrival from London. She had older brothers and sisters and her parents had set up a small fruit and vegetable shop in Hutt Street near where I lived. Our paths often crossed. Rosie was a very conscientious student and she eventually married one of the lads from the Baptist Mission. I lost track of them both when I moved to the Flinders Street Baptist Church. Some years ago I bumped into Rosie and her husband after I had given a talk to a Rotary club in Unley about the Victims of Crime Service. Rose (as she was then known) complimented me on my achievements in life and said she was surprised I'd done what I had, both academically and in my public service career — she'd never thought I was all that bright. She had good reason to think this: during our school days she used to finish in first or second place in her class while I was always well down in the bottom half.

When I was fifteen I had been able to talk to Rosie in much the same way that I talked to my two mates. She was the only girl I knew with whom this was possible. Perhaps this was because Rosie had elder brothers. But it was a novel thought to me — that there were some females around who were capable of intelligent conversation. Later on, of course, when I met my future wife, Mavis, I was immediately attracted by the way in which she and her friend Gert and our group of final-year high school students were able to talk frankly and freely. And this was one of Mavis's attractions to me: here was somebody with whom I could talk and share my thoughts. I was able to articulate the things that were of interest to me and Mavis seemed to understand. But how she came by that ability, I don't really know, because there was only one boy in her family and he was four or five years younger. Perhaps it was something she picked up with her teacher training. All through our lives together, I was grateful for the way Mavis and I could talk and share our innermost thoughts, and luckily we tended to agree on the important, basic values and practices of life. Unfortunately this is a state of affairs that hasn't usually existed between me and the women I've met socially and professionally. When I was in Queensland I never felt I was capable of getting alongside the mentality of the young women I was recruiting for the police service. Of course they were a generation younger than me and they came from a different culture. These were strong barriers to my understanding. I never felt able to fully grasp what they were thinking and how they were likely to respond to my actions. I think this handicap of mine was partly responsible for my failure to convince them that they should join me in reforming the service. And, also perhaps, because they were junior and young — it was asking too much of them.

In my early years at Adelaide High School, my class teacher was an overbearing man who had obvious favourites, many of whom were older than me by one and sometimes two or three years. But then, in my fourth year, there was a change and Fred Burr took over as class teacher. He had a fierce black moustache, was about twenty-five, grinned often, showing his prominent front teeth, and dressed in a most casual manner. He discovered my interest in Marxist economics and went out of his way to foster it. In fact I had no exposure to real Marxist literature at all, but a fellow student had heard his father talking about the dictatorship of the proletariat and the nationalisation of the means of production and this was good enough for us. I'm not sure where Doug Kuss's family came from exactly, but it was somewhere in central Europe, perhaps Czechoslovakia. Doug had dark hair and glasses and seemed a bit different from the rest of us. Doug and I formed our two-man Marxist society more to annoy the teachers than anything else. But this interest was seized upon by Fred Burr. I got on well with him. I think that secretly he was "one of us" — neither Doug Kuss nor I got on very well with the headmaster and I don't think Fred Burr did either. It was a bit late for me to catch up with wasted studies but I did matriculate at sixteen with a credit in economics — the only one in Fred Burr's class to do so. Fifty years later, in retirement, he wrote in a first letter to me that he had noted that my initial university degree had been in economics and he was delighted to think he had encouraged my study of the subject.

I left school with my matriculation certificate and started to look for a job. The Great Depression was well established. I had thought of becoming a teacher, but recruitment for teacher training had been discontinued two years previously and without personal introductions it was impossible to find even a junior clerical position. After writing many letters of application, I secured a job as an office boy at the South Australian Paperbag Company in Leigh Street in the city. I was paid seven shillings and sixpence per week, of which I gave five shillings to my mother. I wasn't a very good office boy. My duties included dusting the boss's office every morning before he arrived, and delivering a large number of invoices and monthly statements on the firm's bike. This kept me busy. However, I twice left the bike in the lane alongside the office when I went to get fresh supplies of invoices. Unfortunately, leaving my bike in the narrow lane was forbidden because one of the partners could not get past in his large car. On the second occasion he scraped the wall and so it was time for me to leave.

The previous year had seen the unplanned break up of our group of lads at the Mission. All left school at age fourteen. Some found jobs as junior labourers in wool-scouring firms, sheet metal factories, or bakehouses; some went interstate hoping to find work. Along with one of my scout friends, Laurie Kitchener, who received support through Legacy, I moved up to the main church in Flinders Street to join its newly formed scout troop.

I can, with sincerity, begin this segment of these memoirs by repeating that traditional romantic phrase: "Long ago and far away I had a Dream one day." It was quite long ago now — sixty seven years in fact — and "far away" in those motorless times that I met my future wife, Mavis Russell.

Just before I left school in September 1932, when I was nearly seventeen years of age, I went to Victor Harbour for a holiday. I had been teaching Sunday School at the Flinders Street Baptist Church and one of my fellow teachers was Brice Russell. With two of his friends, Brice and I set out to hike the 50 miles [80 kilometres] to the seaside holiday town. We took a train to the outskirts of Adelaide and started walking. I don't remember sleeping, I remember joking and laughing and carrying on as we walked. Twenty-four hours after leaving town we arrived. You can do that sort of thing when you are seventeen. The four of us shared an inexpensive bedroom in a boarding house for about a week. Brice and I were then in our Matriculation year at Adelaide High School. Brice's sister, Mavis, and her close friend, Gert, were also staying in Victor and we shared outings with them. My fairytale had begun and has continued to this day. Mavis and Gert had graduated three years earlier from the Adelaide Teachers College. Mavis was then teaching at a small country school in Tweedvale, some distance from the city. Neither of them appeared to be attached to a young man.

I can still recall that holiday together, Mavis was aged twenty-five and had blue eyes and fair hair, and wore casual clothes. She was active, healthy and had, to me, a most attractive personality. Privately I thought the other two non-sibling males in our party were either immature or stupid not to notice her obvious charm. But I was pleased, for their lack of interest in Mavis held no threat to our developing relationship.

By the end of the first couple of days I was already well on the way to thinking Mavis was the most wonderful person in the world. I remember how one morning the six of us went out in a fisherman's boat to check the cray pots. We all succumbed to seasickness. We returned to shore and slowly recovered. I was left impressed by the way in which Mavis responded to the situation. I had had little previous contact with girls and none of those I knew would have behaved in the manner she did. With an obvious absence of self-pity and complaints, she saw much humour in our predicament.

I discovered that Mavis shared my enjoyment of the poetry of Tennyson and Browning. Also, she was familiar with the work of the Reverend Leslie Weatherhead, an English psychologist, who had helped her, as he had me, to gain some understanding of the principles of Christianity. (There were those he hadn't helped, who regarded his teachings as anathema, and who referred to him as Leatherhead.) Brice and I had been teaching Sunday School at Flinders Street Church where Mavis and Brice's father was a deacon and their elder sister the superintendent of the Sunday School. My duties involved teaching my class of eleven-year-olds about a number of miracles — water turning into wine, a few loaves and fishes feeding a multitude, that sort of thing. I was beginning to doubt the absolute truth of the Bible and tended to skip through these parts of the curriculum as fast as possible. But I kept my doubts to myself — it was heresy at Flinders Street to regard the Bible as anything but the literal word of God. Brice seemed to have no doubts at all and his sister the superintendent had been no help when I'd tentatively raised a few questions about Biblical miracles. With Mavis, things were different: doubts and queries could be discussed openly. And Mavis didn't talk down to me, which I appreciated. She was the first teacher I had met who spoke to me as an equal. I immediately thought "here is someone on the same wave length as myself". I enjoyed her company, for not only was she a person whom I admired, but she seemed to appreciate my jocular, male comments. As well, she appeared to give serious consideration to the odd theories I risked revealing in our discussions. Her interest was genuine, for there was no reason for her to seek out my company. I was young, still a secondary school student, a stage she had left well behind. I think that for a long time neither she nor her family saw me as a possible suitor. Yet since that holiday at Victor Harbour she had become the major influence in my life. I was unhappy when I was away from her so I exploited every opportunity to be in her company, and if possible, alone together.

When our holiday at Victor was over, Brice and I returned to school and Mavis returned to Tweedvale in the hills north east of Adelaide. Prior to the First World War, Tweedvale had been known as Lobethal, but anti-German sentiment led to its name change. Later it reverted to the name its original Lutheran settlers had given it. Mavis taught Grades 4 and 5 at the primary school. She lived with another teacher in a shared room and managed to return to Adelaide by bus about once a fortnight. On those weekends when she remained in Tweedvale, she would meet other teachers in the local library, go for walks and perhaps attend a local football match.

When Mavis came to Adelaide, she and I met as part of an extended group — to my considerable frustration. We played social tennis on Saturday afternoons, and frequently had musical gatherings in the evenings. Mavis contributed a great deal to making these gatherings at her home happy occasions for everyone present and, of course, this was especially so for me. On Sunday afternoons Brice and I were teachers at Flinders Street and, with typical Russell family generosity, I was always an invited guest at their Sunday evening meal, followed by church. We went and returned as a group. I was treated very much as one of the family but not until a very long time, as a special friend of Mavis.

Some authorities assert that men are likely to marry women who remind them of their mothers. Maybe so. My own mother sacrificed much to ensure I had a good education, that I could partake in school sports, and that I could enjoy and benefit from scouting. On reflection, I have wondered if on that fateful day when I met Mavis I had somehow discerned that she was that rare type who is less concerned about their own welfare than that of others. All through our long association, I never heard her complain, never heard her say anything adverse about someone else. She always put her family's, and then the community's, needs before her own. She lived with commonsense frugality but with generosity whenever others were involved.

The worst eight months of my life began in April 1933 — yet they should have been my happiest. I was an unemployed eighteen-year-old without any prospects or qualifications except an early Matriculation certificate. I was in love with a twenty-six-year-old teacher in a permanent appointment. In those days there were many unemployed people on the streets of Adelaide. I was just one amongst thousands. There were no monetary unemployment benefits, but ration cards were issued once a fortnight. These bought one some bread, sugar, flour, tea, and meat. The unemployed didn't starve, but there were many evictions of families who could not pay their rent. I spent a lot of time reading in the State Library and helping the caretaker of the church. He couldn't pay me, but sometimes he gave me lunch. As a matrimonial prospect, I didn't rate.

I think I only gained Mavis's acceptance because I was not at first seen by her or her family as a suitor. More by good luck than any kind of management, I had not pressed for that recognition. I rather think all three Russell girls were "man-shy", yet I know they were greatly admired by male colleagues and acquaintances. Slowly it became apparent to the Russells that I hoped for deeper things than friendship with Mavis. And as our relationship progressed, under strict and by now less than approving family supervision, the atmosphere in Mavis's home lost its former congenial warmth. Mavis, however, did not waver in her desire for my companionship. During the January 1934 school holidays, her parents thought it prudent for her to go to Port Augusta to visit distant relatives. These included an eligible young man named Sam, a fisherman who was nearer Mavis's age.

Desperate to achieve at least a little more status in the Russels' eyes, I thought it might be possible to obtain casual work on some of the River Murray blocks picking apricots and later sultanas. So I left home on a cycle with eighteen pence and blankets and my ration card. I pedalled some hundreds of miles calling on blockies without success. I based myself in Barmera, sleeping in an unused shed at the back of the local scoutmaster's house. As I cycled around I met many other unemployed people all seeking casual work picking fruit. The fruitgrowers would put one's name on a list — you could be the twelfth name on the "reserve list" for a blockie who only had work for six hands. Mavis wrote to me but I couldn't reply because I couldn't afford the paper or the stamps. Her letters were warm and encouraging to a young man in despair about his future. I would visualise her being courted by Sam, under parental pressure to be polite. But she since told me that she never had doubts about choosing me as her life partner.

In late January 1934, the Russells got a telegram through to me. The Police Department was advertising thirty vacancies for men under twenty years of age to join the Force as trainee constables. I got back to Adelaide, applied, and joined the 300 applicants who had survived the rigorous medical examination. We then sat for a written paper. I understand I topped this test and was the first of the intake to be appointed.

3

The South Australian Police Force

(1934–1940)

I joined the South Australian Police Force in February 1934 as a police messenger, a kind of cadet. I was on twenty shillings a week, and I lived at home. I wore a uniform that allowed me to ride on the trams for nothing. Life took on hope, meaning, a promise of happiness. I had emerged into bright light at the end of a very dark tunnel. My naive impressions of a policeman's lot were still based on those bedtime stories of the Birdsville sergeant that my mother had told me. It seemed to me that a person could get paid for just doing a daily good turn over and over. And my social life blossomed as I became accepted as a possible son-in-law to the Russells. Mavis was most happy with my appointment and I now became her "steady boyfriend". We entered upon a more customary courtship of regular Saturday nights at the pictures on our own, shared Sunday activities with her family, and occasional weeknight meetings.

But "the job" as it is called worldwide by all manner of coppers, did not turn out the way I expected. About two years earlier, Commissioner Leane had decided to develop a more educated force by recruiting lads with intermediate and matriculation certificates at a younger age than the customary twenty-one years. They would fill in the years with clerical work until they turned twenty-one and could be sworn in as officers. By rotating the cadets within the various branches of the force, it was hoped that they would acquire a working knowledge of each. I believe that Commissioner Leane did not succeed in selling this concept and that he failed to achieve the active cooperation of his officers. Most officers were content with the status quo and saw no personal advantage in the scheme. Perhaps they believed that it would affect their chances of promotion, and perhaps they lacked sufficient commitment to the ideals of British policing. The idea that an individual constable should receive his authority from the community and exercise it on his own initiative ran counter to the easy assumption that all a young policeman needed to do was follow orders from on high. As well, most of the twenty cadets and messengers were mediocre material by secondary school standards; they were certainly inexperienced in leadership roles. A number of lads were from the country and lacking in urban sophistication. However, we were welcomed into the various branches at headquarters in Angus Street — though this welcome, I think, was mainly because we took the position of "the lowest man on the totem pole".

Instead of receiving systematic instruction on procedures, we became the gophers, the typists and tea-getters. This was especially true when we were supervised by civil servants. The young trainee became an assistant to the civilian office boy, relieving him of his more mundane tasks. A few of our number were already touch typists. They possessed a skill so valuable in a force where one-finger typing was the rule that they were kept at this task for their entire traineeships. I arrived full of enthusiasm for community servicing and was immediately made dockets clerk in the commissioner's office registry. All day long, five days a week, I picked up big bundles of dockets in the main office and took them to a small, airless room to file away, or I began the reverse process of finding dockets to match a list I was given. There were five copies of every document, the result of copious use of carbon paper. I managed a reasonable morning's filing, but by early afternoon I was bored stiff. I took to reading the more interesting dockets and so, I suppose, I did learn a little — especially about rape, and murder.

After six months I was moved to the fingerprint/photographic section. I was delighted: at last I would be involved in some real police work. I should have known better. This section was run by civilian photographers who had taught themselves fingerprinting from a classic textbook by Henry Dalton. There were only three photographers and they were jealous guardians of their status as experts. I was assigned to a disabled ex-serviceman, a former policeman who needed a crutch to move. He maintained the criminal records, which were the responsibilty of the section. These were all on 10 x 8 inch ruled cards; details of crimes and convictions were recorded by pen. My job was to obtain the daily list of court appearances and verdicts, find the corresponding cards in the drawers and hand these to the clerk, who would record the details. He would then hand the cards back to me for refiling. I did this for nearly a year. It was deadening. I would try to sneak into the darkroom to watch film being developed, but I received no encouragement. On a few occasions, I got hold of a copy of Dalton which had been left out during the lunchbreak. I read through it quickly. It was easy to follow and the fingerprint classification procedures were well illustrated. But if I was discovered with the book I was shooed away — the secrets it held were only for the initiated. However hard I tried, I could not muster any enthusiasm for my chores with the record cards. Even when the clerk went on his four weeks' annual leave and I was allowed to enter the details myself, I still found the job boring. My wage of twenty shillings was well-earned. The man I replaced earned seventy shillings.

That year there was to be a World Scout Jamboree in Frankston, Victoria. I had kept up my scouting and was now acting as the scouter in charge of the Flinders Street Church troop. I was keen to go to Frankston but decided that I couldn't afford it on my twenty shillings a week. Then I learned that all of the Russell offspring would be going, including Mavis who was in charge of a girl guide troop. This was at a time when I could barely let her out of my sight lest some handsome prince come along and sweep her off her feet … and she was now bound for ten days in far-away Victoria. I was some pounds short of the fee but I had access to scout funds which had been entrusted to me for another purpose. Against all my moral principles, I borrowed the money without consent. I was only twenty at the time, but I was put in charge of the entire Adelaide contingent of scouts: four troops. At Frankston we had a wonderful time, mixing with scouts from all over the world. My contingent put on a display of boomerang throwing before the entire jamboree. Mavis and her sisters stayed with friends in Melbourne, but journeyed to the Jamboree by train every day. I kept as close to her as I could, neglecting my scouter responsibilities. I gave no thought to my misdeed until I returned home and the realisation of what I had done sank in. I went to the person who had entrusted the money to me and ashamedly told him what I had done. He was an old friend and covered for me until I was able to replace the money. I learnt a very hard lesson which has remained with me ever since.

In the following year, April 1935, I was posted to the Police Depot at Port Adelaide for my last year as a cadet. There were forty junior constables living at the depot, receiving basic training before being sworn in at age twenty-one. By this time the creation of the rank of junior constable had replaced Commissioner Leane's cadet scheme. In the main, the junior constables were lads with even less education than the cadets.

We paid for our food out of our twenty shillings a week wage. One of us was appointed cook. The food was mainly edible. We sat in crowded, makeshift classrooms (former dockside sheds) and wrote down in longhand the sixteen Acts and Regulations we would be called upon to enforce after we were sworn in. These were read out aloud by one of the more senior lads. No explanations were given, no demonstrations provided. We were supposed to learn the Acts and Regulations by heart. This was training at its most primitive, but we were all glad to get it for the alternative was unemployment.

Conditions in the depot were equally primative. The kitchen was right next to the stables and hoards of flies migrated between the two buildings. As we were all poor and had to buy our own food, we bought the cheapest possible.

At the depot, we were each allocated a horse — mine was an aged chestnut gelding named Ripple. He was a friendly animal and my anxiety about sitting on his back — sometimes without stirrups — soon dissipated. I was lucky: some of the horses were anything but friendly, they would give you a quick nip or a kick if you let your guard down for an instant. I cleaned out Ripple's stall each morning and groomed, fed and watered him before I had breakfast myself. I saved apple pieces and other titbits for him. After breakfast we carried out riding drills, with and without swords. We did some PT ourselves. After lunch we had lessons in law and police procedure. In the evenings we cleaned saddles and bridles and did some study. I enjoyed my association with Ripple but not much else. There is a lot to be said for the responsibility of looking after a large animal. For the first time in my life, I had a genuine dependant. We were left in no doubt: if our horses became lame, it was our fault.

The senior instructor was an an ex-Indian Army Sergeant-Major, very pukka and proud of it. He wore the Mounted Police uniform of a navy blue jacket with a high collar and silver buttons, white riding britches and spurs. We called him The Rajah, although not to his face. He called us all "boy". He could bellow across the rough, gravel parade ground like a wild bull. But he understood men and he soon had us doing things on horses we wouldn't have dreamed possible. We rode bareback without stirrups. We learned to mount our horses on the run, while they cantered beside us. Out of the saddle we marched and spent a lot of time on drill. We were proud of our marching and worked hard to do our best, even with the local wharfies lined up along fence for a bit of free entertainment.

The depot was residential with two weekends off each month and no evening leave. We were allowed leave on alternate Sundays to attend a nearby church service. For this, Mavis would catch a bus from Torrensville to the city, then another to Port Adelaide, a rough area, where she would meet me outside the church. We would then sit together in a pew holding hands until the end of the service when I would escort her to the bus stop and she would return home. There was no shelter outside the church or at the bus stop. We had only a brief hug when the bus came. For this, Mavis left home early and undertook an hour-long journey alone. No trainee policeman would accept conditions like these today. Except for a small staff to feed and water the horses we could all have been released at noon on Saturday. There were no set duties for the rest of the weekend and we were left to our own devices. It is now interesting to record that none of the lads sneaked off to nearby hotels, nor did we devise any means of smuggling in some illicit grog. We were all well behaved. There were no clandestine initiation ceremonies and no outbursts of violence. The threat of dismissal kept us all in line.

I was sworn in on my twenty-first birthday as a probationary constable for one year, and posted to the Criminal Investigation Branch (CIB) for plainclothes duties. I was one of four so posted. The other three were also former police messengers with the Matriculation certificate. Although I was unaware of it at the time, I was joining a police force loosely based on an English model. In the early days of settlement, the founders of South Australia soon recognised the need for a law enforcement body to deal with bushrangers in the Adelaide Hills, apprehend runaway seamen, provide escorts for the traffic in gold, and protect settlers from marauding Aborigines. There was also disorderly behaviour within the city boundaries that needed controlling. South Australia's founders did not follow the practice of other British colonies of creating a para-military body, an armed gendarmerie, based on the Irish model. Instead they adopted the London Metropolitan Police model, but modified it by dividing the police force into a mounted division for country posts and foot police for the city "beats".

Before Commissioner Leane introduced cadets, messengers and junior constables in the mid-1930s, recruits for the South Australian force were required to be twenty-one years old, fit, healthy, unmarried, with a height of at least 5 feet 10 inches, a completed primary school education and no criminal record. Most of the recruits became honest, decent, trustworthy officers. They were men who, in earlier life, had not become stabilised as tradesmen, or who had become dissatisfied with rural occupations, or were simply unemployed. Many were recent arrivals from the United Kingdom, who had been in the armed services.

When I joined the CIB in 1936 it had some thirty detectives and plainclothes staff and was based in the Police Headquarters on Victoria Square. I soon decided I would like to have my CIB posting made permanent. If this happened, I would be the first to obtain selection this way, since the normal procedure was to select uniformed members who had demonstrated above-average commitment and ability. It would also mean that I would be by far the youngest permanent CIB officer in the place. To this end I worked very hard and made sure that I did nothing wrong in the eyes of my superiors.

The twenty-six months of my cadetship spent at Police Headquarters — observing and listening to office gossip, reading official files, talking to old-timers — had widened my horizons. I now realised that the detection and conviction of offenders was as important — and far more interesting — than being a "kindly" country sergeant. I hoped one day to be a detective-sergeant. At the time, there were only two in the force — one operational and one administrative. Each sergeant had achieved that rank by virtue of his seniority, although a sergeant's written examination had filtered out some candidates. From youth's perspective I soon saw myself as sharp as the best detectives and better than most. The head of the CIB was always an inspector. When I began, it was an officer widely known as "Greasy Mick". He was a unkept, fat man who sat in his office all day spilling cigarette ash down the front of his shirt. His only son was the local representative of the Melbourne-based *Truth*. For some reason, *Truth* always managed to get the inside information on Adelaide criminal investigations. Greasy Mick represented the old order of detectives and was not impressed with the need for education. He made it clear from the start that he didn't like me — although, at heart, it may have been the new system of recruitment that he didn't like, rather than the recruit himself. I certainly went out of my way to ensure that he had no grounds for disapproval. I worked harder and longer than any others in the branch and as a result stumbled across a couple of wanted villains. I had some other successes as well. On one occasion I located some stolen goods in an obscure second-hand dealer's shop. Fortunately, Greasy Mick soon retired and was replaced by a country inspector, William Owen Ignatius Sheridan.

This continued the "Irish" dynasty, although it has to be said the Protestant–Catholic divide that was a feature of some of the eastern states was never very prominent in South Australia. The police force was a public service department available to migrants with little education. It was no wonder that the Irish were over-represented. "Bill" Sheridan was a newcomer to CIB work, but he soon picked up most of the goings-on in the office. By contrast to Greasy Mick, he was courteous and intelligent and I got on well with him. If Catholic members received any privileges, I never noticed it. He treated me fairly, acknowledged any good efforts I may have made and usually approved my suggestions. I couldn't have had a better boss. Also my sergeant, George Walters, was an inspiration to me. However, there was still no systematic detective training. Potential detectives simply served for a few years as plainclothes constables, during which time they sank or swam according to their capacity to learn on the job. There was also a relatively easy detective's written examination which I passed at the end of the second year.

Apart from a superficial check of crime scenes by fingerprint experts, there was no forensic backup available and the development of criminal intelligence units was many years away. A few unsophisticated criminals were identified and convicted on fingerprint evidence alone, but a burglar doesn't have to be very bright to know about wearing gloves. The most serious violent crimes were usually committed within domestic relationships, and astute interrogation routinely resolved these. The cleverest criminals, especially those of the white-collar variety, were probably never caught — if, indeed, their offences were ever reported or discovered. I noted that the most potent weapon in the fight against crime was the detective's capacity to bluff a suspect by acting as if he knew a great deal more than he revealed. This skill was most successful when applied to offenders who actively wanted to confess. A surprising number were first timers. On one occasion, when I was twenty-two, I was alone on night duty when I was called out to a stabbing case. A woman had had a row with her husband because he had arrived home late for a meal. While they were eating the spoiled food, she picked up a carving knife and plunged it into her husband's chest, killing him. When I arrived at the scene the woman was sobbing, saying she really didn't mean to kill the man. Because it was a homicide and I was young, I followed the routine and sent the police driver to pick up my sergeant, but there was really no need: the distraught woman was keen to tell us everything that had happened.

The more astute members of the CIB were extremely good at bluffing. When interviewing suspects who were not first timers, and therefore presumably literate in criminal jargon, the detectives often adopted a heavy, semi-jocular conversational style. I watched this style practised very effectively on many occasions over the years. It has many advantages. For one thing, if the interrogator goes too far with his insinuations, or more direct accusations, and wishes to retreat, he claims: "I was only joking. You weren't stupid enough to think I was serious?" This was also often the mode of conversation amongst the CIB staff themselves, and it also appeared in discussions with bookmakers and other racecourse cronies.

The detective's ability to bluff was aided by a symbiotic relationship with the print media. In Adelaide at this time there were three newspapers — a morning and evening paper and the aforementioned independent weekly, *Truth*, which specialised in sensational stories. Each of these papers had full-time journalists ("crime reporters") who were employed to obtained "scoops" from detectives. The price of these scoops was good publicity for the detectives. There was a positive, practical side to these stories — they weren't entirely motivated by a desire for personal aggrandisement. These frequent mentions helped build up an image of the officers as astute interrogators who could quickly detect a falsehood and could outsmart suspects with cleverly devised questions. Believing this, many offenders abandoned hope before the interrogation had even begun.

There was another technique which some detectives used to good effect. One member of a two-man team would become enraged and threaten violence without actually administering any. The second detective then posed as a more sympathetic officer who advised the suspect to confess. I understand variations of this tactic are occasionally employed today. With suspects who were not of working-class origin — and especially if they came from one of the professions — the interrogators were sometimes ill at ease, although those suspected of sexual, especially homosexual, offences did not seem to cause any such awkwardness, regardless of their social standing.

I had many good opportunities to observe the more effective detectives in action because I had been attached to the operational sergeant's small team. We investigated the more serious cases. This was a plum job. I don't know why I was picked but I was soon using my stenographic skills to provide what amounted to the first records of interview used by the South Australian Police. I had learned shorthand at school and was the department's fastest writer (120–140 words per minute); I was also a reasonable typist, although not the best. One of my colleagues from my days as a police messenger was even better and could type at forty words per minute. My sergeant ensured that I was present and taking notes at all important interrogations. I would then type these up and they would form an integral part of the prosecution's case. Sometimes I would be the one who gave this essential evidence in both the Magistrates' and the Supreme Courts. On occasions my shorthand notebook outlines would be checked under cross-examination. I became an accomplished prosecution witness.

In this way I relieved the sergeant and others in his squad of the boring chore of one-finger typing of long documents. This also meant that an opportunity to manufacture false evidence was lost since I was not prepared to commit perjury in order to obtain a conviction. In any case reference to "Detectives Underwood and Remington" (the two brands of typewriters in the CIB office) to bolster cases for the prosecution was rarely employed. I was never aware of it actually happening, but jocular comments from time to time by some of the staff suggested that there may occasionally have been a slight rearrangement in the sequence of question and answer to strengthen the police case.

One of the duties of a junior plainclothes man in those days was to supervise the operation of the totalisators at racecourses. The workers in the tote would sell tickets through a window until just before a race. In order to ensure that no ticket-seller took a ticket for himself after the start of a race, there was a plainclothes policeman on duty inside the tote. The police also kept an eye on the calculation of dividends to ensure that the right amount of money was paid out. It was dreary work. One Saturday, while inside the tote, I noticed a young lady at the window buying a ticket. She looked younger than the statuatory twenty-one years. I went outside and identified myself as a police constable. The girl confessed to being nineteen years of age. I took her name and address and informed her that I would have to report the matter. What happened next is something I only learned about indirectly. The girl went straight to her father, a prominent member of the Jockey Club's committee. The father approached the senior sergeant on duty to see if the matter could be fixed.

"Who's the constable?" the sergeant asked.

"Whitrod."

"No chance."

Detectives of that era were also greatly aided by the legislative consorting provisions which made it an offence to consort with convicted or reputed thieves. In the popular imagination, criminals congregated in "thieves' kitchens", places that were half brothels, half sly grog shops. Here they would drink beer and plot crimes. If undesirable types could be prevented from congregating like this, the theory went, the crime rate would diminish. Conviction for consorting carried a penalty of up to six months' gaol and there were probably five or six such convictions a year, just enough to keep up the pressure. CIB officers would note any suspicious meetings and issue warnings. If the consorting continued over a period of months, then the person involved could be charged, but more often he would be "squeezed". After, say, five warnings, the person involved was considered ripe for a charge. He would be aware of his position. Some CIB officers would then squeeze him for information about the activities of other criminals, offering to defer the charge if he cooperated. It was a useful device, although based on a strange view of the underworld. In fact every Salvation Army officer in town was chronically guilty of consorting, but the Salvos were never squeezed.

Entry to the CIB opened up a new world of masculine activity to me. Women police then were few in number and had a very restricted range of duties — they were mainly concerned with the welfare of women and children. There were no women attached to the CIB. But they occasionally accompanied detectives when females were involved as victims, witnesses or suspects. The women police officers did not wear uniform and were largely untrained in crime investigations. They were warranted members of the force, but were never known to arrest anybody. The ages of the detectives ranged from thirty-five to fifty-five; all were well dressed in woollen suits and ties, all wore a felt hat, shoes were polished. Since they were all tall and worked in pairs, with a habit of studying closely any strangers when they entered a hotel bar or a racecourse, they were easily identified as plainclothes police. I sometimes wondered just how they managed to be so well dressed on their salaries. It became clear to me that if I wanted to achieve acceptance as a full-blown detective I would have to emulate their dress sense. I was lucky. I made friends with a Mr Sheehan, the leading cutter for Ingersons, then the top men's tailoring firm, and he ensured that my suits were of fine material and well cut, for a medium price. They were so good that some of the older detectives asked me where I got them! The Whitrods paid for them out of my clothing allowance and a bit of scraping.

Two characteristics of CIB duties were immediately obvious to me: the freedom of action, and the strong bond of mateship that existed in the pairs of detectives. After a year living in the depot under closely supervised, semi-military discipline, I was attracted to the manner in which the men were given reports of various crimes to investigate, and then left alone to get on with the job. There were no duty statements and a minimum of record keeping. Daily diaries were maintained and scrutinised weekly by the administrative sergeant but I never knew of any check on the validity of the entries in them. It truly was a Golden Age for the detective staff. Those who were competent and conscientious (about half of the staff) worked; the others — the incompetent and the lazy — got by without rebuke. In most detectives' offices in those days, there was a "hard man" or someone who passed as such. A former Victorian footballer was our "heavy". All state Forces found it advantageous to have one on tap for those occasions — rare in South Australia — when a particularly dangerous criminal needed to be interrogated by a detective whom he respected. This usually meant "respected" physically. There was a certain status attached to this role and supervisors tended to be lenient in their duty allocations to recognised hard men. Our hard man so arranged it that he spent a great deal of duty time attending race and trotting meetings where he enjoyed fraternising with bookmakers and trainers. I know he had difficulty in passing the sergeant's examination for promotion, but on the fourth attempt he was successful. In my eight years I never knew him to mount the witness box to give evidence.

There was no procedure for reviewing cases that had come before a court. "Not guilty" (NG) cases were never examined to see how the conduct of the prosecution could have been improved. The "NG" verdict was always put down to the contrariness of juries. We never received advice from the staff of the crown prosecutor on how we might have handled an investigation any better. Although there was no departmental library, and no incoming journals, the CIB was well served by one of Commissioner Leane's innovations. He organised the preparation of a *Reference Book* which contained details of the sections of all the state and federal acts which were relevant to state police responsibilities and powers. This book was hard-backed, but loose-leafed, so that amendments which came out regularly could be inserted. As well as the relevant legislation, there were details of up to three leading cases on any significant point. But this single book was hardly a substitute for a departmental or branch library. I immediately subscribed to the *English Police Journal* and later to the new *Journal of Criminology*. At some personal cost, I hunted around the secondhand shops for an old edition of Archbold's *Criminal Pleadings* and eventually located one. Archbold was the standard text on English law; it laid down what was necessary to prove a charge and how to frame an indictment. One could learn in Archbold, for example, that it was impossible to steal fish in the sea, since they belonged to no one. Fish in English rivers were different. Prior to my purchase of Archbold, the South Australian police had simply relied on precedent: an indictment would be worded in the same manner as a previous one. After I'd introduced *Criminal Pleadings*, the younger members of the CIB began to argue the merits of recent court decisions when assembling for the 9.00 a.m. and the 2.00 p.m. musters. It was rare for any of the older men to participate.

There was no annual scrutiny of our efficiency. Management by Objectives was several decades away. We persevered with obsolete routines such as the 7.00 a.m. duty at the East End Markets on alternate days. Apparently many, many years earlier, some fencing activity had been detected at the market, but for the eight years that I patrolled there between 7.00 and 9.00 a.m I detected none. Nobody else reported any stolen goods being traded either. The practice meant catching the first tram in to the city at 6.15 a.m. and then wasting two hours strolling around. Everyone at the markets recognised us. The market patrol was a chore quickly transferred to the younger members, and since our time was expendable there was no motive to eliminate the ritual. Similarly, the arrival each morning of the Melbourne express at 9.15 a.m. was monitored by having the alighting passengers scrutinised by a senior CIB man. Again, in my eight years no criminal was recognised. However, it was a duty done willingly by our ex-Victorian heavy, because he and his family resided nearby in a city hotel. He always stood prominently on the platform where he could be noticed. Perhaps it had some good PR result but information from Victorian criminals who had made their arrival undetected was that they had got off the train a few stations up the line and caught a local train into the city. There was no suggestion box at the CIB. Everyone was satisfied with the status quo. The state was relatively free of major crimes and the overall crime rate was not increasing; there were no irritating civil liberties bodies; the opposition party in Parliament did not dare raise any criticism of "our policemen"; and the Rationalists and the Communists received little public support. On the other hand, the South Australian Police Association was unaggressive and also unimaginative.

Mavis and I tended to join those individuals and groups with a similar philosophy to our own, such as the University Branch of the Christian Student Movement. Before our marriage, we had spent several stimulating weekends with this group at a holiday house in the hills. There was a great deal of free discussion on a variety of religious topics and some very funny games. We both admired our chairman, Bill Salter, a final-year medical student whom we were later to come across in the Oxford Group. While I was a police messenger I had became dissatisfied with the sermons at Flinders Street. I discussed my discontent with Miss Edith Lee, a church member and head of the Chidren's Welfare Branch. She suggested that I talk to Ivan Menzies, a Gilbert & Sullivan actor, then in a show in Adelaide. I went to see him, and listened to his description of the principles and practices of the newly formed Oxford Group in England. I found him convincing. The Oxford Group had been started at Oxford University in 1928 by an American Baptist Minister called Frank Buchman. He recruited young, athletic types, and the group developed a manly, cleancut image and quickly spread throughout Europe and America. The group's insistence on absolute standards of honesty, unselfishness, love and purity, as well as its team support, appealed to Mavis and I, and so for a time we participated in its activities. Then in 1935, when I was posted to the Police Depot, the Group decided, without any consultation with us, that it was God's will that Mavis and I join separate teams. This arbitrary decision did not go down well with Mavis's independence, nor mine, and so we drifted to the fringes of the movement, where we have remained ever since.

There was a short time, years later when we were living in Canberra, when we became friendly with some young men who were committed to the ideals of the Oxford Group. We joined them in some of their activities, and might have again become serious members ourselves. However, when the founder, Frank Buchman, came to Canberra for a visit, he was accompanied by a group of dedicated spinsters. They told Mavis she was to attend meetings in the afternoons at 4.00 p.m. She pointed out that this was the time our children would be coming home from school, and that she had a tea to prepare. These family responsibilities were not accepted by the middle-aged, thin-lipped spinsters as reasons for non-attendance and so, despite much peer pressure, the Whitrods again withdrew from Group activity. Mavis and I continue to regard the principles of the Oxford Group — now known as Moral Rearmament — as being of the highest order; its members live frugally and are a friendly mob, but the group's practices still reflect the values of its founder, an American bachelor Baptist minister. As well, individual consciences tend to be swamped by the group mentality, and this is much influenced by the professional full-time workers.

Just before being sworn in, I asked Mavis if she would become engaged to marry me, although force regulations required me to first serve three years as a single man. She said that I had first to obtain her father's permission. I did this and at my twenty-first birthday celebrations we announced our engagement. We were the first of the younger members of the force to do so, but we were soon followed by the older of my contemporaries. I had achieved a permanent posting at the CIB and it was probably because of this that I was given permission to marry after thirty months instead of the required three years. We were married at Flinders Street Church where Mavis's parents had also been married, and we had a splendid reception afterwards provided by Mavis's parents at a fashionable city restaurant.

Mavis's bridesmaids were Gert and her younger sister, Jean. Mavis looked radiant and I was the happiest man present. My CIB sergeant and some other police were there to share my happy event. We had scraped together enough money to have a short honeymoon after which we returned to a rented flat at Glenelg. The honeymoon, however, started as bit of a disaster. I had booked us into the Normanville pub and we caught a bus to the seaside township some 40 miles (65 kilometres) south of Adelaide. The pub, it turned out, didn't really cater for boarders, although they must have occasionally put up the odd drunk for the night. There was only one bedroom with a dilapidated bed strung with a sagging wire mattress. The food was dreadful. The company in the public bar was uninviting. We decided to move to Victor Harbour where we knew we would find congenial lodgings. But we had no money. I had arranged for my fortnightly pay cheque to be sent to the Normanville post office and so we stayed in the dreadful pub from Saturday to Friday waiting for the arrival of the wherewithal to pay the bill. The money arrived and we left. The publican was happy to see us go. In Victor Harbour we stayed in a guest house we knew, Clifton, and were very content.

Until recently, I have never thought about the impact of marriage on Mavis. The prevailing regulations required her to resign her position as a qualified teacher as soon as she married. She then took on, as a full-time job, the small task of keeping a one-bedroom flat clean and preparing meals for the two-hour breaks I had for lunch and dinner. We lived on the corner of Anzac Highway and Durhum Street near the Glenelg beach, but we knew no one in the vicinity. Mavis's old friends were still teaching and she must have felt the isolation of that small flat, and the loss of a satisfying career. My salary was less than hers had been so she had to exercise much frugality. We couldn't afford the entertainments we had enjoyed before we were married. The first three months must have been difficult for her. At first we couldn't afford a radio. I cannot remember Mavis mentioning anybody she had talked to during the day, and we did not then have a telephone. She never complained. She always greeted me with a smile and an appetising meal. She listened sympathetically to my tales of job woes and small successes, but in return I never gave her much listening time. I left home in the morning at half-past eight and I often didn't finish work until nine-thirty at night, although I came home for meals twice in this period. It was a lifestyle that quite suited the older detectives. Their children were no longer at school; their wives had their own circles of friends; they often managed to spend their evening shifts in the pictures (free entry with a police pass) or at the greyhounds, trots or boxing. Or they could go quietly home where a departmental telephone would summon them if anything urgent arose. Young constables had no telephones so they had to remain close to headquarters. I would patrol the central business district in the evenings looking for break-ins. But there was not much crime to be detected in this casual fashion.

Mavis and I hoped to find a more permanent home. But, except for the sum of £100 which Mavis had saved over the years from her salary, we had no assets. We talked of the possibility of buying a house on the small deposit of £100 and then raising a mortgage. It was still Depression time in Australia and money was scarce. Neither of our families could help. We eventually located a friendly builder who built us a nice house at South Plympton on the tramline, which was very convenient for getting to and from work. The house was built for £1000 and our builder accepted the £100 as the first instalment. The house had a Mt Gambier freestone front, three bedrooms, a sleepout at the back, a bathroom with a gas heater and electric light in every room. We started life in our own home with very little furniture indeed. But we initiated a small example of chain migration: soon other young policemen were buying houses in the area, attracted by each other's company and the convenience of the tramline straight to Victoria Square.

We had also spent money on our first luxury — an Irish setter pup, Kerry, who became our devoted follower. I had always had a dog at home in Halifax Street and, although this was not a Russell tradition, Mavis readily agreed to Kerry's purchase. The three of us frequently went for long walks together on the alternate Sundays when I was off duty. With the help of our groomsman, Max Dawson, who had once been a scout of mine when I was a scouter at Flinders Street, we dug up horrible onion weed, planted a lemon and apricot tree and some grapevines, and built a fowlhouse. Mavis was always a keen gardener and homemaker and, despite becoming increasingly larger in body size due to pregnancy, shared in all of our activities. She was an excellent cook and made a specialty of Cornish pasties of which I became her best fan. Mavis's biological and nutritional studies ensured that our meals contained all the nutriments needed, and her frugality meant that very little was wasted.

My salary of seventy shillings a week just covered current expenses and fortnightly mortgage repayments so we were always financially hard pressed. Since we seldom went out, we did buy an inexpensive radio. When the time came for Mavis to go hospital, we could scarcely raise the taxi fare. We had decided upon the Memorial Hospital at North Adelaide for it was reputed to have the best maternity wing. Subsequently all of our three children were born there. Although we had a minimum of furniture, one of our first purchases was an ice chest in which to keep milk fresh for Andrew, who was born a year after our wedding and six months after we moved to our first home. Mavis was thirty-one when Andrew was born. So we decided that she would be looked after by the best obstetrician in Adelaide. We told him about our financial situation and he agreed to accept time payment of his account. I remember visiting Mavis in the maternity wing with Kerry — to the delight of the nurses — when Matron was absent from the ward.

4

Lessons from the war

(1940–1944)

ALL through the late 1930s war had been looming in Europe, but I don't remember this making much impression on us in Adelaide, even when Hitler invaded Poland and war was officially declared. It was the retreat from Dunkirk in June 1940 that suddenly brought home to us how badly things were going for England. There was a surge of popular feeling, resulting in young men volunteering for military service with little more thought for the future than a belief that they ought to go and help their mates in a crisis. England, for many of us, was an extension of Australia. The British were our mates. They were in desperate trouble, but we were sure that, with our help, they would be able to defeat the enemy in six months or a year. However, not everybody felt like this: few of my peer group at the CIB nor the males in the Russell social circle felt any obligation to volunteer for service. Yet for me there was a strong urge to go to the aid of Britain, the only nation standing up for the democratic principles we all said we believed in. Perhaps my long association with scouting and its English origins may have affected my assessment. Perhaps Mavis's similar association with the Girl Guides and its emphasis on loyalty to the King may have been behind her calm acceptance of my decision to join the RAAF.

I volunteered, but there was a six months' callup delay during which time I attended weeknight refresher courses in maths and classes in elementary navigation. Mavis, who was more learned in maths than I was, provided some extra tutoring. During this period we decided that we should provide Andrew with a brother or sister just in case anything happened to me. For me the six months passed agonisingly slowly and it was a tense time at home since Mavis and my family were facing an unknown future, but she remained calm and full of common sense. We made what plans we could.

In February 1941 I reported for duty and left our South Plympton address. I would be away for over four years. At home was my pregnant wife, a very young Andrew, and Kerry, our dog. Unlike some employers, the South Australian Police Department did not make up the salaries of its staff who enlisted, so Mavis had to survive on the wife's allowance portion of my RAAF Aircraftsman Gr. 2 pay. We decided that we would invite my father and mother to live at our home during my absence and they came to stay with Mavis. Our second son, Ian, was born while I was still training at a Mt Gambier base. I was unable to get leave to visit my wife in hospital. On completion of my training, I was promoted to pilot officer — a rank, not a job description — I was a navigator. With my promotion came a small increase in salary.

In early November, I was posted abroad and Mavis, Andrew, and our infant son Ian, in a pusher, somehow managed to get to the railway station to farewell our contingent. There was also a small team of my mates from the CIB. Mavis and I had only time for a quick, sad hug. She was smiling bravely as the train left but she later told me that our four years of separation were a very difficult time for her. Nobody knew what lay ahead, which was just as well for the farewelling relatives and friends. In my own group of twelve navigators who had trained with me, eight were killed and two became prisoners.

Mavis had the worst war by far. She woke each morning to a life without my help. She had two small children, a lower income than she'd enjoyed when single, she had other people living in her home, she noted with some concern the daily newspaper lists of casualties and, without transport, she had to struggle up the high steps of trams with the two very young children and a shopping basket. Wartime conditions meant she had to hunt around for scarce fresh food, carefully husbanding the food and clothing ration coupons. All this without any companion with whom to discuss any matters of concern.

On the other hand, I was in a new environment. I spent most of the four years of war in front-line squadrons. Operational aircrew in Europe reversed the usual serviceman's view of war: "a few moments of great excitement and months of boredom". There was much for us to do all the time. In 1942 and 1943, we flew Catalinas from Gibraltar on patrols over the stormy mid-Atlantic that could last anything from sixteen to twenty-two hours. We would fly out to sea as far as six hundred miles to meet convoys coming from the United States. We did this every third day. Since Cats carried two pilots but only one navigator, these were arduous trips for me. I had to know where we were at any moment in the event that we had to report the location of hostile shipping, aircraft or submarines. I suppose I spent about half my time in the air doing the calculations that would tell us where we were. I had to work out how strong the wind was by watching the tops of waves or by dropping flares and calculating the drift. As well, I had to take my turn at radar duty and try to make visual contact with the conning towers of submarines that might have been missed by the radar. On these operations, we had to be awake and ready for briefing a couple of hours before takeoff and it needed a couple of hours after the mission to debrief. One could go thirty hours without sleep. We rested on the second day, and then prepared for the next flight. Towards the end of my year at Gibraltar, I became quite jittery and found I couldn't sleep much before a mission. At times I had no sleep for forty hours straight.

When flying out of Gibraltar we sometimes gave similar cover to Malta-bound convoys. This was less difficult but fraught with danger from the anti-aircraft fire of the American destroyers who shot at everything. As well, the Germans had installed heavy guns on the southern side of the entrance to the Mediterranean, so we had to be very careful in the vicinity of Gibraltar. Some of our aircraft disappeared when nearing base, presumably as the result of anti-aircraft fire. Mysterious disappearances were especially threatening since there were many possible causes, and we wanted to know if there were any new precautions that we should be taking.

Apart from providing navigation, survival was my prime concern. I shared a room with my skipper, Dick, another Australian. He was unmarried. If I showed any moroseness because of absence from the family, Dick organised some activity, such as playing tennis or sharing a half-pint of weak English beer. He helped me through the worst periods. We became close mates and went on leave together. I had someone I could talk to who understood my situation. Things were different for Mavis, who was battling along on her own.

My other operational tours were in the North Atlantic and in the Indian Ocean. Navigating in the Arctic, escorting Russian-bound convoys, proved to be challenging — first finding them in thick cloud when my astro skills were useless, and then getting back to base at Akyrerie in Northern Iceland. At the time, flying boats were only equipped with magnetic compasses, and the proximity of the North Magnetic Pole meant that the compass was particularly sluggish in responding to changes in the aircraft's heading. At the time, the allies were very keen to support the Red Army on the eastern front. Any German division that could be tied down in the east meant one less division on the western front. Stalin extracted a high price for this service in terms of aircraft parts, fuel and other necessities of war. The convoys carrying this material had to sail through the North Sea and into the Arctic Ocean, eventually docking at Murmansk in northern Russia. Our job was to fly over the convoys looking for enemy battleships and submarines operating out of occupied Norway. The weather was usually atrocious, making it very hard for us to see anything, but this also meant that we too were very hard to see. We were rarely shot at.

In retrospect, I think the war taught me several valuable lessons. I discovered that I could master a complicated technical instrument like the Mk9 Bubble sextant to give me a position within a 4-mile triangle after ten hours of ocean flying, despite the chronometer's inaccuracy. My self-confidence grew to almost match that of the rest of the crew whose lives were at stake. They had great belief in my capacity since we always "got there" and "got back". I did receive squadron assessments of "above average".

The war, of course, dragged on far longer than any of us thought it would when we volunteered. I found that the best way to cope with separation from my family was to put life into two compartments: home life and war life. For the most part I lived in the war life compartment, and I became inured to the war. I just accepted that it was the present state of affairs. I suppose I rationed the amount of time I allowed myself to think about Mavis and the boys. I think most aircrew with families did this. Anyone who mused too long or too deeply on their distant loved ones became moody and depressed. Mavis wrote every week and usually her letters got to me; however, none of the parcels she sent me arrived, not one. I wrote back, although not as regularly as Mavis did.

I never doubted that I was flying with the best pilot in the squadron who would get us out of any scrapes, nor that I was with the top wireless operators, gunners and, of course, our excellent Belfast-trained flight engineer. I learned to trust our crew. We were a "family" and known on the Squadron as "Dick's crew" — a description we were proud of. I didn't actually swagger in the mess but I didn't pay homage to any other crew either. It was a nice feeling to know you were regarded as one of the best. Our RAF officers' mess was dominated by the squadron crews. We talked, argued, drank, played shove halfpenny, and engaged in more violent pastimes. There were ground staff there — the engineer officer, the intelligence team, the met forecasters, the padre and the doctor. They were made welcome in any discussion/drinking group, but the padre and the doc were especially regarded as "dwellers on the fringe". They were seen as useful but not essential in getting a crew over a convoy. The last two were my age and my rank. They called aircrew by their first names as we all did, but they were set apart because they never achieved that degree of acceptance, being always "Padre" and "Doc". I liked them both. We occasionally talked on equal terms about anything. Gradually I lost my Murrays Lane cringe when addressing medical doctors and ministers of religion. Ever since my Gibraltar days I haven't accepted any "social distance" between us, although I have noted that in Australia these two professions seek and receive more status than they do in England. The others in our crew were all volunteer RAF sergeants. Over the four years, I grew to admire their fine characters. I thought that they were superior in many ways to their officers, especially those officers who were permanent RAF. One of the less attractive aspects of the officer–men divide was that the two pilots and I had almost no contact with the rest of the crew after a mission had been flown. We might have been together for almost twenty-four hours sharing the dangers and deprivations of the patrol but, once back on solid ground, the sergeants retreated to their own mess and quarters and we to ours. It was very English.

On the other hand, I had found a very warm "second home" in the United Kingdom whenever we went on a week or so's leave while our Cat had an engine overhaul — as it did about once every six months. I had been adopted by an aristocratic family who lived on their estate just outside Winchester. The Lady Lilian Austin, a sister of an earl, offered me hospitality when she discovered I had no family or friends in Britain. Roundwood was a large country house, and even in wartime there were ancient servants and a nanny. Paintings of Hussars in full dress uniform adorned the walls. At Roundwood my socks were darned, and Lady Lilian would always write to Mavis after a visit to reassure her that I was well. I think I was the only young man to stay there who had not been to Eton College. Lady Lilian knew I was an Australian policeman but I received only the most gracious treatment from that family. I quickly noted and learned some of the social graces that had been missing from my own upbringing. This helped greatly later on in my career when I was in close contact with the royals.

Lady Lilian was friends with the local wartime doctor. He was a Harley Street specialist who had been bombed out of London and had come to Micheldever, near the estate. He was about fifty and from an entirely different social world. We became "mates". Whenever he heard I was coming he would somehow acquire a crate of local beer and have it installed in "my" room. This was a guest bedroom set aside mainly for my use. Lady Lilian, who was an ardent reader and had a weekly order at Foyles, would also place alongside my bed a collection of books which she thought would interest me. I was not quite one of the family but I was a very welcome guest. I had come from a background which encouraged the concept of "the class war" and my High School studies of Marx and the capitalist system had strengthened the thought that the British aristocracy was unnecessary and did not, in any way, justify its privileges. Lady Lilian's caring and responsible attitude, not only towards me but also to the estate workers and their families, considerably modified that view. Later on, when I spent time alone yarning and joking with Prince Philip as we sat birdwatching in the front seat of the aged Whitrod Holden sedan, I gained further understanding of the class situation in England. It wasn't as one-sided as I had thought: *"noblesse oblige"*: meant that the better nobles certainly accepted their obligations towards the proletariat.

I was not aware that my visit to Roundwood immediately before my posting to the Middle East would be my last. I expected to return to England as I had done from my other postings. So I left two pairs of silk-woollen thermal underwear in an attic. These had been issued to me in the Arctic, but I had never worn them: they weren't very Australian. I would certainly not need them in the Middle East. But the war ended and I went home on a freighter from Aden. In the 1960s, when I was a student at Cambridge, Mavis and I paid a visit to Roundwood. I asked Lady Lilian about my long johns. They had been taken over by her brother. The Earl of Sunderland still wore them when the weather was cold.

One of the other lessons I learnt from the war is that life really is unfair. I'd had my suspicions that we aren't all dealt the same hand of cards. But the war really reinforced my belief that we don't all start off equal and we don't all have equal opportunities. I felt then, and still do, that many worthwhile contributions to the community go unrecognised. Some people receive public awards that they deserve, but many don't.

This was driven home to me when I was in Gibraltar. Dick and I became friendly with a civilian type whom we used to meet playing tennis on the navy's courts. He said his name was Don

Darling. Dick and I got to like him and we met occasionally. We didn't know much about his background. And then one day he asked us if we would like to accompany him on a trip to Algeciras, the town across the bay in neutral Spain. He said he'd shout us lunch at the pub over there. So the next time Dick and I had a spare day we joined up with Mr Darling and proceeded through the border post, Dick and I presenting our Air Force identification and Don Darling his civilian passport. We walked around the shore of the bay towards Algeciras. On the way we stopped very casually at a small cafe and Don suggested we have a cup of coffee. Inside the cafe Don said that he wanted us to play the part of tourists being shown around southern Spain. We drank some excellent coffee and then Don disappeared for a quarter of a hour with the cafe proprietor with whom, he said, he had a small bit of private business to transact. When Don returned, he took us to the main part of Algeciras and we lunched very well on the terrace of a hotel, surrounded by Spaniards and some other fair-haired types whom Don pointed out to us as German officers on leave. They looked at us and we looked at them. And then we returned to Gibraltar.

We had a few more outings with Don. We learned about a "Spanish" trawler that had slipped into Gibraltar harbour and unloaded some cargo. We thought this was a bit odd — ships from neutral countries did not normally do this. We talked about this with Don who told us that the vessel also visited the French Mediterranean coast where its crew performed a few duties "for us". We didn't pursue the subject.

After the war I discovered that Don Darling worked under the code name Monday. He was the southern organiser of the famous MI9 escape route over the Pyrenees. He organised for escapees from prisoner of war camps or shot-down airmen who had managed to escape from France into Spain to reach Gibraltar. I suspect that the cafe owner may have had a small dinghy with which to row escapees to our side of the harbour. As well as Monday, there were Saturday and Sunday and the MI9 escape route was very successful. But the Germans were nevertheless able to infiltrate the organisation and send through their own agents posing as downed allied airmen. In this way, the Germans learned where the safe houses were and then shot those people who had been helping the escapees.

By chance we met one of the British airmen who had crossed the Pyrenees in winter with his mate from a bomber crew who had been shot down over Holland. They had made their way to southern France and then over the Pyrenees by the smugglers' route. One man had dislocated his ankle on landing and the injury had worsened and become gangrenous. He had received some medication from friendly doctors along the way, but had walked for three weeks on a green and painful foot. When he arrived at Gibraltar he was taken to our mess to await a plane home. He was in considerable pain. When I think back on the sacrifices made by the Dutch and French Resistances in giving help to allied air crew and escaped POWs, it seems to me that we really owe them a great debt. I know that some of their contributions have been acknowledged, but often honours are given for very minor things compared with the dangers involved in helping an airman from another country. True enough, the airmen were on the same side as the Resistance, but the lives of not only the active men and women of the Resistance were at stake: whole families could be shot. Yet throughout the war that escape route kept operating. A few years ago I read that the chief organiser of MI9, who had become a member of parliament, was assassinated by a car bomb while on his way to the House of Commons.

Another incident that confirmed the idea that life is less than fair occurred when Dick and I went for an exploratory trip in a British submarine operating out of Gibraltar into the Mediterranean. We only went for a while, but I was completely frightened the whole time, although I hope I didn't show it. Dick wandered around asking technical questions about engines and speed and horsepower. I couldn't muster any enthusiasm at all. But I really was impressed by the courage and the sheer guts of the submarine crews who went to sea time and time again. In this case it was a medium-sized sub under the command of a Lieutenant Spring-Rice. Spring-Rice was a young man of about twenty-three or twenty-four, tall, fair-haired, athletic, charming to talk to. Dick and I got on well with him and we benefitted from our stay on his submarine. He got us safely back to Gibraltar and I have never been so grateful to be on dry land. About a week later, we were flying out of Gib towards Malta and saw Spring-Rice's submarine coming back towards Gib on the surface. It was only a few miles out in a safe lane. He saw our aircraft and signalled to us on the Aldis lamp: "Good hunting, birdmen." And I thought about how much courage was involved because he himself had survived a number of attacks from aircraft. In fact, Spring-Rice did not return from his next trip: his submarine was sunk somewhere in the Med. I feel a loss, a personal loss, that that type of man had given up his life, while back home wharfies were going on strike, demanding higher wages for the task of loading munitions for our soldiers in New Guinea. And I'm afraid that whatever little interest I had in the ALP disappeared when I learnt about that. For some years after my return to civvy street, every time I read of Eddie Ward getting up in Parliament and making one of his speeches, I used to think what a loss it was that Spring-Rice had gone.

Thinking back about Spring-Rice's Aldis lamp message to us brings to mind another three-word message that I haven't forgotten in fifty-eight years. This was a message that was flashed to me by the commodore of a convoy of oil tankers in the Atlantic, making for Malta. The convoy of twenty large tankers, manned by merchant seamen, had set out from the West Indies carrying oil fuel. They would have been given a close escort until they reached "the gap" in the mid-Atlantic. The American destroyers would have turned back before the convoy reached the waiting British warships. There was no air cover possible so far out to sea. It was here that the U-boat packs would have been patrolling. They had sunk ten vessels from this convoy — half the fleet.

I can't imagine a more frightening experience than being a merchant seaman in the mid-Atlantic on a large oil tanker exposed to U-boats waiting to torpedo you. If you are hit, the vessel either catches fire immediately or you can be thrown into the sea where you suffocate on the oil that spreads out and gets into your lungs. It was a dreadful prospect. And the remaining ten vessels would have seen the other ships go down one by one in the middle of the night.

They would have seen the flames and heard the screams. But they couldn't have stopped to pick up survivors, as this would have given the U-boats stationary targets. They would have had to steam on, leaving their mates to drown or die of burns.

In this case, we left Gibraltar and were the first aircraft to give the convoy cover after the ordeal. It was early morning when we picked them up and began to cruise around looking for U-boats. The commodore of the convoy sent us a signal: "Thanks for coming." We stayed with them as long as we could and then left when another aircraft from our squadron arrived and took over. Our squadron was required to give the convoy close cover all the way through the Straits of Gibraltar and on to Malta.

Dick and I picked them up a few days after our first encounter as they were nearing Gibraltar. We flashed the captain a message: "Meet you in Gib." The tankers arrived in Gibraltar harbour at about midday and by tea time the crews were ready for shore leave. Dick and I went down to the docks and met the captain and his mate. The American ships, unlike the British ones, were completely dry. No alcohol was carried on the American vessels, so we offered the Americans dinner in our mess. It was a bit late when we arrived, but we scrounged a bit of a meal and had a few drinks. When our bar closed at ten o'clock, we loaded up with some more grog and retired to Dick's and my quarters. The four of us drank whisky and sherry until the early hours of the morning, by which time the dockyard gates were closed and locked. So the captain and his mate stayed the night, sleeping on the floor. One or two of us became sick as dawn approached, so our room was a bit of a mess in the morning, but we got up and showered and shaved. Dick and I were due to fly late that afternoon, so we took things fairly quietly, seeing our American friends off at the gates of the camp.

Later that morning, Dick and I were carpeted in front of the Wing Commander — "Uncle Case", as we referred to him. He was a regular RAF type: domineering, a pain in the neck, a bully. I never felt at ease in his presence. The war was providing Uncle Case with a big career opportunity, to achieve promotion. I thought he was a phony, that he did not have the commitment to action that the other air crews had. Years later, when trying to analyse why I couldn't get on to the same wave length as Joh Bjelke-Petersen, I found real parallels with Uncle Case. I think Joh wanted the state of Queensland to benefit from his administration, but I also think he was even more interested in the Bjelke-Petersen family benefitting from it. I don't doubt that Uncle Case wanted the Allies to win the war, but he wanted the war to effect his own advancement. He tore strips off Dick and I for the party we'd given our American friends. He was outraged that we'd left our room in such a mess that our batman had complained to the head batman who had complained to the adjutant who had complained to him. As a matter of fact, Dick and I didn't get on at all well with our batman. I suppose he thought us tight-fisted, but we refused to tip him as the English officers tipped their batmen. It didn't surprise us that he'd complained. The wing commander subjected Dick and I to his normal diatribe. We received one of these every four or five months for some misdemeanor or other. We took it in good order, but what annoyed me was that Case could so completely fail to understand the relationship, the bond, that had developed in just in a couple of Aldis messages between a convoy badly beaten up by U-boats and the first aircraft to reach them. But Dick and I felt good about our hospitality, and felt hostile towards Case. My own hostility has lasted a long time.

I always felt that the merchant marine crews never, never got the recognition that was due to them for the effort they made during the war.

5

Homecoming

(1944–1953)

IN early 1944 I had finished my second tour of duty. My squadron had been flying out of Mogadishu in Somalia, looking for U-boats in the Indian Ocean. There were a few around. The war in Europe was entering its final, land-based phase and the larger German submarines were being sent round the Cape of Good Hope and into the Indian Ocean to aid the Japanese. These were 1200 tonne vessels equipped with small gliders. The U-boat would sail into the wind on the surface, towing an observer in the glider. He could spot a likely target at a far greater distance than was possible with the U-boat's radar, which was almost at sea level.

I was war weary. I had completed my two tours of duty and was still alive, but England now had little use for Australian navigators skilled at coastal surveillance. I wanted to go home. I applied for discharge and was told to return to Australia on a thousand tonne tramp steamer that was due to sail from Aden to Fremantle. The captain welcomed me aboard and gave me his own below-decks cabin. He would use his day cabin next to the bridge. We set sail across the Indian Ocean that I had recently been patrolling from the air. I probably knew more about the U-boat menace than the captain, so I kept an eye on his course. We steamed to the south-east, away from the worst areas. The trip home was uneventful — boring, even. Every evening at sundown I would join the captain in a small gin sling. He had a limited supply, so we only drank one at a time.

I spent a frustrating fortnight in the Fremantle disembarkation centre, waiting with hundreds of others for a place on a troop train to Adelaide. But I managed to ring Mavis. By today's standards, the quality of telephone transmission over the thousand miles of wire strung alongside the East–West railway line wasn't good, but it was the first time we had heard the sound of each other's voices in almost four years. At last the train pulled out of Fremantle. It took two or three days to cross the Nullarbor Plain, stopping every now and then for meals. These were served by the side of the track, the food doled on to each man's plate. Eventually I arrived at the Keswick Barracks in Adelaide where I was given two weeks' leave. Outside the barracks I noticed a taxi discharging a couple of soldiers. As they got out, I got in. The driver said he was happy to take me back to the city where the streets were full of high-tipping American soldiers. I said I wanted to go to Plympton, all of three miles away. The driver insisted he was going nowhere but the city.

"All right," I said. "We'll go to the city watch-house, where I'll report you for failing to fulfil the obligations of your taxi driver's licence."

"Who are you?" the driver said.

"Detective Whitrod." Without further comment, the taxi driver took me home.

It was a wonderful feeling to be back. I am sure Mavis rightly had expectations that her lifestyle would now revert quickly to its happy prewar state. But, after the euphoria of the first twenty-four hours, I found myself confused, bad-tempered and depressed. After four years of male company, I could not fit into a domestic environment with two young children who did not know me and who did not carry out my orders. My father, quiet and easy going, was the significant male in the household. It was to him that my sons turned when confronted with this loud, irritable stranger. Ian didn't know me at all, and it is unlikely that Andrew retained any memories of the father he'd briefly farewelled when he was a little over a year old. I don't think my relations with my sons ever completely recovered from this early childhood separation. Later, things were quite different with my daughter, who had a father at home from the beginning.

Looking back, I don't think I had any real idea at the time of how my years in the airforce had affected me, or how my presence now affected my family. For four years I had had a batman to carry out routine domestic chores. In the officers' mess, I had eaten as much as I liked of whatever was on the menu and then got up from the table, leaving the clearing and the washing up to others. Suddenly I was expected to take some responsibility for household chores and to consult others on how I should spend my time. In my years away, I had had very little social contact with women; the squadron had been an all-male preserve wherever it operated. Now I was in a household stamped with the presence of my wife and mother.

I must have made my family miserable. During my first week at home, I would go into the city for hours and walk down the main streets just hoping to bump into a familiar RAAF face. I would return late for the family's evening meal, having drunk too much, muttering: "I'm off to bed." I must have been a great disappointment to Mavis, but her only response was to treat me with even more tender, loving care than before. Nowadays there are all sorts of diagnoses and treatments for post traumatic stress disorder, but then it was regarded as pure moodiness.

We decided that Mavis and I should go away on our own for a week on a second honeymoon to a favourite guesthouse near Mt Lofty in the Adelaide Hills. But after the first day I could no longer stand the quietness and the isolation. I was jittery and full of complaints. I pleaded with Max Dawson, my old friend from the Flinders Street scouting days, to come and join us. Max had just been discharged from the army. He was reluctant to join us, but I needed a man to talk to — someone who had gone through the same sort of experiences I had. Max had been a medical orderly in New Guinea where his unit had sometimes continued with surgical procedures while under attack, operating by the light of kerosene lamps when the generators failed. We three spent the rest of the week just tramping around the hills and talking. I gradually felt more at ease. Without the help of Mavis and Max, I could easily have gone further downhill.

I returned to the CIB and was faced with a job that now incorporated new regulations and procedures. Rationing and the blackout had been introduced while I was away. There were US troops all over town and responsibility for keeping them in order had to be shared with their military police. Although many of my old mates were still in the CIB, there were many new faces — strangers with whom I had to learn to work. I felt old and worn out, and too cynical to once again tackle departmental tasks with enthusiasm. I was given a welcome home night by my workmates. Beer was rationed, but somehow a fridge-full was found. We met in a room above a fish shop in Grote Street which had been some sort of workshop and was reached by a steep flight of stairs from a door in a side lane. The festivities were boisterous and full of horseplay: neck-ties were cut in half with scissors, the crowns of felt hats were bashed in. I'd known some pretty wild nights in the officers' mess during my service, but I found this sort of thing adolescent. I felt that in the years I'd been away I'd grown up far more than my contemporaries who'd stayed in Australia. I returned home that night in a cross mood: I'd made the mistake of wearing my best tie.

But someone in the Detective Office made a brilliant decision when they paired me with a younger officer, Ted Calder. Ted was an excellent mate with whom to work, and I gradually got back into harness. He was somewhat boisterous and a renowned practical joker, but his sense of humour ran to things that were a bit more sophisticated than tie-cutting. Ted's good humour helped to restore my own. He shared my ideals of policing, was enthusiastic, hard-working, and competent. He was well-liked and knew his way around the town — an asset I had lost during my five years' absence. I believed we were an excellent team. I began to act normally. Life at home improved. We helped my parents buy a small cottage, and they left us to ourselves. I took Kerry, our setter, for some long runs on my bicycle. I teamed up with an old workmate, Jack Vogelesang, to build a weekend shack at Encounter Bay. We bought a block of land for £40 and spent another £40 building the shack during our four weeks' annual leave. It was just one big fibro room, but it was a great place for a cheap holiday: the kids could play on the beach and there was good fishing to be had on the rocks.

Mavis and I thought we would like another child, and in November 1945 Ruth was born. With her coming I somehow managed to shake off my remaining mental trauma and became a useful parent, providing some relief to Mavis. At one stage, Ruth got sick and I can recall spending long hours beside her cot humming lullabies to get her to sleep. I began to take on the family tasks that I had found so irksome in the earlier months. Mavis's attitude to me never altered during those troublesome times; she had never failed to smile at me, and give me a warm hug.

I began to regain my old ambitions and so started part-time studies in law at university. I realised that if I was to catch up with the men who hadn't been to war, I'd need to have something extra on my record; a degree would be ideal. The government's rehabilitation scheme for ex-servicemen was quite generous. I could have studied law full time, but the living allowance would not have been as much as my policeman's salary and, now that I was back into the swing of things, I was enjoying being a detective far too much to give up the job. As it was, I became the University of Adelaide's first part-time law student. The CIB still worked its old impossible hours and so I found that getting to lectures and the library was difficult. When I was on night patrol, I often managed to duck into the Law Society's office where the library was open until late. In those days it was necessary to look up cases individually. No one had yet collected similar cases into convenient volumes. As usual, my time with the family suffered. I completed two years of part-time study, mainly at Honours level. I ran into no real resentment from my police colleagues for trying to become a university graduate. I think it was looked upon as just another example of Whitrod's eccentricity. Quite a few of my colleagues routinely got time off to play Australian Rules football, so there was a sort of precedent.

I began to agitate in the CIB for less rigorous working conditions. These demands were modest enough: six nights off a fortnight instead of the traditional four, a better pension and the like. There were now more young married men in the CIB who wanted time at home with their families, and who didn't get their fill of pleasure from attending race meetings on duty. I didn't want to risk my career prospects in the CIB by agitating too hard and was careful to take a quiet, reasonable approach; even so, Inspector Sheridan called me into his office and advised me not to become too radical. So I stood for and was elected the CIB representative on the Police Union executive. We started moves for a better pension and my union status gave me some defence. Without being a boss's man, I tried to be diplomatic. We had no success over our demands for shorter hours, but we were successful in having a form of superannuation introduced. I argued that, as many policemen lived in accommodation provided by the department, they had no house of their own when they came to retire. A lump sum payment would make it possible to buy a house. I also produced statistics to show that the average life expectancy on retirement for a policeman was only three and a half years. A lump sum payout would be very much in the interests of his dependents. I helped put our case to the government's chief secretary who, like the Premier Tom Playford, was an ex-serviceman. We got on well together. Overall, my industrial activities didn't seem to affect my standing in the branch. Everybody below the commissioner stood to benefit.

I was selected by the commissioner on the advice of the CIB chief to represent the Police Department in an important radio debate on juvenile delinquency. When we were on air, it seemed to me that the three other panelists were tackling the problem in a very general sort of way. I managed to talk about the experience of growing up poor in the inner city. I talked about going to school and selling newspapers in the city. Many juvenile delinquents, I said, came from the same background as myself. I also managed to quote some statistics that showed that catching offenders when they were young made them less likely to re-offend than if they were only caught after their life of crime was well established. A day later, a letter appeared in the *Advertiser*:

> Yesterday evening [19.05.47] at the weekly debate over Station 5KA "Adelaide Speaks", one of the four contributors was Detective Whitrod,

> the other three being Dr Constance Davey (psychologist), Mrs Amy Wheaton (University Lecturer in Social Sciences) and myself. I consider Detective Whitrod's contribution was outstanding, and was an excellent illustration, of the ability, perspicacity and wisdom of the young police officer of today, as compared with his predecessor of a generation ago. (F.G. Hicks, barrister, Adelaide)

The radio appearance was probably one of the things that brought me to the attention of certain senior members of the intelligence community. Another may have been the Chief Watchman case.

One day my mate Ted and I were called in to the Inspector's office, where we found him in the company of a prominent Adelaide barrister, Jack Alderman. Mr Alderman was the owner of a racehorse, Chief Watchman, the favourite for the Adelaide Cup which was to be run in a few days' time. He had been told by his trainer of an approach by an investor who wanted the horse nobbled. The investor would make a killing by backing the second favourite at a larger price. At the time, I was only a detective constable and Ted a plainclothes constable. Clearly this case should have been allocated to more senior members of the force. But it seemed that Mr Alderman was asking for our services because he believed we were not only competent but also trustworthy. The inspector appeared to agree with him. Only later did I realise the significance of that agreement. The barrister, who was frequently involved in criminal trials, was well-informed about the members of Adelaide's small underworld and their activities. Maybe he knew something about why some of the more senior CIB staff managed to be so well-dressed. It was a nice compliment for him to ask for us to do the job. Ted and I planned our moves with care. In those days, drugs were rarely used to slow down horses. In this case, the proposed scam involved giving the animal a large feed shortly before the race. It would have to run on a full stomach. We arranged for the trainer to ring the investor from the Glenelg Police Station. While they discussed the scam, I listened on an extension and took shorthand notes. Sophisticated phone-tapping with recording devices had not yet been developed. A search of the investor's home on the Friday morning when we arrested him netted more evidence. Then followed a long, bitterly fought Supreme Court hearing at which Ted and I were cross-examined by leading counsel at some length. The investor was wealthy and had friends in high places and had engaged the services of a top Queen's Council. I half suspected that the QC dragged out the cross-examination, not because he thought he could get his client off, but because he was being paid a handsome fee on a daily basis. Either way, corroboration between Ted and myself proved to be solid evidence. The fact that the whole telephone conversation had been taken down word for word as it happened must have carried considerable weight; I was immune from any suggestion that my memory might have been at fault. I was slightly worried that the jury might contain an investor who would be unduly sympathetic to the accused, but I knew that any small-time punter on the jury would know that it was the likes of himself who ultimately paid for any successful bit of race-fixing. The jury believed our version. The investor was convicted and imprisoned.

Details of the hearing were circulated widely by the media and followed closely by the race-going public. Ted and I received high compliments from the crown prosecutor and from our inspector. But some months later there was an unexpected development. A South Australian judge, Sir Geoffrey Reed, had been appointed the first Director General of Security. At the same time, Adelaide lawyer Bernard Tuck, who was known to have worked in army intelligence during the war, had quietly sold up his practice and left town, perhaps to become one of Reed's deputies. These gentlemen also seem to have been impressed by our performance.

One evening, out of the blue, I received a telephone call.

"I don't suppose you know who I am. My name is Bernard Tuck."

"I know who you are," I said.

"How come?"

"Your father was the minister of the West End Mission when I used to go there."

"Oh, that's right. Have you any idea why I'm ringing you?"

"Yes."

"What am I ringing you about?"

"You want some good investigators."

"How did you find that out?"

"I worked it out."

"Well, you're the only one who's done so."

I had no hesitation in joining the Australian Security and Intelligence Organisation (ASIO). The organisation's work seemed to me to be of national importance. I received a small rise in salary and access to a motor car (I had been taught to drive by my Arab bearer on the airstrip in Mogadishu, though I never undertook a test). Mavis noted my enthusiasm and unselfishly agreed to the change even though the new job meant moving to Sydney where we had no friends or relatives. I had to leave quickly, so Mavis was left with the task of selling the house, packing the furniture and bringing the family to Sydney.

A senior officer of ASIO called recently to refresh my memory of the legal restrictions on publishing material concerning my service with that organisation, so I am forced to confine myself in this narrative to personal information.

I purchased an unsuitable house on a hill at Rockdale; it was infested with a plague of fleas. We called in the fumigators a few times, but we never completely got rid of them. The hours I had to work in Sydney were awesome: ten to twelve hours a day for six and often seven days each week, and sometimes overnight. For me it was exciting work — I was in charge of a team of field investigators. But Mavis had to locate a school for the boys and a kindergarten for Ruth. She had to find shops and walk there almost daily, supervise the homework of the boys who were now on a different school curriculum and handle my outlandish hours. On one occasion when she had been awake all night with Ruth who had the measles, I tried to get time off to give her a hand but met with no cooperation from the only other person authorised to handle my classified material. Much of my time was spent on surveillance duties. Because couples were less conspicuous than two men, our teams were mixed. I spent many long boring hours in close physical proximity to my attractive ex-WRANS teammate, keeping watch at night on various houses. Luckily Moya and I were good friends, equally dedicated to our job, and there was never any suggestion of a closer relationship. Mavis never exhibited any resentment about our pairing. Jealousy is unknown in her repertoire of emotions.

Despite my inability to help with the family responsibilities, Mavis managed to keep up with family traditions such as celebrating birthdays. She walked some miles each day to and from kindergarten with small Ruth. Mavis encouraged me late at night to build a dolls' house with scrap timber because Ruth wanted one for Christmas and there were none for sale in the shops. Ruth was delighted with what Father Christmas brought her.

ASIO's Sydney headquarters were in a disused wartime brothel, Agincourt. It was an ideal building, four stories high, built of solid sandstone and surrounded on three sides by a naval dockyard. I had been given a small team of experienced investigators, mainly ex-New South Wales police, and all former servicemen with good records. We were all about the same age. I had as my deputy Leo Carter, a former F/Lt RAAF pilot, one of the state's early police cadets and a champion boxer. There were several others of the same calibre. I was fortunate. They accepted me although my knowledge of New South Wales and its personalities was almost zero. This was my first experience as a manager of a team of adults and, in retrospect, they taught me much. They were all highly motivated, intelligent, physically fit and mature. Our task was to identify and locate the chief organiser of a wartime Russian espionage net. In the year I was in Sydney we did not succeed, but the team covered a great deal of territory exploring the limited leads we were given. I was impressed with my team's contribution, so much so that I have tended ever since to use them as a model of what can be achieved. As their leader, I had the opportunity to observe other leaders in a wide range of responsibilities. It seemed to me that I needed to discard my naive assumption that people were somehow automatically slotted into positions for which they were best suited. I had to distinguish between the position and the person.

I assessed some of the leaders as capable of carrying out the tasks assigned to them and producing valid results. In such cases, the person and the position were almost identical. But there were two other categories. These were some managers in positions for which they were incompetent and produced few if any results. Then there was one manager who was in a category all by himself: by deception, he produced invalid results. For a long while these went undetected because they were unquestioned.

In my subsequent dealings with people of managerial status I gave first priority to their personality, with its individual strengths and weaknesses. In my experience there are a number of people in public life who are "square pegs in round holes". They have usually gained office through nepotism, through the political advantage their appointment gives their selectors, or merely through that old bugbear, "seniority". I suppose the other big lesson I learned in Sydney was that I must be more aware of, and responsive to, the emotional needs of staff. My South Australian Police Force and Air Force days did not prepare me for the circumstances of personal stress that one or two of my staff had to face. We believed we had very little time in which to complete our task. This placed considerable pressure on us all. And, of course, no senior member of the organisation came to my aid when the Whitrods were hard-pressed and without support in Sydney.

My performance in ASIO did not go unnoticed and, in mid-1951, I was promoted to a desk position at headquarters in Melbourne. This meant another shift to an unknown city. I went ahead and purchased another unsuitable house at Moorabbin, a new Melbourne suburb. Without demur, Mavis successfully sold our house in Sydney, packed up our furniture, and brought the family to Moorabbin without assistance from me. Luckily the new job only required usual office hours, so I came home for tea at 6.00 p.m. and was off duty most weekends. We set about normalising family life for our children. We joined the local Baptist church, which we found had no youth groups, so I formed and ran a scout troop and persuaded a workmate to form a cub pack. Andrew went to one and Ian to the other. Mavis formed and ran a guide company and I persuaded another female colleague to form a brownie pack for Ruth.

Mavis arranged for the boys to attend a secondary school and found a primary school for Ruth. With yet another new school curriculum, Mavis spent time helping the boys adjust to the different requirements of their homework. In the wintry Melbourne evenings, she knitted warm pullovers. This was a skill inherited from her thrifty mother. Our family was always well-equipped with woollen gear. We found we did not share the fundamental approach of the local Baptist fellowship and made few friends there. Mostly our friends were parents of scouts or guides, and their children often spent some time at our house.

On weekends, the Whitrods would tour Melbourne beaches, occasionally swimming or exploring the teatree fringes of the sand dunes. Mavis did her best to develop a flower garden on the swampy land I had bought, and I tried with dismal results to do the same with vegetables. With Mavis's encouragement, I built a fowlhouse for some chooks, which gave us enough fresh eggs for family breakfasts.

6

Canberra, first time

(1953–1969)

IN 1953 I was invited to apply for the job of director for the Commonwealth Investigation Service (CIS) in Canberra by ASIO's new director, Brigadier Charles Spry. He thought I might be able to facilitate greater cooperation between the two organisations. At the time there was a lot of ill-feeling between them. The post offered me an opportunity to have my own command and gave me freedom to introduce modifications and new ideas into an organisation badly run down and widely regarded as incompetent. During the war, the CIS was Australia's equivalent of MI5 and regularly exchanged information with the British and Americans. But both these countries came to regard the CIS as inefficient and unreliable. When the British began planning to use the Australian desert for nuclear weapon and missile tests, it was thought that Australia should have an enhanced security organisation. Rather than attempting to upgrade the CIS, ASIO had been formed and given the CIS's intelligence role along with all its interesting subversive activity files.

This bypassing had left bitter feelings in the gutted remains of the CIS, especially since Robert Wake, one of the CIS seniors, had abandoned them to become a top dog at ASIO. For most of the senior officers left in the CIS, this was added injury for they did not trust him. They considered Wake to have been a disloyal supplier of information to Dr Evatt when he was shadow attorney-general in the federal Parliament. Many people wondered — and some no doubt still do — how Wake came to be selected for this very important appointment in ASIO, especially since the army top brass also regarded him as having a murky past.

When I was in ASIO, I read many of the old CIS files. I concluded that the American and British envoys had been right in urging the prime minister to create another counter-intelligence body (that is, if the rumours about CIS's unreliability were correct). Rumour had it that the creation of ASIO was insisted upon by the British and Americans as the price for remaining in "The Club" and continuing to share classified information. The CIS files I read contained information of doubtful veracity by ASIO standards. Most of it had been collected by untrained fourth division clerical assistants, who were supervised by office clerks. The officers in charge of each state office also came from this background of clerical experience and often clung to wartime honorary ranks. With their restricted work record, it is understandable that their knowledge of the legal system was minimal. If these state chiefs needed legal advice, their practice was to seek help from the state offices of the Commonwealth crown solicitor. Their better staff members — and some were very good — had been poached by ASIO. Whenever any really serious inquiry was necessary, the CIS called in two seconded detective sergeants from the New South Wales police. For a number of reasons, it suited many Commonwealth departments to have this investigative service of mediocre competency available to them.

Senior Commonwealth public servants could call on the CIS for help if there were any incidents of theft or fraud by their own staff or by their clients. When these senior bureaucrats eventually received a report, they could decide for themselves what they would do about it. If they had initially notified the police, they would have lost control over the result of the investigation. A decision to prosecute might have been taken even though the bureaucrats thought inaction to be a more appropriate response. The lack of skilled investigation by the CIS was held to be secondary to the possibility of downplaying a report if it reflected adversely on departmental management. As well as the CIS, many Commonwealth departments, such as Customs, the Postmaster General's Department and Supply, had their own internal inquiry units. These were again staffed by fourth division employees and supervised by untrained clerks. There was little coordination among them, and it was only if things proved difficult that they would seek assistance from the state police.

There were a number of factors operating against my being able to improve the efficiency and reputation of the CIS. I could not arrange the wholesale dismissal of permanent public servants merely because they did not measure up to my standards and I could not replace their supervisors for the same reason. The CIS had no independent mandate that would enable me to act on my own initiative; we had to wait until it suited another department to utilise our services. Life at the CIS proved to be challenging, exhausting and, too seldom, rewarding. In the postwar years, the Commonwealth was expanding into new fields and territories and I didn't relish the passive, waiting-to-be-called approach. I thought that there ought to be immediate opportunities for the CIS to develop as an independent investigative body.

It took me a little time to recognise the motivations and the power of those permanent heads of department known as the Seven Gnomes. These bureaucrats ruled their separate and independent Australia-wide fiefdoms from Canberra. They had become well-ensconced during the war, met regularly for lunch and knew far more about their departments than their parliamentary bosses ever did. They guarded their domains fiercely and resisted any other empire building, especially by a young branch head from outside the service.

I needed to do some thinking and there was a scarcity of sympathetic counsellors with whom to discuss my ideas. I was not a member of the Royal Canberra Golf Club, nor did I play bowls at the Forrest greens. I was not yet a member of the Commonwealth Club where interdepartmental matters were resolved over long lunches by the key players. I had no Melbourne or Sydney school ties with useful contacts. I had no tertiary qualifications. I attended a small non-conformist chapel and not St John's or the Manuka Catholic Cathedral. I was not even a Rotarian. My highest police rank had been detective constable. My RAAF experience was irrelevant because most senior Canberrans had spent the war in Essential Services far from danger, and clearly considered those who fought to have been naive.

Every Commonwealth public service officer was aware that the CIS had been rejected for its incompetency, and as a consequence they regarded me not as a saviour but as an undertaker. I was now a branch head in the Attorney-General's Department which was itself run by a long-time academic lawyer, Professor Ken Bailey. He and I got on well together but, like all lawyers, he preferred the status quo, always sought a precedent for any of his decisions and preferred caution to courage. He selected a financial support section which reflected just those attitudes. This meant that any proposals of mine for extending activities or increasing expenditure automatically faced a barrier of firm opposition. I had to base such proposals on specific ministerial or Cabinet directives and so relieve the department of any responsibility. I noted that branch heads in other departments operated in a much more financially relaxed climate, especially those who were able to offset costs by some form of revenue raising. I never once exceeded my budget allocation, a rare achievement in Canberra where some departments and branches deliberately exceed theirs to justify an increase in the following year.

We nicknamed the assistant secretary (Administration) "Negative Neil" because of his automatic rejections or long deferrals of approval. Bailey always insisted upon the assistant secretary's consent before he would himself sign as head of the department. Those of my recommendations which did survive this frustrating procedure had to wait many months before they could be implemented. This problem arose partly because I had no lobby group in the community to back me up by pressuring the federal government or individual members of it to endorse my moves. Nobody really cared what happened to the CIS or its uniformed section, the Peace Officer Guard (POG), and any proposals of mine were suspect if they were likely to intrude upon anyone else's territory.

The leadership of the POG Association was unable to share my vision of a national law enforcement organisation which included its members — they were so demoralised; such a future appeared to be a fantasy land to them. I understood their response. The POG was created by the then attorney-general, Billy Hughes, in 1917. Hughes had failed to persuade the Queensland police to arrest some demonstrators at Warwick Station. In frustration he formed a small Commonwealth police force to enforce federal laws, but had called them peace officers rather than police officers in an attempt to placate the states. The POG was given the same powers to arrest and detain as the ordinary police of whatever state they happened to be in. Towards the end of the war there were about five-thousand POG officers throughout Australia. They were almost completely untrained and were looked down upon by their state colleagues. The POG was also treated as second class by its own supervisors. And those supervisors were still in place in the CIS.

The CIS investigators didn't hold a much higher opinion of my vision of an efficient national police force. Their industrial representation was provided by a central union which covered all fourth division employees of the Commonwealth Public Service, a huge category which included everyone employed by the Commonwealth who hadn't matriculated. The union was reluctant to support moves which might be to the detriment of its other members in the various departments and agencies. I felt very much alone in seeking to introduce major changes in such a hostile environment — an environment strange to me politically and geographically. If I had been over forty years of age instead of under, I doubt that I would have persevered when I realised the odds against my success.

But things changed, and the first change was probably the result of the prime minister's wife's insistence that her husband be provided with adequate protection from cranks and other would-be assassins. Mr Menzies had already received death threats. The leader of the opposition, Arthur Calwell, had been shot at. Many of the postwar migrants to Australia came from cultures with a rich history of political assassination. When in England, Mrs Menzies had been impressed by the 24-hour-a-day escort provided by Scotland Yard. Unable to persuade the prime minister to ask for greater protection in Australia, Mrs Menzies went to the president of the Senate. The president instructed me to make the necessary arrangements despite the expected lack of cooperation from the prime minister. I really wasn't prepared for this assignment, but I accepted it and started to look for a suitable bodyguard.

I was not very impressed with the calibre of my outdoor CIS staff. I finally decided on a comparatively new member of the POG. This was Howard Farnsworth, a retired detective sergeant from an English county force who well understood the nuances and significance of such escort duties. Howard's authorised but discreet presence in the outer office of the prime minister at Parliament House, especially when the prime minister indulged in quiet whiskies late at night with his cronies, began our crawl back to respectability. Howard handled visitors to the prime minister with respect while at the same time thoroughly checking their credentials. He never stepped out of line and proved to be a useful adjunct to the prime minister's staff. Somehow he managed to remain on-side with the journalists. Slowly, Menzies began to accept the new level of cover.

A second step towards recovering the CIS reputation was the royal tour of 1954. Some preliminary Commonwealth planning occurred under the chairmanship of Alan Brown, one of the Gnomes and head of the Prime Minister's Department. In these early plans, the CIS was given a very minor role. Then I arranged to be appointed to the committee as security adviser. This was a new development in Canberra thinking and required some diplomatic approaches. I used the Farnsworth arrangement with the prime minister, and my police and ASIO qualifications to justify it. I ensured that, in the new handbook for circulation to all state governments, it was noted clearly that the Queen and the Duke were Commonwealth guests. This had not been made obvious in earlier documents. The direct implication was that the Australian government had the overriding responsibility for the success of the tour, and this included the physical well-being of our guests. In the preliminary plans it had been left largely to the states to make protective arrangements, but now I travelled with the Commonwealth committee members to all states "to coordinate arrangements between the Commonwealth authorities and the states".

The state police forces were upset, but my plan had the backing of the Commonwealth. It was helpful that the Commonwealth, amongst other things, was providing all royal tour transport: the aircraft, cars, vessels and communication. Arrangements for the large party of overseas press travelling with the royals were also a Commonwealth task. Still, the states resisted this encroachment on their traditional responsibilities and it took some delicate balancing over a number of royal tours for me to be accepted as the principal adviser. I took a fair battering from the state officers in the meantime, for police are touchy about trespassers in their patch. One of my most profitable moves was to appoint one of my inspectors as a liaison officer with the overseas press. I noted that the palace kept a close eye on articles in the British and other overseas papers, and amongst themselves would mention any that were favourable or critical. I kept close company with the senior household staff, and got on well with them. I gained the impression that the royals, too, were interested in the home press.

This liaison arrangement had not occurred elsewhere. The inspector tactfully made access for the overseas journalists much easier, and speeded their movements through crowded venues. The tone of the articles in the British press became more favourable, both to the royals and to Australia generally. The household gave us credit for this and later the inspector and I were presented with pewter tankards by the overseas press "in recognition of our assistance". This was apparently a reversal of their treatment by police elsewhere. The palace let it be known that they approved of my innovation.

I accepted personal responsibility for the safety of the royals and went everywhere with them. Prince Philip would frequently dash off on some unofficial activity if he had free time, often accompanied only by his private secretary, his personal detective and me. The Prince discovered that I shared his interest in wading birds, and whenever an opportunity presented itself, he would get me to drive him to some isolated spot to photograph Australian migratory waders. On one occasion his equerry rang me at a Perth hotel at midnight asking me to pick up Prince Philip at 5.00 a.m. for three hours' birdwatching. I did not know Perth. I rang the secretary of the state Ornithological Society, who was unknown to me and then in bed, and had trouble convincing him that I was not making a hoax call. I accepted his advice to go to Pelican Point some miles up the river, arranged for a car to call for me at 1.00 a.m., found my way to this destination, made a quick security check, returned to my hotel, had a shave, picked up the Prince and took him to Pelican Point where he had to wait for thirty minutes for the tide to turn.

We got back to the royal yacht *Britannia* at 8.00 a.m. where the prince quickly breakfasted and changed and at 9.30 was present at the official farewells. When my turn came, the Queen thanked me and said in jest "Don't keep my husband out so late!" In turn the prince presented me with a copy of his book on *Birds of the Antarctic* inscribed "To Ray Whitrod with many thanks P.P." The use of my first name warmed my heart for it was an indication of our unusual relationship. When in the company of others he always used the formal surname only, calling me "Whitrod" — the English public school form of address. I liked Prince Philip a lot. He could tell flattery a mile off and was often quite short with local dignitaries who were putting on airs and graces because they were entertaining royalty and their neighbours weren't. When the royal couple's eldest son, the Prince of Wales, was sent to Timbertops in Victoria to complete his secondary education, the Victorian Chief Commissioner naturally assumed that he would be responsible for the young prince's security. I queried this with the Prime Minister's Department who cabled the palace. The reply merely said: "We would prefer Whitrod's man."

Another opportunity to expand the CIS came when a replacement was needed for the New South Wales seconded police officer on Norfolk Island. I proposed that I should send one of my own officers, since Norfolk Island was not a state responsibility and operated under a Commonwealth administrator. There was the usual waffle, but my offer was accepted by the Prime Minister's Department. There must now be over thirty such Commonwealth officers on duty at overseas posts.

My plan to transform the CIS was to give it a vision of itself as a possible national police force. Such an idea had been debated at the pre-Federation conferences in the late nineteenth century, but Kingston had said that it was too early to raise that proposal and it had been shelved. Now there was an expanding number of Commonwealth activities that required some law enforcement protection. The forging of Australian currency emerged from time to time as a national threat. There was no coordination of investigations nor accumulation of expertise except for an individual officer of the Royal Mint who gave it part-time attention. The invention of photo-reproduction techniques was changing the whole nature of counterfeiting at the time: the would-be forger no longer had to be a skilled engraver. I approached the Mint and they agreed to have one of my officers stationed with them to specialise in this area. The smuggling of gold was also a problem: there was considerable money to be made by illegally shipping gold to countries whose paper money was of dubious value. Subsequently this led us into a number of important investigations, some of which involved trips to Ceylon and India, and established our international connections.

A further opportunity for expansion occurred when the chief engineer of the Snowy Mountains Hydro-Electrical Authority (SMA), Sir William Hudson, discussed with me the gambling, hard drinking and minor troublesome behaviour in the single men's quarters in the construction camps in the high country. Many of the SMA employees were skilled migrants from northern and southern Europe, so there were also occasional ethnic clashes. The nearest state police were at Cooma, quite a distance away from the construction camps. In winter, the intervening roads were sometimes impassable.

Sir William thought that a continuous uniformed police presence was required to maintain orderly conditions. He asked for our help. I had got to know some of the SMA staff on the occasions when our scout troop spent Easter hiking in their territory. The SMA officers appreciated my scouts' disciplined behaviour and their care for the environment. And since we were well able to look after ourselves in tough conditions, we weren't seen as potential search and rescue customers, unlike some other tourists. The regional managers often went out of their way to offer us little privileges like a free hot evening meal in their canteens after a day's strenuous climbing around cold Island Bend.

I suggested to Sir William that we form an SMA patrol of about twenty men to be employed by the authority, but sworn in as Special Peace Officers, which would give them state constabulary powers. They could be commanded by one of my experienced inspectors, whom I would second to the SMA. We would train them and give any backup support they needed. This plan was accepted, but it was always a ticklish job since the officers were operating in strictly New South Wales police territory, in some cases making use of state legislation to keep control. However, by and large, this arrangement worked to everybody's satisfaction for many years and I think it likely that Sir William would have conveyed that assessment to the prime minister, Robert Menzies, who was personally interested in the progress of the Snowy scheme.

So far all of my ventures at improving the reputation of the CIS and its associated lowly Peace Officer Guard had prospered. I tried one more idea — I introduced guard dogs to improve the efficiency of the POG at the Weapons Research Establishment near Adelaide and in other classified areas. We had large numbers of Peace Officer Guards on duty at these establishments, but often the officers had little to do except guard buildings and their classified contents. I thought we could do these jobs just as well, if not better, by using fewer men paired with trained dogs.

We decided to use German Shepherds, but because of a wartime restriction on the import of new bloodlines, the dogs of this breed in Australia were developing problems. I got Cabinet approval to import a pregnant bitch which was donated by the New Zealand police who used German Shepherds extensively. We began a systematic breeding and training program along New Zealand lines, and soon had the German Shepherds on regular duty in New South Wales, Victoria and South Australia (although not at Woomera because of landholders' opposition). In one instance, one of our tracker dogs and his handler were able to assist the New South Wales police in apprehending a much-wanted prison escapee who had been hiding for some weeks in rough bushland in the Blue Mountains.

We had less success with Mrs Menzies. She didn't like the dog we brought in to guard the prime minister. In those days, the Lodge's gardens were surrounded by a simple hedge. On two sides, the hedge was surrounded by fields. A man patrolling the grounds on foot could easily miss an intruder hiding in the bushes, but a trained German Shepherd dog would soon sniff him out. I had some difficulty persuading Mrs Menzies that, since the dog was on a lead at all times, it would pose no threat to her cat. She wasn't convinced, but I pointed out that we already patrolled the governor general's extensive grounds with a dog and had had no complaints. She reluctantly allowed the dog and its handler into her garden. Within a week, her cat was missing. I was immediately sent for.

"The dog's eaten my cat," Mrs Menzies told me.

I said I thought this was unlikely, but that I would make all possible inquiries. I told one of my sergeants to take six men and door-knock the surrounding area and also to check with the National Capital Development Commission to see if a dead or missing cat had been picked up close to the Lodge. These enquiries drew a blank. Three days later, I received a phone call from the POG man at the Lodge's gate.

"Director, we've found the cat."

"Good on you. How is it?"

"Dead."

"Where was it?"

"Behind some bushes, just outside the grounds."

"What did it die of?"

"Don't know, but there are teeth marks in its stomach."

"Don't tell Mrs Menzies. Take it to the nearest vet and get an autopsy."

The nearest veterinarian was a chap called McKay in Arthur Circle. My man took the cat to him, but wasn't able to get an autopsy done until the next day. I rang McKay myself around midday. The cat, he said, had died of natural causes — there had been something wrong with its liver.

"And the holes in its stomach?" I said.

"Maggots," the vet said.

"And you'll certify that the cat died of natural causes?"

"Certainly."

I drove to Arthur Circle, picked up the signed cause-of-death statement and drove straight to the Lodge.

"Your cat's dead," I told Mrs Menzies.

"I knew it," she said. "Your dog's eaten it."

"Mr McKay has certified that it died of natural causes."

"McKay! He's a butcher. I wouldn't believe a word he says."

I backed out with as much dignity as I could muster. Up to that point I had achieved good standing with the prime minister's wife, but no longer. Mrs Menzies had considerable influence with her husband and I was concerned at this development, but I don't think I needed to worry. I only spoke to the prime minister occasionally and, as far as I know, we got on well. I was an admirer of his contribution to our country's well-being. Luckily he was in turn a great admirer of the royals and I was made aware that on several occasions Prince Philip had said some nice things about me. It took some time to re-establish friendly relations with Mrs Menzies and we never patrolled the Lodge's grounds with a dog again.

Fortuitously, I experienced further progress towards making peace with the Gnomes. One of them, Sir John Crawford, and his wife lived near us and their only child, Janet, joined my wife's guide company at Manuka. We met infrequently but I think that Sir John and his wife were grateful for the encouragement and fun that their daughter received. Sir John was a former scout and appreciated my contribution. Later, when I left for New Guinea, he presented me with two valuable reference books after I had told him of my ignorance of the territory. One was by Charles Rowley, whom I then got to know personally and found most helpful. Sir John was also aware of my academic studies and I hope that at their lunch meetings he would have passed on to the other Gnomes his assessment that I was not just another rednecked copper.

Since I was stuck with the main body of CIS personnel, people I regarded as mediocre investigators, I sought to give them better leadership. Whenever a vacancy occurred through the retirement of one of my deputies in a state office, I managed to persuade the Commonwealth Public Service Inspector to let me fill it with an outside appointee, usually a competent, well-respected state detective inspector or sergeant. This meant that in most cases I could then rely upon both official and unofficial cooperation from the state forces. As well, I used an earlier friendship with the commissioner of the Tasmanian Police, Bill Delderfield, himself a former South Australian police inspector, to receive an invitation to address the Annual Police Commissioners' Conference of Australasia, which that year was meeting in Hobart. Although I attended only one session, and this as a guest, the invitation was nevertheless a big jump in acceptance by the state commissioners. Since Bill Delderfield was the host, as the chairman of that year, he could issue such invitations. There had been one or two special guests in the past but mainly for some specific purpose. The Commonwealth had never participated before. My speech about Commonwealth aspects of law enforcement — which I was careful to keep non-threatening to the sectional interests of my audience — was well received, so I gained an invitation to give a similar address (I made it a report) the following year in Wellington. There were social activities involved at these gatherings which gave me a chance to assure the state officers that I did not constitute a threat to their areas of responsibility. I offered to ease any difficulties that they might encounter in dealing with Commonwealth agencies — some of which were a little uncooperative with members of state police forces.

I later became a full member of the annual conference and attended twenty-three in all, missing only one when I was overseas. I soon noted that most of the formal work of the conference had been completed beforehand by the departmental secretaries and, in the main, reports were minimal and proposals undisturbing — all that was needed from the delegates was endorsement. The main benefit was the yearly socialising of the heads of the forces and the consequent reinforcement of friendships. At least that was the *modus operandi* of those commissioners who had risen up through the ranks. With the appointment of Brigadier McKinna in Adelaide, General

Porter in Melbourne and myself as head of the Commonwealth force, two factions developed among the conference participants. The three of us were interested in introducing businesslike management practices into our forces. The other commissioners were very much in favour of the status quo. They had risen through the ranks and were now comfortably positioned. The world was their oyster, so why change it? Why indeed when, in some cases, the world was supplying an income considerably greater than that normally earned by the head of a police force? At the time I had little understanding of how entrenched corruption was in the eastern states and I don't think McKinna or Porter were any better informed. Nevertheless, Porter and McKinna were more skilled at conferencing than the other commissioners; they personally did their homework and knew their subjects better than the old brigade. They were both experienced commanders from the war and had held managerial jobs in civvy street. Their perspectives and values were strange to the others. They presented their arguments forcibly and eloquently with no kowtowing to long years of law enforcement as a main argument. Formerly, it had been New South Wales with its large numbers that was seen as the unofficial leader — a position which its representative happily accepted and expected. This started to change.

Once McKinna and Porter had joined the conference, I found that I was no longer the lonely expositor of change, forced to couch my proposals in the humblest of terms in order to get a hearing. I had a number of national propositions which I now thought might be approved with the backing of these two former senior army officers. I was keen to have a national statistics unit to collect, collate and analyse crime trends in this country. This suggestion was taken by some state police commissioners as a way of unnecessarily providing their critics with data on which adverse comments could be made.

It was well known in police circles that an informal system of recording offences, traditionally called "in Paddy's Book", was current in the eastern states, and maybe elsewhere. This procedure required the initial report of an offence to be entered into an unofficial pocketbook. If there was a successful result, such as an arrest or the recovery of property, the details would then be transferred to an official form. This enabled the manipulation of relevant figures to produce commendable police clearup rates in annual reports. I was keen to do away with Paddy's Book. There was considerable opposition to my idea. But South Australia and Victoria were forceful supporters. I first raised this proposal in 1961, but it was not until two years later that the conference gave me the responsibility of organising and chairing a committee, comprising representatives from the state forces and the Bureau of Statistics, to implement the concept. It is interesting to note that the response of the Australian Bureau of Statistics was only lukewarm, but I talked to the deputy chief statistician who I knew through hockey and he agreed to have one of his staff serve on the small national committee I was forming.

I feel sure my limited knowledge of statistics, gained during the six years I spent studying part-time at the ANU for an Economics degree, helped me overcome some resistance because the participants of the annual conference (and their departmental advisers) knew even less. Nevertheless, I had to make compromises and the program which eventually received approval from the conference was a modified version of my original proposal. There were lots of teething troubles, particularly when we were considering what offences to include, how offences were to be defined and what criteria were to be used to determine the clear-up rate. We distributed a small book containing the guidelines to be followed in obtaining and compiling the data. Problems continued, but with tact and perseverance the Uniform Crime Statistics program got under way.

In the area of Uniform Crime Statistics, Australia lagged behind Europe, and the extent of our proposed coverage was still small compared to Canada. My committee recommended that the scheme initially cover only seven major offences — homicide; serious assault; robbery; rape; break and enter; fraud and motorcar theft — and we were interested to discover that the United States had also selected those categories. For a number of years, beginning in 1966, the Bureau of Statistics published in its *Commonwealth Year*

Book the limited but still useful data collected by our program. I understand that, in later years, the procedure was modified, allegedly because of its inadequacies. I remain convinced that in achieving this initial agreement, substantial progress was made in publicly providing reasonably valid information on the crime situation. Later, when I moved to Queensland, I managed to reduce opportunities to fake crime returns in the metropolitan area by arranging for all incoming telephone complaints of offences to be centrally recorded on tape. Each complaint was allocated a number which was then used on the actual crime reports. In addition, I made it possible for patrol officers to dictate by telephone to stenographers at the Operations Room details of offences detected by or reported to them by members of the community. I arranged for an independent auditor from the New South Wales Office of Crime Statistics to visit Queensland for a week each year to examine our procedures and audit our returns. My annual report to Queensland Parliament therefore carried the signatures of a financial and an operational auditor. During the seven years I was Commissioner of the Queensland Police Force, the figures showed a small improvement each year, although we still remained within the main range of British-type police clearance rates. The auditing procedure was abolished when my successor, Terence Lewis, took over. His first annual return showed that Queensland had made a dramatic leap to a high clearance rate. No one questioned this increase.

As far as I am aware, no other Australian Police Force has emulated my action, nor has there been any attempt to extend the Australian Bureau of Statistics' Victim Surveys to discover if offences reported by victims are actually recorded in the police database. All we know is that there is a big discrepancy between the number of offences experienced by victims and the number recorded by the police. There has been some research into the reasons why victims do not report crimes to the police, but there is no research that I am aware of that seeks to correlate victims' actual reports to police with subsequent police records.

When I proposed the gathering of Uniform Crime Statistics at the Police Commissioners' Conference, the low level of debate clearly indicated that both the commissioners and their advisers, the departmental secretaries, were ill-informed about possible challenges to law and order in the coming years. They were unable to assess which ways of meeting these challenges were best. I had some discussions with General Porter and Brigadier McKinna about how to improve on this situation. We agreed that there was little point in attempting to offer education to the present office-holders, but that there was merit in working on their probable successors. Victoria withdrew from further discussions because Porter was already doing something about it in his force, but he indicated that he would support our proposals. So South Australia and the Commonwealth recommended that there should be a Senior Police Executive Workshop, lasting for four weeks. The workshop would cater for representatives from each state or territory, chosen because they would probably become the next commissioners. McKinna and I were to organise the workshop. The first two weeks would be in Canberra, where participants would listen to such experts as we could muster and discuss with them the coming challenges to law and order. Then there would be one week in Melbourne, looking at what Victoria was already doing, followed by a week in South Australia to examine McKinna's plans. The conference endorsed the proposal, and planning for the workshop commenced.

I was able to select a panel of experts from the Australian National University whom I knew personally. From listening to lectures during my own courses I knew who could give talks providing the latest advice on their topics to these senior police in a style which would not be boring. I recruited Mick Borrie, George Zubrzycki and Des O'Connor. I put these academics "into the picture" with regard to the purpose of the workshop and was pleased with their response.

They set out on what I now know to be an unwinnable task: to interest these pragmatic deputy police chiefs in an intellectual task: thinking about the future. In retrospect, I realise that the attitude of the deputies was justified and that I was too optimistic. The New South Wales representative was Fred Hanson, who became the next New South Wales police commissioner. Try as my academic friends would to interest him, he sat most of the time looking out of the window. He was not the only one — Athol Wedd from Western Australia was similarly uninterested in the proceedings, and there were various others. They had their own priorities, and these were not affected in any way by this attempt to intellectualise the police forces of Australia. In those days, commissionership of a state force offered rich pickings, with little or no possibility of any illegalities being discovered. However, the workshop provided many opportunities for socialising out of hours.

Another strategy I used was the provision of better and longer training for my recruits and the organisation of national workshops to which state officers were invited. I argued for the need for our own permanent school and, with some diligent hunting around, located the vacant quarantine barracks at North Head in Sydney and received Cabinet approval to occupy the site. It was an ancient collection of wooden huts, but with some scheming we managed to make it usable. The school was opened on 10 April 1959, and it fitted in nicely with my vision of creating a Commonwealth Police Force. This had officially come into being in 1957 when assent was finally given by federal Parliament to my draft bill. For several reasons, this act was not proclaimed until April 1960 when I was appointed the new force's first commissioner.

In just four years, my original plan to transform the discredited CIS and POG into a national law enforcement organisation had made useful progress. I had laboured long over the draft legislation before submitting it for departmental approval. I had backed it with convincing factual detail. I had confided in, and won the support of, significant Gnomes or their principal advisers in an effort to minimise opposition from those federal ministers whose territory might be encroached upon. I had gently explained to senior state police that I was not setting out to create an American-type FBI and had showed them those sections of my draft bill which restricted our activities to purely Commonwealth interests. In this way I hoped to reduce resistance from backbenchers in the federal Parliament who were vulnerable to state lobbying. I am not sure how much success I achieved. Certainly, when the bill was being debated in federal Parliament, all government members supported it, so that it passed with a large majority. But that support may have been due to the discipline of the government's whip. Since I kept well clear of politicians, I did not pick up any suggestions of concern from government members.

On the other hand, the well-known radicals in the opposition, who were probably still smarting from the outcome of the Royal Commission on Espionage, set out to strongly attack the proposed "creation of a national police force". They may well have done this purely from Australian Labor Party principles, although socialist philosophies elsewhere favoured a strong, central law enforcement body. My recollection is that the prominent ALP parliamentarians — Evatt, Ward, Cameron and Haylen — were well-briefed on comments by the director of the American FBI, J. Edgar Hoover. Now discredited in the United States, Hoover had not wanted a national police force in his country, since it would have challenged his own empire. As well, the ALP spokesmen were able to correctly describe members of the CIS and POG as not conforming to the standards of state police in physique and training. Much of this detail came from another ALP member, Jim Fraser, who represented the Australian Capital Territory. My suspicion is that Fraser, in turn, was provided with this information by members of the ACT Police Force, who saw themselves as liable to being swallowed up by the proposed new force. With hindsight, it is possible to understand the alarm with which corrupt state police forces and their political allies would have viewed the creation of a national force. At the time, the state forces were the final arbiters of investigation. In Queensland and New South Wales, the top politicians would not have seen a problem in the head of the homicide branch being bent. The head of a homicide branch is a key man in state corruption as he is able to cover up the tracks of underworld, or police, executions. We now know that in the eastern states some informers who were prepared to give evidence about drug traffickers and their connections to the police simply disappeared. I had little understanding then of how some underworld groups might have influenced the policies of political parties.

Mr Eddie Ward, the member for East Sydney, made a strong onslaught on my proposed appointment as the first Commonwealth commissioner, claiming I had already displayed vindictiveness towards Labor, was bitterly opposed to Labor policies and that I was poorly qualified to be given this appointment. Someone, probably also Sydney-based, had fed Ward this material for he was able to go on and announce that I had acquired land at North Head to establish a training centre, and that I had been going through the state police services picking out the best officers and offering them higher salaries. Interestingly, during my years with the CIS and the CPF, I came across traces of association between Sydney CIS staff and key ALP figures. The minister defended me, saying that I had served the state and Commonwealth governments well, and I was now being slandered and defamed. The minister went on to explain again that the new force was concerned only with applying Commonwealth legislation and protecting Commonwealth property. It was not "the secret police" referred to by the opposition.

The bill was not as all-embracing in its provisions as I would have liked. I kept it as simple and minimal as possible. I had thought about introducing some legislation that would help me overcome problems of corruption but, even in those days, I realised that this might provoke further opposition. I decided to rely upon the lesson I had learnt in ASIO — if I could stimulate my staff to grasp a big enough vision of the important challenges embodied in their appointment, if I could secure their full commitment to achieving that vision, and if I could obtain satisfactory working conditions, the staff might stave off the temptations which were bound to develop.

I remembered that Chief Kelley had managed to achieve a transformation of the Kansas City Force when he was appointed after the exposure of the notorious Prendergast municipal machine, and I realised, too, that it had taken him twelve years to accomplish that transformation. Kelley had then gone on to replace the dubious J. Edgar Hoover as head of the FBI. Over the years, the field staff of the FBI had rightly earned a reputation for being incorruptible. It seemed to me that this was partly due to the prestige of their office, and I wondered how I could raise our reputation, both locally and internationally. Each year the English Home Office awarded the Queen's Gold Medal to the author of the best article on a police topic which the Home Office selected. It was open to serving officers of the United Kingdom and the Commonwealth. In international police circles, it was regarded as an accolade of standing. I submitted a paper with a *nom de plume*, and was delighted to be informed I had won. As far as I know, this was the first time the medal had gone to an Australian policeman. I was presented at Government House with the inscribed medal by the governor general, then Lord Casey. He entertained me to tea and was interested both in my paper and in my plans for a Commonwealth Police Force. I left that meeting feeling that I had recruited a supporter, and a powerful one at that. My paper was then published in the English *Police Journal* which has a worldwide circulation, and I hoped that this success might contribute to our recognition by other police and associated academics as a modern police force.

The bill had one interesting innovation for a *Police Act*. It empowered me to recruit at any level. Traditionally state police could only offer recruits appointments at constable level. I needed desperately to bolster my head office staff with officers who had sufficient intelligence to handle some of the new challenges which would face the force.

It was because of this new provision that I was able to recruit Kerry Milte at superintendent level. Professor Stanley Johnson, then head of Melbourne University's Criminology Unit, recommended Milte who had topped his examinations for a law degree and had then impressed Johnson with the outcome of his postgraduate year in criminology. Milte was tall and well-built and, at the time, aged only about 23 years. He had been raised in the disciplined environment of a Melbourne Fire Brigade station.

Recruiting someone so young at superintendent level raised eyebrows and some opposition, which I overcame. It was only by offering Milte a superintendent's salary that I could match the money he was being offered by several big law firms. I did not explain to all and sundry that I wanted someone to create a central crime intelligence unit since there wasn't one nationally or in the states. There was an obvious need for one and Canberra was well-placed to provide a home for it. There was no model for us to use, so I initially set Milte to working on an elementary intelligence section for our own use. Milte proved to be a good choice, although he and my deputy, Jack Davis, a former New South Wales Fraud Squad member with an Honours degree in law, did not hit it off. I think this was purely a clash of personalities, combined maybe with a little jealousy. After I resigned to go elsewhere, Milte also left and went into private practice. Then I heard he had become associated with Senator Lionel Murphy who became federal attorney-general in the Whitlam government. I have little doubt that Milte was the architect of Murphy's notorious raid on ASIO headquarters in Melbourne in search of concealed files about terrorists.

In 1962, with approval from the Commissioners' Conference, we were able to introduce a Commissioned Officers' Course at Manly to which, each year, all states except Victoria would send about two students. I was very careful in selecting staff for the course. The course went well and, as far as I know, continues on in some form today. At the 1966 Commissioners' Conference, approval was obtained for a sub-committee to be established to investigate the setting up of a National Police Planning and Research Unit, but we made slow progress for a few years until, in 1969, I was appointed chairman of a committee of representatives from the Commonwealth, Victorian, Queensland and New South Wales forces. We met on a number of occasions in Canberra, and this time Inspector Barlow of the Queensland force gave me considerable support for the concept. The sub-committee agreed that the research unit's main objectives should be to examine present police practices and procedures in order to provide recommendations on how to increase efficiency and plan for development. We decided that the basic costs should be shared by the Commonwealth and the states, and that each force should provide a liaison officer to cooperate with the unit. We felt it was important not to duplicate or conflict with the National Institute of Criminology. These arrangements were subsequently implemented.

One of the people remaining in my memory from those early

Canberra days is the governor general, Sir William Slim. I met him quite a few times and I was most impressed with the man. Slim dealt personally with letters from ordinary Australians that had been written to him as representative of the Queen. Apparently this is an old English custom: when all legal avenues have been exhausted, a citizen may appeal directly to the monarch. In Australia, this means the governor general. Slim read every letter that was sent to him, although his secretary, Murray Tyrrell, would already have dealt with most of them. Many of these appeals to the governor general were made by people who were mentally deranged, and it was often obvious that there would be no point investigating their claims. However, Slim was adamant that before a letter was consigned to file, it was necessary to be convinced that there was no merit in the appeal. So the governor general arranged for any appeals which looked as if they had substance to be sent to me as director of the Commonwealth Investigation Service. As a result of our field inquiries, it became evident that there were some people in the Australian community who would be possible threats to the safety of the Queen when she was in Australia or to the governor general himself. On one occasion, our officers on the gate at Government House intercepted a man who had driven up from Sydney to demand an audience with the governor general. When the guard commander asked the man what time his appointment was, the man indicated that he didn't need to make an appointment: he was in Canberra to bring the governor general to account. The guards talked to the man quietly and asked him into their office to sit down while they made the necessary arrangements. While they had the man preoccupied, a guard made a surreptitious examination of his car and discovered a loaded rifle and spare rounds of ammunition. The man was taken to see two Commonwealth doctors who certified him as temporarily insane and committed him to Kenmore psychiatric hospital in Sydney. There he soon recovered and was released.

A year later the man again arrived at the Government House gate. Luckily the same guard commander was on duty at the time and he immediately identified the man. Again the man was found to be carrying a rifle and ammunition. He was recommitted to Kenmore where he soon made a full recovery and was released. Our inquiries revealed that the man was a marine engineer whose vessel docked once a year in Sydney. Here the man hired a car, bought a rifle and set off to Canberra because he was convinced that the governor general was not doing a proper job.

It was the existence of people such as the marine engineer who gave us the idea of producing a small loose-leafed photo album carrying pictures and details of people who posed a threat to prominent Australians or visiting overseas VIPs. This *Black Book*, as it became known, was invaluable during royal visits and during such high-security exercises as the visit of the American president, Lyndon Johnson. Johnson was the first American president to visit Australia and I remember driving with him in a car with an open roof from the centre of Canberra to Government House. We arrived at a large intersection where a crowd of people were waiting. So thick was the crowd that the car slowed and Johnson, who was a consummate politician, ordered the driver to stop. He stood up and spoke to the people. I noticed a face in the crowd that belonged to one of people depicted in the *Black Book*. He was the author of a number of very threatening letters which detailed what he would do to visiting VIPs. The man was moving towards Johnson. I tried to get out of the car, but the crowd was so thick that the front door was jammed shut. I tried to get Johnson to sit down, but he wasn't paying any attention to me — he was enjoying the adulation of the crowd. I saw the man from the *Black Book* reach up to Johnson, shake him by the hand and say, "Welcome to Australia, Mr President."

Later I remarked quite casually to Johnson that I thought the crowds were larger than those on the Queen's previous visit. Johnson said quite sharply: "Son, don't tell me, tell the press." It wasn't my job to tell the press anything. But if I had done so, I would have told them that the crowds were actually smaller than they had been on the Queen's *first* visit.

During Johnson's visit, I became quite friendly with his own Secret Service team who, I learned, were actually Treasury officials rather than members of the FBI. But their leader told me something I didn't know about the FBI's head, J. Edgar Hoover.

"You're in a good spot to broaden your horizons," he said to me one day. I asked him what he meant.

"Do what Edgar Hoover does," the Secret Service leader said, and went on to describe how Hoover kept a large album filled with details of affairs, adulteries, tax evasions and anything else that could be used to blackmail influential Americans. Hoover, the Secret Service leader assured me, always managed to get what he wanted in Washington. His budgets were always approved. "You could do the same thing in Australia — it wouldn't be too difficult."

I said I was sure the ploy would work perfectly well, but I wasn't really interested in building my own empire in quite this way.

The other American president I came into contact with was John F. Kennedy, whom I met on a visit to the United States. He really impressed me and I found him a very engaging person. What struck me was the very easy camaraderie that existed between JFK and his Secret Service escort team. They shared jokes and generally seemed to be on warm personal terms. The Secret Service team were very keen on their job. They were much more professional in their work than the two Scotland Yard men that I'd known over the years from royal visits. I had been at the White House talking to the escort team about tactics and movements when I was asked to join them on their next run with the president. About an hour later, I joined them in their close escort car for a trip shadowing the president's limousine. On our return to the White House, Kennedy left his car and walked over to me and said: "Welcome, Aussie. I'm glad to have you with us." We chatted for some time and then the Secret Service team and I followed Kennedy into the White House. While I was having lunch in the Staff Mess, the leader of the escort team told me that the president had invited me to travel on Air Force One whenever I was with the Secret Service. I thought that was a great privilege; many Americans would have given a lot of money to say that they had travelled on Air Force One. Shortly after I returned to Australia, a packet arrived from the White House. It contained a certificate signed by the president which stated that I had been an invited guest on Air Force One and a photograph of the President signed "To Ray from John F. Kennedy". A couple of years later, I was quite disturbed when I heard that Kennedy had been assassinated. I had been aware, of course, of his father's anti-British sentiments when he was the American Ambassador in London during the war. But John F. Kennedy spoke to me as if Australia and the United States were cousins; I felt welcomed by him and I noted that that sort of conversation would not have occurred if a strange officer had appeared in the royal escort team when the British monarch was in Australia.

When I had been offered the directorship of the CIS, Mavis had sensed how keen I was to take on this responsibility and so, despite our having become settled in Melbourne, she had agreed to another move to another strange city where we, as usual, had no relatives or friends. I went on ahead, but this time — having learned from my two previous mistakes — only took a rented house. With perseverance, Mavis sold our "white elephant" without loss, packed the furniture again and brought the family to Canberra. Once again, she made the routine calls on the headmasters of the local schools and got the children settled in and adjusted to the new school curriculum, before she searching for and buying a home for us. Mavis found a house in the best residential suburb in class-conscious Canberra. She obtained it at a price which so impressed our land agent that he immediately offered her a job on his staff. This invitation she declined, and we settled down to the task of getting our family arrangements back to normal. The local guide company was short of a leader, as was the local scout troop, so we both volunteered, and our children joined our units. Both the guides and the scouts flourished, and did so for the next eleven years. We set new standards in Canberra for guide and scout cooperation. In New South Wales (which for scouting purposes included the ACT), there was a split between these two "kin" organisations and we found this disconcerting. So we arranged joint training for leaders of both organisations, as well as social activities, and when our own scouts and guides held their annual camps we often managed to have combined campfires at night.

We joined the local Baptist church and discovered an intelligent, progressive fellowship. The church had a lively youth group which, amongst other activities, fielded two men's hockey teams, one in senior grade. Andrew and Ian were soon involved, and not long afterwards I was invited to be their goalkeeper. The three Whitrod males turned out each Saturday afternoon, and Mavis and Ruth loyally came as barrackers. After the game the family usually went to a picture show at Manuka, and then had a snack at a nearby cafe. From 1954 to 1964, Mavis gave all her time to being a homemaker. She was always there when the children came home from school. She listened to their accounts of the day's events, tactfully offered wise counsel, ensured we were all properly clothed and fed, offered warm hospitality to the other children of our neighbourhood who were less well cared for, maintained a nice garden in poor soil, and made friends with our neighbours. A former guide, now a professor of Economics in Canada, wrote recently saying that the Whitrods had provided her with a second home while she was growing up in Canberra, and added that she had always been warmly welcomed and her views were listened to with respect — a rare thing for children in those days.

Mavis also carefully balanced our financial books which was not easy despite my reasonable salary, for one-third went in tax and there were mortgage repayments in addition to the costs of raising a family. Each Christmas we all returned to Adelaide by way of an eighteen-hour drive. This could become very boring, and Mavis helped entertain us all by getting us to sing campfire songs and other old tunes.

When each of the children were in their Matriculation year, Mavis would spend more time than usual helping them with their assignments. Her knowledge of French and maths was most valuable. If the children appeared stressed, she would provide comfort by just being available to listen or by making a cup of warm cocoa in the cold Canberra weather. She was a most resourceful mother to our kids.

All three eventually matriculated, but Ian was the first to leave home. He was interested in becoming an engineer and so enrolled in an Adelaide University course and boarded with his grandparents. He was seventeen when he left. Although Mavis encouraged him to go, I know that his departure left a large ache in her heart. She had "lost" me for four years, but I had returned. I think, somehow, she sensed that Ian would be leaving for good. But several times, Ian, feeling homesick, returned from Adelaide unexpectedly, driving his old car. He would arrive in the early hours and just go to sleep in his old bed. I can still remember how Mavis, absolutely delighted, would tell me "Ian's home". He could only stay a few days each time but they were most happy occasions for Mavis and me. Andrew left when he married, and a little later Ruth went into residence at the Canberra Hospital to train as a sister. Our once busy, active, comfortable home was now mainly a place of memories. Both Mavis and I kept up our active interest in scouts and guides, but now they were all other people's children.

About this time I had completed my Economics degree at the Australian National University, which had taken me six years of evening lectures and time at the libraries, and had started on a part-time Master's Degree in Sociology. I was lucky in having very good lecturers at the ANU. George Zubrzycki and his team made me welcome. We had been in Canberra some ten years, and while I had been to a number of overseas and interstate conferences, Mavis had stayed at home. I talked to her about the possibility of undertaking a postgraduate course in Criminology at Cambridge. We found that we could manage this financially if I went on a year's leave without pay, taking all my long service leave in a lump sum to pay for the boat fares. We would also need to swap our Canberra residence for one in Cambridge, and it would be necessary for Mavis to secure a casual teaching job in England in order to meet our everyday costs. These were big challenges for a fifty-six-year-old mother who had left teaching twenty-six years earlier, and who now was morally entitled to a long, non-working overseas holiday.

Carl Jung has a theory of meaningful chance — in other words, not all events happen at random. Somehow we were able to meet all of the necessary conditions, and left Sydney for England on a cheap passenger liner. Ruth made a special trip from Canberra to see us off and, from her meagre savings as a first-year student nurse, bought Mavis a magnificent opal ring and me a most serviceable fountain pen. She inspected our little cabin and tearfully said: "Bon Voyage — You have it all wrong. It's children who leave their parents not vice versa." I was most upset. If I could have reversed the program I would have done so. I am sure Mavis felt as homesick as I did, but she consoled me more than I comforted her. Our loved daughter's remark made me feel guilty. We were failing her in that her familiar place of security and support would not be available for a year and we would be on the other side of the world if she needed us. We need not have been so concerned. During the year we received a cabled request from a future son-in-law for permission to marry Ruth. Mavis was delighted that Ruth had followed her own example and asked her intended to seek parental approval. We told Ruth that we sent our sincere congratulations to them both.

I had prepared for the four-week voyage by taking a new textbook on criminology with me to study. Mavis purchased a typewriting manual and each afternoon spent two hours in our cabin practising touch typing on an old portable machine I had brought with us. Mavis became a competent touch typist. She would have been the only passenger with a serious study program.

As soon as I met my fellow students at the institute, I knew my postgraduate year at Cambridge would be an interesting and useful one. About twenty people had enrolled. They were mainly English, recent Honours graduates in law, but there were psychologists and social workers as well. About half of the students would have been about twenty-five years old, but there were others in the group who were older and had some practical experience. I was the oldest and I soon chummed up with the next oldest, Ian Barsby, the headmaster of a junior borstal. We would spend afternoons taking long walks along the Cam, swapping life histories. He had been a fifteen-year-old London Sea Scout who had helped man a small yacht that had sailed to Dunkirk to pick up survivors. I think he approved of my two RAF tours but, with traditional English understatement, he only hinted at it. He was most knowledgeable in the areas of juvenile delinquency and education techniques, two of my weaker subjects. We would arrange our walks to allow time for a pint of bitter and a discussion of the material presented to the class, before returning for the twilight lecture. I liked Ian very much. He invited Mavis and I to stay for a weekend at his borstal and there we met his charming wife and two tall sons. I discovered we had much in common. I had never been in a borstal before; this one was more like a residential country high school than a prison. There was no high fence around it. On the crisp Sunday morning of our stay, we all walked as a group warmly clad to the little Anglican Church nearby. Ian was on good terms with the young vicar whose sermon, I thought, was better than most I had become accustomed to back home. I thought I could have fitted into that environment if I had been single and had had a reasonable job.

For work experience during a vacation, Ian and I went to a self-governing junior boys' borstal near Glasgow where we lived in, as did the borstal supervisor, George Wilson, and his wife. This borstal only contained about thirty lads (Ian's had about a hundred) and here they were locked in. It was fascinating. We sat in at one of the "trials" of one of the fourteen-year-old inmates who was found guilty by his fellow inmates of recklessly damaging one of their precious canoes. They awarded some penalty (the nature of which I have now forgotten) and the offender appealed to the supervisor because he thought it excessive. I did too. George reduced the penalty. He told us that the boys were very hard on each other. He often had to soften an inmate-imposed sentence, a task that usually put him in a good light with all the boys. I found the week very demanding. A number of the boys were apparently not seeing much of their dads on visiting days (if, indeed they ever saw them at all) and were hungry for adult male company. Ian and I were quickly accepted and I told them tales of Australia. In the evenings, a night duty staff came on and we were free of responsibilities. George Wilson was a connoisseur of single malt whiskies, and he would drive us around to little pubs whose shelves boasted a fine array. These were pre-breath testing days, luckily. George had advanced ideas for his borstal, but I heard some years later that it was closed down by public demand after one of the boys had murdered a small girl.

Another time, I spent a week with Tommy Koh, a lecturer in law from Singapore, and Al Moreton, an American attorney, at the then recently opened Grendon Underwood Psychiatric Prison for lifers. During the day we had the run of the prison, but at night returned to the outside world. We were well received by the prison staff and participated in their morning conferences. Grendon Underwood was conceived as a therapeutic community in which everybody was involved: prisoners, warders, medical staff and anyone else who had gained access to the gaol. Several of the lifers were there because of the killing of young homosexual boys. They tended to be more intelligent than the average prisoners and we had a number of useful discussions with them, both as a group and in one-to-one unsupervised sessions in the cells. We were told that many of the prisoners were pleasant blokes to talk to, but could take offence easily and were known to have "turns".

"Don't worry," we were told. "We will be within reach."

Tommy and Al confided in me separately that they were scared while inside the walls. I did not let on that I didn't feel all that comfortable myself.

In the third term, Al Moreton and I went to Blackfriars Shelter in London. We were supposed to spend a working week living in the shelter, a home for homeless men. The place was dreadful — it was near the Thames in an area of total urban decay: broken-down, rat-infested, deserted warehouses and slums. It was still winter, so the shelter was full to capacity, the summer exodus to the country not having begun. The shelter smelt. The drunks and derelicts smelt. Al and I were meant to dine with the men in the soup kitchen. We arrived on Monday, but by Wednesday we were both fed up. Al Moreton was an assistant district attorney in the United States; I was the head of a national police force: we decided there were limits to participant observation. We discovered a pleasant pub where we spent many happy hours and ate decent meals, although we still slept in the shelter at night. But even though Al and I wagged it a lot of the time, the experience was a good entry into a world that I had only known from the point of view of a cop.

For the year, Mavis and I had an upstairs furnished flat in central Cambridge in exchange for our Canberra house. Mavis obtained a casual teaching job at a small village, called Melbourn, some 20 miles (30 kilometres) away. Every cold, bleak morning she rose at six-thirty. We would have breakfast and then she would trudge off some distance to catch a bus. She arrived back home at five-thirty and set about preparing our evening meal.

Mavis found the return to teaching, after an absence of twenty-five years and in a different system, a challenge. She never complained, and somehow managed to provide her class with stimulating education and a wider vision of the world. The English education system didn't impress Mavis very much; the custom of allowing teachers to apply for jobs in any school they fancied meant that some schools attracted a very competent body of staff, while others, in less attractive locations, made do with the also-rans. During term breaks, other students in my course went home but Tommy, the Chinese academic lawyer, and Eric, a Ugandan reform school head, had nowhere to go and little money. Neither of them was then married. Mavis warmly invited them to our flat for meals which she specially cooked for them, and we shared our stories of homesickness. I watched with interest how they both succumbed to Mavis's charm in the same way that I had done nearly thirty years beforehand. Somehow, quite naturally, she had bridged two different cultures and a generation in obtaining their friendship. We called ourselves "remnants of the British Empire". Eric said to me one day, "Ray, back home I would give not one cow, but two, for a woman like Mavis."

Lest you think I make too much of Mavis's conquests, I recount the following. In 1969 we were in Papua New Guinea. A newly arrived Indian academic joining the Waigani University called on us. She said that she had heard the Whitrods were in Port Moresby. For many years she had wanted to meet us. She explained that she was a friend of Professor Kibuka in Uganda. He had confided in her that he hated all white people — all except Australians. He knew Australians were different because he had met the Whitrods.

One afternoon, Tommy said to me that he had been asked to pass on a request by one of his countrywomen students that I spend a little time in dalliance with her. I had never met the girl. She had said to Tommy that she thought his Australian friend was "interesting". I was a bit flattered by this request but Tommy advised me not to make too much of it. Tommy said that in his culture, having sex was a more casual affair than the British style. Reluctantly, for the following reason, I didn't take up the invitation. I still have an occasional nagging thought that I missed a great opportunity to do some important fieldwork — important to trainee navigators, that is. When we were being taught how to swing an aircraft's magnetic compass, we were told there were three factors to manipulate. These were A, B and C for Chinese. When one of the squad had the courage to ask why "C for Chinese" the instructor scornfully answered that it was a reminder that this was a factor operating athwartships on the aircraft, and was unlike A and B, which were fore and aft. When the trainee still looked puzzled, the instructor said, "Everyone knows that Chinese vaginas are horizontal and not vertical."

Our squad was stunned. As far as I know, we were all Adelaide lads and none had as much as spoken to a Chinese girl, let alone explored such mysteries. It didn't make biological sense, but then in films that we had seen in peace time there had been some very bandy Chinese girls, and prewar the RAF had been stationed for many years in Singapore, and so … If I agreed, I thought, I would be able to write to Doddy, the only other survivor of our squad, and say, sort of offhandedly, "You remember that we were told …" But now I will never know until I get to Heaven. Judging by the movement of Angels, gender doesn't seem to be important. But how will I recognise Kerry, and Sandy One and Sandy Two, and Reddog and Bluedog, if they are neither dog nor bitch? The Bible is uninformative on this point, but then the clerics who wrote it were unlikely to be doggy people.

It is interesting, although probably not relevant, that clerics chose for their icon, a crooked piece of dead wood, whereas one would expect "shepherds" to select a sheepdog. Perhaps the idea was too controversial — maybe the Presbyterians wanted a Scottish terrier ("Jock") and the Baptists a retriever ("Splash") or may be the "crook" was simply an artifact from history. But a dog in the pulpit could provide some entertaining diversion if the sermon was boring.

Mavis and I were befriended by a Fellow of Johns, the Reverend Dr Alan Welford whom I had met previously at the Psychology Department of the Australian National University. Alan and his wife, Ruth, were most kind, inviting us to private dinners in his quarters at the college, and explaining the nuances of Cambridge University life. Ian Barsby and I were dined also by our psychiatric lecturer, Donald West. He was a small, well-dressed, very intelligent lecturer on "deviant" behaviour, and he was an acknowledged authority on homosexuality. He was about my own age. I thought his lectures were very objective and well balanced; the man intrigued me. Ian and I went to his cottage on the outskirts of Cambridge and were introduced to his male partner. It seems extraordinarily naive now, but it had not occurred to either Ian or me that West himself might have been homosexual. This was my first experience of being involved socially with practising homosexuals. I think having got to know Donald West before learning about his sexual preference made it easier to then accept him for what he was. Up until then I had just had the normal copper's view of homosexuals: I thought they were a limp-wristed blot on the landscape. The shock of learning about West caused me to revise my own attitudes. I began to realise that, for some people, homosexuality was more normal than heterosexuality. To that extent, my acquaintance with West was very good for me — it rubbed off one of my bad patches. Ian and I had a very pleasant evening in a thoroughly civilised Cambridge household. Donald West also introduced us to some fellow authors whose books were set as texts to be studied on the course. I had never expected to meet these giants, and was surprised to find that they were interested in hearing of my work and reflections on Australian criminology. They invited my comments on their publications. They may have been kidding a colonial, of course, but my ego got a boost.

I was delighted on one occasion to be dining with Robert Thouless, whose book *Straight and Crooked Thinking* had given me pleasure and knowledge when I had read it back in Australia some years earlier. He treated me as an equal, and ever since my "academic cringe" has almost vanished.

I had promised Mavis that, directly after my exams, we would have some weeks' holiday in Scotland, a country which she had always wanted to visit. We could afford this because I had arranged for the two of us to travel back to Australia for nothing by working our passage as English teachers on a migrant ship. Suddenly I received a telegram from Canberra saying that my deputy had suffered a heart attack and I was to return home immediately despite having four weeks' unused leave. I replied with the arrival date of the migrant ship and was told that this was not acceptable: we would have to fly home — at our own expense. I also lost the leave. At any other time I would have argued against this ruling, but I was keen to get back to campaign for the establishment of a similar Institute of Criminology in Australia, so I didn't want to rock the boat. Mavis has never chided me to this day about the cancellation of a visit to Scotland that she had yearned for, and earned.

We returned to a childless house that required far less housework than it once had. We both got back into scouting and guiding, I resumed study for my Master's degree and Mavis began a four-year part-time Diploma course in Horticulture. I was preoccupied with proposals at work, scouting and studies. I had returned to Australia strongly convinced that one way to upgrade not only the Commonwealth Police Force, but all Australian police forces, was to provide opportunities for selected officers to emulate my Cambridge experience. Since, unlike me, few police officers — if any — would be prepared to pay for this education, perhaps the solution was to establish an Australian Institute of Criminology. If my memory is correct, Sydney and Melbourne Law Schools already provided some criminology teaching, but from what I had been told by their students, these were very much home-grown courses and lacked the sophistication and practicality of the Cambridge version.

I was aware that some opposition to establishing an institute could be expected from those who hadn't experienced the Cambridge approach and, of course, also from those who opposed any expansion of Commonwealth activity and from the Negative Neils who would have to fund it. I didn't know anyone of significance who could share my task of securing both federal and state agreement.

In 1966 I put together the outline of a campaign to obtain this approval. One idea was to have a trial run, a residential seminar, with federal and state participants. This would identify the deficiencies in the preparation of senior officials in the Australian criminal justice system, and would demonstrate how a national institute of criminology could overcome these deficiencies at a reasonable cost. For the police, supplementary courses at the Staff College should take care of any matters not covered in the seminar. All my spare time in 1967 was devoted to selling this "trial run" idea to a number of doubtful senior executives — "doubtful" since they had never found any need for this type of knowledge themselves and each one believed he was competent in his job. I was forced to do a lot of lobbying but eventually, with blood, sweat and tears, the Seminar on the Control of Deviant Behaviour in Australia began in residence at Bruce Hall, Australian National University, on 30 January 1968.

This was the title I had selected because it did not preempt what I hoped would be the outcome — a unanimous recommendation by state and federal participants for the establishment of an institute. The seminar was a major coup which has not been repeated. Each state and territory, as well as New Zealand, was represented by directors or senior executives of police, courts, welfare, prisons and the probation services. There were a total of twenty-three participants, including two from the Provost and Legal office of the RAAF, with myself as director. The seminar finished on 23 February with a Parliamentary dinner for all participants given by the Attorney-General of the Commonwealth, the Hon. Nigel Bowen. He asked what conclusions had been reached, and was told by his guests that there were two principal recommendations: an "institute" should be established, which could possibly be a joint governmental venture, but would preferably be part of the Commonwealth Attorney-General's Department; and there was a need to develop statistical facilities to handle criminal data. The attorney-general said he was attracted to the joint government approach and asked the state representatives to make such a proposal to their own governments when they returned home. Each state representative said that he would, and the attorney-general said that he would arrange the Commenwealth's participation right away. I subsequently furnished him with a full report on the seminar which set out the recommended functions of the proposed institute and nominated the types and numbers of staff required. By and large, these recommendations were followed when the institute began operations.

Later on, when we were refining the implementation of the seminar's conclusions, it became apparent to me and to my federal and state colleagues that the research responsibility we had envisaged would be better met by separating the practical aspects from the theoretical, especially for the police aspects. So we then pushed for the establishment of a National Police Research Unit, and in time, as I have already mentioned, this appeared, under joint federal and state control, in Adelaide. The unit concerns itself with the nuts and bolts of policing: telephone intercept technology, speedometers, the best cloth for winter uniforms.

Some time later, when I went to say goodbye to the Commonwealth attorney-general on the eve of my departure for Papua New Guinea, Nigel Bowen said to me: "What will I do now that I am losing my ideas man?"

The first time in Australian history that a prime minister had gone to a war zone was Harold Holt's visit to Vietnam in 1966. I decided to go to Saigon a week ahead of the prime minister to check our security arrangements in person, flying into Saigon from Singapore. The plane arrived over Tan Son Nhut airport at about 20 000 feet and began circling down in a tight spiral. I asked the steward what was going on. He said any other form of approach would expose us to ack ack fire. As it was, there was still the possibility of rocket fire. The airport was absolute chaos: men and machines everywhere, choppers taking off and landing incessantly, ammunition being carted about.

I already had a Commonwealth policeman stationed in Saigon,

Ray McCabe. He was in charge of security at our embassy and was one of the few men I had who could speak French. I'd sent him a signal giving my time of arrival and asking him to book accommodation for me. He met me at the airport and drove me into town, explaining that he'd had a bit of trouble finding somewhere for me to stay as the city was full. He'd been in contact with the manager of the Intercontinental who was a friend of his and the manager had his eye on a room currently occupied by a French foreign correspondent who was due to spend a week in the field. The room, Ray McCabe explained, should be free the next day, but the first night of my stay was going to be difficult. I told him I didn't really mind where I stayed for a single night; I was used to dossing down under wartime conditions. Ray McCabe said that was good, because he'd managed to organise a small room over a bar. But first he suggested we had a drink at a cafe that had been a favourite of the French Foreign Legion during the colonial days. It was a simple place with long wooden trestle tables. We ordered two beers, and then another two — the night being hot and steamy. The beer came in intriguing leather tankards. Ray McCabe said they dated from the time of the Foreign Legion. I said I'd like to purchase a pair of them as souvenirs, if this were possible. Ray said he'd call at the place in the morning when things had quietened down and make the manager an offer.

We then drove to the place where Ray had secured a bed for me. We entered a small bar attended by a bright-eyed girl. Ray pointed upstairs and she indicated that we should go up. Ray took me to a small, simple room with bare boards on the floor, a shower in one corner and a bed with a copy of *Playboy* lying on it. There were a few hooks on the wall, but no other furniture. I told Ray the place would be fine for one night and he left. I had a shower and retired to bed. But my sleep was fitful; all night long there were sounds of people coming and going, laughter, giggles and heavy traffic on the stairs. At about seven in the morning I went down to the bar where the girl gave me a knowing smile. Two or three other young women also smiled sweetly. Ray McCabe turned up ready to drive me to the Intercontinental. As we were leaving the bar I said, "What was that place?"

"Actually," he said, "it's one of the Yanks' favourite brothels. But even there, I had great difficulty getting you a room."

I went to the Embassy and met the Ambassador. He said, "I'm glad you've come, Ray. We've got a little problem. It's nothing to do with your work, but we've got no one else who could handle it." The Ambassador said that a recently arrived diplomat had been driving quite slowly through the crowded streets of Saigon when he had knocked a small boy off a cycle, injuring him. It appeared to be a genuine accident, not anybody's fault, the sort of thing that happened quite often in the city's chaotic traffic. But the diplomat had obeyed the standing instructions for incidents such as this one: he hadn't stopped for fear of an ambush. The Ambassador said that Ray McCabe had made some inquiries and discovered that the boy was in a hospital in a fairly rough part of Saigon. The Embassy was keen that someone should visit the boy and make contact with his parents to assure them that all medical expenses would be taken care of. Ray McCabe and I drove to the hospital. It consisted of two long rooms with beds in them and not much else. The place was dirty and the overall impression was one of extreme poverty. The nurses looked poor, the families of the sick and injured looked poor. We located the boy and Ray spoke to him in French, reassuring him that he would be looked after. I checked with Ray some time later and he reported that this had been done and a small amount of compensation had been paid.

I returned to the air conditioning of the Intercontinental. The place was indeed full. It was pretty clear that most of the long-term guests of the hotel — Americans and other foreigners — had Vietnamese mistresses in place. I checked over the rest house by the river where Harold Holt would be staying and met the local security people. The place looked about as safe as it was possible to get in Saigon. There was still the possibility of a stray shell hitting it, but there was nothing I could do about that. Shells could land anywhere, as I found out when I got back to the Embassy. Ray McCabe said: "I've got some bad news for you. You won't be getting those leather tankards."

"Why not?" I said, thinking they might be too expensive.

"The place got hit by a shell last night. The cafe's gone."

I returned to Singapore, met up with Harold Holt and accompanied him and his team back to Saigon. We flew by helicopter to a number of places where Australian troops were stationed and we visited another hospital — this time in the country. At that time, the roads in the area were reasonably safe in daylight if you were in a military convoy, but the countryside itself — where the hospital was — could roughly be described as no man's land. The hospital was for civilians, but it was run by Australian staff, about five doctors and ten nurses working on a six-month rotation. It was little more than a couple of large huts. All the catering and much of the dressing of wounds and general nursing was being done by the patients' families. The prime minister thanked the Australian medical team for the job they were doing — and indeed, they were doing a wonderful job under horrible circumstances. I asked one of the sisters if a patient with a leg amputated below the knee was the victim of a land mine and she said that he was.

"Is he one of ours or one of theirs?" I said.

"Who cares?" she said

It was customary in Saigon that VIPs leave small gifts with those who have looked after them. The prime minister had brought his assistant secretary for Finance and Administration with him and this man was in charge of the swag of goodies. One of the local white mice, as the Saigon police were called, had attached himself to me as a sort of liaison officer because he could speak some English. He said something to me about a gratuity. I told him the assistant secretary had all that under control. But my contact said that none of those gifts would ever reach him, his welfare was in my hands. I said I had no money and he looked very disappointed. I checked up on what the police were paid. It was almost nothing. It seemed to me that they simply couldn't have existed on their salaries alone; bribes and tips of one sort or another would have been essential. The system itself negated the prime precondition for a non-corrupt police force: that the job be sufficiently well paid for there to be no need for illegally accepting money from other sources.

7

Papua New Guinea

(1969–1970)

LIFE was proceeding normally in Canberra when I was asked by an old colleague who was about to retire from the Police Commissioner's job in the Territory of Papua New Guinea (TPNG) to help find him a replacement. I promised I would but I was unable to attract any worthwhile applicants, perhaps because the Royal Papua New Guinea Constabulary would soon be facing the turmoils of independence. I told Mavis that this was a critical stage for TPNG, since it was vital to develop a law enforcement structure that would be able to cope with the new stresses, before the country became independent. We agreed that I should volunteer, so in 1969 we transferred to the Royal Papua New Guinea Constabulary. We passed the necessary medical tests despite our ages, and with sadness Mavis again sold our family home.

I was very busy in TPNG and Mavis quickly found tasks that needed to be done. She organised the wives of native police into basketball clubs, taught them swimming in the hitherto prohibited (for them) barracks swimming pool, and helped to teach the wives, who were mainly village girls, how to buy appropriate goods cheaply from the trade stores. The wives were shy and unaccustomed to such friendly relationships with Australian people, but Mavis won them over. Our excellent houseboy, Manassa, started teaching Mavis pidgin and she corrected his English. We found Manassa's church less stuffy than the local Baptist church, which was still dominated by a colonial outlook. Once when I was away in the Sepik, Mavis discovered an intruder in her bedroom. Our guard dog, Pepi, was barking in the passageway and Manassa ran to her. The intruder fled. After that, whenever I was absent, Manassa chose to sleep outside our bedroom door, and Pepi was allowed inside at night time. Manassa and Mavis formed a very happy domestic team, and I know he appreciated her "colour-blindness".

I still entertained some illusions about the world. My much earlier reading of those absorbing novels by Edgar Wallace of the Nigerian adventures of "Sanders of the River" and of the doings of his young Assistant District Officer Bones, with their enforcement team of Askaris, had left behind a rosy image of the life of a colonial law enforcer. But Edgar Wallace, despite his expertise in solving criminal mysteries, had overlooked the underlying difficulties of such an arrangement, even in the then-stable Nigeria. I was largely ignorant about the situation in TPNG, but I quickly learned that the Territory was already undergoing major social change. A constitutional reappraisal was imminent. This was a political reorganisation being pushed by Canberra but resisted in some TPNG quarters as premature.

From the policing aspect, these changes were being made against the backdrop of a criminal justice system that was an amalgamation of western legal philosophies applied by force to a tribal society composed of over 700 linguistic groups. Its enforcement employed the continental principles of policing: the suppression of lawbreaking by regulations imposed from above. This form of policing had been used by the British colonial administrations in what could be termed "occupied territories" such as India, Ireland and Africa. Police in these regions were actually armed gendarmerie who made arrests on orders from superiors. I regarded this model as unacceptable except as a temporary measure. For me, a police job is a vocation — one which helps provide an essential feature of democracy: the maintenance of law and order by common assent to a process in which individual constables make their own decisions.

I had much to learn. In the short time before my departure, I had tried to read some of the material available in the libraries of the

ANU, which meant that I arrived in Port Moresby with that dangerous commodity, a little knowledge. I had been unable to track down any account of a police force making the transition from the role of the gendarme to that of the London bobby. That apparent absence of literature should have rung alarm bells signalling the futility of my solution for the future policing of PNG. Some years later I did come across fragmentary references to the pioneering work of Sir Herbert Dowbiggin in what was then called Ceylon. He had very successfully moved its police from a Royal Irish Constabulary model to that of the English civil police system. But it had taken him from 1913–37 to achieve this. Dowbiggen had turned the Ceylonese police into an almost unarmed body in which the truncheon was the main weapon. He had created a detective branch, installed a photographic section, put a greater emphasis on education, and involved his policemen in maintaining peace in their communities. All of this was well before their independence, when Ceylon became Sri Lanka. At that time, there was a theory that policing naturally passed through three stages of development: local, armed gendarmerie, London bobby.

If I had known of Dowbiggin's work when I went to New Guinea, and known how long it had taken him to achieve his results, I am not sure that his time-frame would have deterred me. Middle-aged coppers about to receive their Master's degree in Sociology tend to be a little arrogant, stubbornly clinging to their own judgments, and making little of their ignorance. And I knew very little of local customs. Take my interest in dogs as an example.

Not long after we arrived in Port Moresby, another small family moved there from Australia. They had young daughter who was feeling the loss of her usual playmates. Her father came to me one day and sought my help in recovering the family pet, a daschund dog which had gone missing. His daughter, already unsettled, was greatly upset by its disappearance. He had advertised, offering a reward, without result. I spoke to one of my inspectors. "No chance," he told me. He explained that fresh meat was a delicacy in TPNG and that daschunds fitted nicely on a cooking spit. He said: "That dog would have been cooked and eaten before it was missed." I don't know how the father explained that to his young daughter.

On a Saturday afternoon not long afterwards, Manassa, who had been weeding the front garden, brought in a young native whom he had found crying on the roadway. Mavis immediately set about treating the very nasty wound on the lad's leg. He objected and talked in pidgin to Manassa. Manassa explained that the native did not want the wound dressed until it had been seen at the police station. I drove him down in our little family car and the duty inspector told me he would attend to the matter. Later I rang him. He said that everybody was happy. He had telephoned my neighbour whose large dog had bitten the lad. The neighbour had come to the station and paid the lad the equivalent of one of our dollars, and the lad had then gone off to get the wound treated. The inspector said that this was the usual custom. I learned that some ex-pats encouraged their large dogs to attack "wandering" locals (our lad claimed he had been on the road in front of the house). Mavis and I thought this custom was unfair and wondered what could be done about it. Of course, these days, with marauding gangs of rascals in Moresby and other towns, fierce dogs are regarded as legitimate protection.

I have already mentioned the dearth of published material about countries that had changed their policing philosophies. I searched for accounts of any former colonial region that had gained its independence. I noted that Jamaica was not far from Mexico City, where the next Interpol Annual General Meeting was to be held in October 1969. As it was my turn, in company with another commissioner, to represent Australia, I decided that a side trip to Jamaica was in order. The Territory's administrator was kind enough to approve three days in Jamaica in addition to my attending the AGM even though I had only been at my post in Port Moresby a short time.

In Mexico City, an official from the Australian Embassy called at my hotel and told me that our ambassador would appreciate my help in getting the local police to investigate a break-in at his office that resulted in the theft of a number of typewriters. When the embassy reported the offence, some detectives called and demanded a large sum of money to help them begin their investigations. The ambassador refused to pay. I made enquiries among my North American colleagues and was told that this was customary in Mexico, but I could not discover where the money normally finished up. I told the embassy what I had learned and suggested they take it up with the Mexican government, which was under an international obligation to provide protection to foreign embassies. I doubt that this was much help to the ambassador, but I had been preoccupied at the time of the official's visit to my hotel. I was busy learning the Mexican Two Step. Despite taking the precaution of drinking only bottled Coca-Cola, I had made the error of brushing my teeth with hotel tap water. That was sufficient for me to pick up the dreaded local diarrhoea. Despite medication, I was incapacitated for a week. As soon as the Interpol AGM finished in Mexico City on a Friday afternoon, I flew to Kingston, the capital of Jamaica. By the time I had gone through Customs and Immigration and booked into a hotel, it was too late to contact the local police. Early on Saturday morning, I called at Police Headquarters where I was expected but personally unknown except for my honorary life membership of the International Police Association. My welcome was friendly enough but I had picked the worst weekend to discuss official business. The country was celebrating the results of the previous day's re-election of its popular president. There were ample parties but little information. I returned to TPNG not much the wiser.

I had originally given myself five years in which to make a useful contribution to the resoution of TPNG's difficulties. I was fifty-three years of age, in good health and thought I could last until sixty; Mavis had turned sixty herself but had a strong body. I tried to gauge the current situation and, against a five-year allowance, work out the best strategies to adopt. I found my prospects were bleaker than when I had started on the restructuring of the former Commonwealth Investigation Service. In Canberra, it had taken me some years to win over a majority of the Gnomes. In TPNG, the Gnomes were the *kiaps* — the district officers and their assistants, and whilst the Gnomes numbered only seven, the *kiaps* were a whole united clan placed strategically throughout the Territory. I learned that my role as commissioner was anomalistic — that while I was the titular head of a three thousand-member force, only those members stationed in the towns were under the directions of my officers; all the others were *kiap*-controlled.

I discovered that many of the constables had been recruited from amongst men who had served the standard two years' corrective detention in a *kalabus* for grievous assault. These charges generally arose from the traditionally approved custom of settling arguments between males with a slash to the shoulder with a large knife. Afterwards, both victim and offender would call in at the nearest police station and report the offence. The offender would plead guilty and be sent to the *kalabus* where he would be medically checked, placed on a nutritious diet, taught simple bush carpentry skills or engine maintenance, taught pidgin or English and paid a small wage.

The *kiaps* were graduates of the Australian School of Pacific Administration (ASOPA) in Sydney. They had joined as career officers when young, having been selected from a large number of applicants. After two years' specialist tertiary education, they were more knowledgeable in TPNG matters than my inspectors. Many of my senior police had been accepted into the RTPNG force having only obtained the rank of constable in Queensland or elsewhere. Some were former British servicemen without any police background. Coming to TPNG had earned them a sudden jump in rank, so the training and experience levels of my senior men fell far short of those of their Australian counterparts. A cadet scheme designed to produce high-ranking indigenous officers was already in place and when Independence finally arrived, one of the first cadets became the new commissioner.

The *kiaps* as a class impressed me. I thought that they were even an improvement on the British colonial administrators in that they were not as class conscious. They had done much for the Territory. They all spoke pidgin and motu, the two main vernaculars, whereas only the best of my men had taken the trouble to learn any native language. The *kiaps* appeared not to have feathered their own nests at the expense of the local people although they had ample opportunity to do so, being the main distributors of Australian funding. I gave myself little hope of ever winning the *kiaps* over to my argument for a more democratic policing service. With evidence on their side, they could argue that TPNG traditions provided for "big heads" to become leaders after much community consultation. It seemed to me that there was a good possibility that Independence would merely result in control moving from the *kiaps* to the "big heads."

I discovered that the unsatisfactory state of the TPNG's criminal justice system had not passed unnoticed by the Commonwealth and that a few years earlier (before the thought of imminent Independence) a high-powered symposium had been held in Canberra. This had been attended by an anthropologist, judges, administrators and law teachers. I noted that no police and no community representative had been invited. As far as I knew, no one was researching the topic of the future policing system. I talked to the vice-chancellor of the university at Waigani, Dr John Gunther, but "policing" had only low priority access to the limited funds available. I did not know of an appropriate specialist such as a forensic anthropologist or a sociologist police officer who could carry out such a study, except myself and I was too busy with day-to-day affairs. I obtained the approval of the administrator, David Hay, whom I had known previously in Canberra when he had been a diplomat, to invite Brigadier McKinna, commissioner of the South Australian Police Force, who had served in New Guinea during the war, to discuss with me some improvements to the TPNG situation. McKinna came to Moresby and we discussed the possibility that there could be local disturbances of some size after Independence, especially in the Highlands which had a history of clan fighting. McKinna recommended, among other things, the early establishment of a mobile, specially trained unit, which could be despatched to trouble spots to augment the local police detachments. This proposal disappeared into the appropriate administrative channels and I am unaware still of its final disposition.

There was a problem in staffing the Force. Many of the young men entering the Force could now read and speak English, unlike their older colleagues. This meant that only the younger members were able to read the instructions and other memoranda from headquarters. Because of this, the older men were losing the respect habitually given to age by their juniors. On the other hand, when a police patrol was sent out on its own into the bush, it was the older members who were experienced in bush craft and who were respected by any villagers they came across.

I was concerned by an earlier statement by the Territory's crown solicitor who reported that "the present system of administration of justice did not grow from below to satisfy a popular demand, but was imposed from without, and was contrary to popular practice". This seemed to me to negate the very heart of English style democratic policing but, as far as I knew, the solicitor's views were based only on anecdotal evidence. If the police were to operate with the consent of the community, then it was clear to me that we ought to find out more about any conflict or confusion this "imposition" of foreign values actually caused. I later picked up a reference by the anthropologist Peter Lawrence, a recognised authority on this region, who said "the New Guinea process of social control rests on principles diametrically opposed to those underlying our own legal system". Lawrence concluded that attempts to impose Australian law on TPNG societies invited one of two reactions: rejection, or change of social structure.

I noted that in TPNG there were many differences of opinion on the relative seriousness of particular offences. Members of the judiciary were Australian, with only a few assistant magistrates recruited from the local population. In the police force, all the constables were locals, but the senior officers were almost all white Australians. The principal body of law defining criminal offences in Papua at the time was the 1899 Criminal Code of Queensland, but the principal part of the legal system in regular contact with Papuans and New Guineans was the Native Regulations. Some activities, such as adultery and sorcery, were not crimes under the Code, but were crimes under the Regulations. In the allocation of penalties, the judiciary were required to consider the sense of resentment and outrage on the part of those injured and of the public. No one else seemed interested in exploring the way cultural differences affected the perception of crime, so I sought approval from the ANU to undertake a survey of views on the seriousness of common crimes as part of my Master's thesis. As informants, I selected some three hundred young English-speakers of both sexes in the TPNG — 75 at the Administrative Staff College, 106 new recruits at the Police College, 31 second year students at the university, 46 students at the Teachers College and 98 serving soldiers of the Pacific Island Regiment. For the Australian sample, I selected 30 recruits at the Queensland Police Depot, 101 male cadets at the South Australian Police Academy, 100 RAAF servicemen and 66 psychology students at the University of Queensland. The results were interesting. There was a good deal of agreement on the degrees of seriousness, with some of the groups showing a similarity by occupation as much as by nationality. Those subjects with some tertiary education, for example, viewed civil disorder more tolerantly than others. The Queensland psychology students differed from all other groups in their view of the seriousness of homosexuality. Violent crime was considered less serious by the TPNG participants, while Australians regarded offences by juveniles as less serious. The TPNG replies showed that they viewed stealing more seriously than the Australians, but both university groups were more tolerant than their countrymen.

While these group differences were interesting, I found on probing TPNG individuals that these totals disguised even deeper disagreements. For example, I asked my TPNG informants why they regarded "burning the Australian flag" as nearly as serious as a murder, when the Australians considered it a very minor misbehaviour. The TPNG people explained that the Queen's spirit resided in the flag and that burning it was akin to killing the Queen. I asked why non-payment of council rates was regarded in TPNG as being as serious as stealing, when Australians considered it a very minor offence. My informants explained: "If we don't pay our rates we can't pay for a road to our village. We all use the road. Those who don't pay their rates are stealing from us." The ANU examiners accepted my thesis. My survey was carried out thirty years ago, and I do not know how the large social changes which have occurred in the TPNG since then have affected local assessments of the relative seriousness of crimes. As far as I know there has been no replication of my study. I recently discovered that Professor Brian Inglis thought highly of it.

During my varied career, I've met a number of public figures — some impressive, and some not so impressive. The most impressive person I met in TPNG was the Roman Catholic archbishop of Port Moresby, Dr Virgil Copas. Virgil and I met quite accidentally one afternoon and I was taken by the very pleasant and concerned manner in which he talked to me about the problems of New Guinea. He was an old hand: he had been archbishop for almost ten years, and before that he had been a navy chaplain and then a priest in Darwin. He was a man of about my own age, sparsely built with a very pleasant, unassuming face. When he entered a room, he did so without any ostentation — nobody paid him any particular attention or homage, even the members of his own church. But when Virgil talked to you, he immediately focused on what you were saying and was very soon on your wavelength, picking up all the nuances and feelings behind your statements. He gave me a lot of good advice about the ways of the people, both black and white, in TPNG. On the odd occasion when I felt a bit fed up, Virgil lent a sympathetic ear. We didn't meet all that frequently; Virgil came to our house for the occasional meal with Mavis and me and a couple of times he asked me down to the archbishop's "palace" next to the cathedral.

The cathedral was a fairly humble affair and Virgil had set about raising funds to make it a bit more like a major place of Christian worship. But he had wanted this done in the native style rather than the normal Roman fashion, full of statuary. Virgil had given instructions to the architect to incorporate local New Guinean features into the renovations. So the front of the building had been given an imposing, decorated facade in the Sepik style. Sepik men are known as excellent wood carvers and house designers.

I wasn't at the unveiling of the front of the cathedral, although I wish I had been because it soon became apparent to the onlookers that the designer had incorporated a number of Sepik totems that had very erotic meanings in the local culture. These were typical of the Sepik buildings, but Virgil had to quickly engage in some diplomatic maneuvering to get them disguised in a way that made them acceptable to the European Christian community.

Virgil was a very learned man. He had a doctorate in divinity from Rome and was well-read in most philosophies. He was able to suggest reading to me that helped me understand some of the local customs and cults — especially the cargo cult belief system which was still prevalent in some parts of New Guinea. Virgil's assistant was an Irishman who had formerly been a Macquarie Street eye surgeon. He became a priest and had come up to TPNG to work with Virgil and to provide free eye treatment for the natives of the region. The two men worked well together; they were committed people who really had the good of their fellow men at heart. They understood the region far better than many of the civil administrators who still saw TPNG as a sort of de facto Australian colony. I liked the Irishman; he and I got on well together even though we didn't meet all that often. I think he had gladly sacrificed all the privileges of his Australian practice, but what he did miss, it seemed to me, was a drop of Irish whisky. And since he couldn't afford whisky on his priest's pay, this was a longing not often satisfied. About once a quarter I gave a small afternoon tea party to the other departmental heads in Port Moresby at which both tea and grog were served. I always ensured that the whisky bottle was spirited away by Manassa while it still had a fair amount left in it. The next day Manassa would drive down to the "palace" with the bottle wrapped up in brown paper and marked "medical supplies". And whenever I saw the Irish doctor he always said, with a solemn face and a twinkle in his eye: "That medicine was well applied."

When Virgil had served ten years in Port Moresby, he retired to Kerema on the south coast of Papua, a place even less pleasant than Port Moresby. He spent most of his remaining years there until ill-health caused him to move to a small unit on the Gold Coast of Queensland. I understand he died a short time ago.

In my working life, both as a policeman and an air force officer, I have been the subject of regular reports on my performance and personality and I suppose that these have all been stored away somewhere. But one report that I have always regarded with a great sense of pleasure was an unexpected tribute by a stranger who described me in a letter he wrote. His name is Kev Roberts and this is what he said:

> At about the time of the moon landing, I was one of a handful of Europeans (whites) working in a remote location on the island of Bougainville. Initially, it was my job to wire up a very small diesel generator to light the first half dozen portable accommodation blocks on a coconut plantation called Loloho. Soon, the small workforce was the vanguard for the many hundreds of specialists to follow, where eventually, the quiet little bay would be transformed into a busy shipping port, and the immediate hinterland would be carved into another shape by huge bulldozers. Even small hills were flattened and pushed out over the white sandy beach until the magnificent coral reef that lined the bay was completely and forever covered in debris from the land.
>
> Understandably, despite being forewarned by government that this was to happen, most of the natives were appalled at what was going on. Up until this moment in their lifetime, they were very simple people, not far removed from what we would describe as stoneage, and to see their fishing grounds and other locations destroyed before their very eyes, was unfathomable. Their worst enemy during the previous thousand years would not do such a thing to them, as their land is a common entity that provides life to all. Naturally, they were incited to riot. They had no idea or understanding of the white man's definition of progress …
>
> This civil unrest attracted attention from many areas, the media included. I happened to be standing near the beach one morning as a bulldozer began the task of flattening a small hill. Angry natives came from everywhere and began shouting at the huge machine to stop its destruction. In desperation, a native woman then broke rank and placed her infant child in the path of the bulldozer in a final attempt at saving the situation. This action was captured by a cameraman and the dramatic

photo was published worldwide. It was then that the police force was called upon to be on special alert and the riot squad was flown in from Port Moresby.

At this early stage, a wet canteen had been built on the beach that extended out over the water. From this magnificent position, the yet-undamaged section of the reef could be viewed in all its glory. I happened to be in this little canteen when a very tired and drawn man entered with a few others. I had no idea who they were and assumed them to be media representatives who had just bounced their way up the goat track that stretched all the way along the coastline from the grass airport at Kieta.

One particular man among the newly arrived visitors seemed to be the point of focus of everyone present and they bombarded him with a multitude of questions. From this I deduced that he was probably a politician of sorts as I can't recall that he was dressed in uniform. He answered each question in a very cool and calm manner, yet at the same time, any fool could see that he needed to rest.

After some time spent watching him converse with the mob, and feeling slightly sorry for him, I approached him and asked him over to the corner of the room on some pretext, probably to view the reef. He immediately accepted as it was an excellent opportunity to rid himself of the henpeckers.

I forget the exact conversation, which lasted for only a few minutes, but I spoke of diving and exploring the immediate area, the size of the crays that I had eaten, and the general beauty of the area. I ensured that the contents of the conversation did not include one snippet of controversy. He immediately relaxed. Within those minutes, I knew that I was speaking to a very genuine human being. A very caring person who seemed to have the empathy of a mother. It was with great surprise when I later learned that he was Papua New Guinea's Commissioner of Police. His job was not to mould the policy of the new country, his job was to police that policy, no matter what the politicians had decided.

Many months afterwards, when I had returned to the big smoke of Port Moresby, I happened to be waiting at an intersection when a large black vehicle pulled up beside my grubby little utility. I noticed that it was a government limo with heavily tinted windows. Suddenly, the rear window wound down to reveal the familiar face of a person who was now dressed in the uniform of the Commissioner of Police. He flashed a huge smile and tipped his cap at me. In surprised recognition, I gave a silly nod in response and seconds later, we parted. In retrospect, after such a brief meeting, many months earlier, only a gentleman would bother to do that. Ray Whitrod was such a gentleman.

A few years later, it transpired that he was far too human and genuine to survive in the corrupt and sordid world of Queensland politics. As a flower soon dies when the earth is fouled, he was cut, packaged and trashed before many Queenslanders could ever get to know him.

While in TPNG, I had a firm thought that I should seek to develop in my Australian colleagues a better understanding of policing problems in the territory. It seemed to me that in the near future TPNG would want to send locals to Sydney or Melbourne police headquarters to train as police experts in such things as fingerprinting or ballistics. If the state commissioners were more aware of the TPNG problems than I had been before my appointment, their responses were likely to be more favourable. The venue for the Australasian Police Commissioners' annual conference rotated around among the participant nations. While the TPNG commissioner had attended many of them, he had never before invited his colleagues to the Territory. In my own experience, members had travelled to New Zealand twice but never to Port Moresby. I decided to invite the commissioners to the Territory. I obtained the support of David Hay, the administrator, and then did some lobbying among my Australian colleagues. I had thought that the possible reason for the reluctance of my predecessors to offer to host the conference in TPNG was a lack of confidence in their ability to run such a conference, or just possibly that such a conference might have meant the loss of a "holiday" down south in more pleasant conditions.

As soon as I began to canvass the possibility of a TPNG conference, I ran into strong opposition from the commissioners' wives and their civilian secretaries. I had known that the host always provided a separate entertainment program for spouses, but since the Whitrods could not afford it, my wife had seldom attended a conference so I knew little about these activities. I had not realised that one of the attractions for the ladies was several days' shopping at large department stores where discounts had often been arranged.

Rather than Port Moresby, which in many ways closely resembled Townsville or Darwin, I had decided that I should offer Mt Hagen as the site for the conference, as this would give maximum exposure to TPNG problems. But I could not arrange suitable shopping — especially when it came to gifts for children and grandchildren. There were native artefacts of course, but these apparently didn't appeal.

Although I did win over the commissioners and we held the Conference at Mt Hagen, quite a few of the wives did not attend. We had what I assessed as a useful week's conference in the Highlands, with visits to nearby villages where we were graciously entertained at a "sing-sing". At the "sing-sing", the locals performed in splendid head-dresses with mainly only grass skirts below. The benefits of this conference were not apparent during my short stay in TPNG, but I like to think that it did later influence the state commissioners' favourable responses to requests for the secondment of their senior officers to assist the PNG constabulary after Independence.

I found my more relaxed policing philosophy was contrary to the stiffer views of the *kiaps*. I was in conflict with their proposal that police should be used to force landholders off their traditional land in Bougainville. I told the administrator that there ought to be a less violent way of achieving their removal and that if the police were to be seen as the protectors of the local people, every avenue that might lead to a peaceful resolution ought to be explored. The *kiap* approach may well have been correct, but I had trouble accepting it. One of my problems in TPNG was that I had not developed any close working relationships. I was clearly a new arrival and an outsider. To the "old hands", I was a too-clever academic from the comforts of a Canberra office who had never been on patrol. They thought that I failed to appreciate that the principle of the separation of powers did not and could not exist in many parts of the country simply because of the lack of manpower. I had met the public defender, Peter Lalor, and liked him and his philosophies but our relationship was only in its early stages. As I've said, I liked the Catholic archbishop who was dedicated to TPNG and a mature thinker knowledgeable in the TPNG culture, but in only a year we hadn't yet achieved the deeper mutual understanding and trust that comes with long acquaintance. At about this time, I received a telephone call from John McKinna asking me to consider applying for the commissionership of the Queensland force. The Queensland Police Minister, Max Hodges, flew to TPNG to personally invite me to apply.

I decided that I had little hope of bringing about much improvement on the TPNG front in the next four years. I had suffered several attacks of malaria which Mavis nursed me through; the hot muggy climate was harder on our ageing bodies than I had expected; Mavis was missing contact with our children and grandchildren; we had not made any close friends with Port Moresby residents for our philosophies were not mutual; and I had realised how little I did know about the complex scene. Economists have a concept, *opportunity costs*, which requires decisions to be based not only upon the benefits of choosing one particular option, but on the loss of benefits if another option is chosen. I was being offered an opportunity to implement a set of recommendations to improve the Queensland Police Force which had the unanimous endorsement of the Queensland Cabinet. This appeared to me to present a better opportunity for real progress than an isolated campaign to prepare TPNG police for Independence Day, especially since my moves were being resisted by a substantial number of influential administrative officials. There would be other benefits: a move south would bring the Whitrods closer to their family, away from malaria and within easier reach of medical specialists and better living conditions. So, after a preliminary refusal and some long talks with Mavis and Kim Beazley Snr, who happened to be in Port Moresby, I accepted the minister's invitation.

The administrator, David Hay, appreciated my situation and accepted my resignation with a kindly worded regret. I was touched to receive a letter from the secretary of the TPNG Officers of Police Association asking me to reconsider my resignation as his members would very much like me to stay. Before we left, Mavis found a suitable position for Manassa and a safe home for Pepi, our faithful watchdog. When Mavis first told Manassa we were leaving, his eyes filled with tears and he retired to the kitchen and sobbed. Manassa, like Eric Kibuka, obviously regarded Mavis as a two-cow lady.

I now realise that I was a poor choice for the TPNG commissionership. I was not acquainted with local customs and current administrative practices. I was inadequately briefed, mainly because there was no authoritative material on which to base predictions of social change or on which to make decisions about the coming upheaval. The politics of the situation made the Commonwealth feel justified in seeking to grant independence as soon as possible. The reality was best understood by the *kiaps*, who argued that it was coming too soon. When first asked to help, I had tried to poach a younger police administrator from the states' forces, but I could not attract anyone in whose capabilities I had faith. I had been it, by default. My predecessor, Bob Cole, had been a man I much admired. He had a fine war record in the TPNG regiment; he had been a senior *kiap* and was able to hold his own with other senior *kiaps*, he spoke fluent pidgin and had a most cooperative wife: he was an excellent choice for the job. But Bob Cole was understandably thin on police practices and philosophy, especially for urban areas, and these looked like being trouble spots in the near future. The Coles had decided that they should go south to retirement — and they were younger than Mavis and me. Perhaps a better arrangement might have been to invite Bob to stay on for a year with me in a protracted handover. His TPNG knowledge would have ensured that my London philosophy was modified for local application. In fact, I now think that I was wrong in attempting to introduce these principles, no matter how modified, at that time. Perhaps we could have worked out some kind of variation on the "bastard" Canadian system where the Royal Canadian Mounted Police provide an armed gendarmerie for country areas and a national police centre, while Canadian municipalities appoint their own constables in the English form.

But it is easy to use hindsight to formulate alternative scenarios. As it was, we left Papua New Guinea and I soon found myself at Brisbane airport where Sergeant Ken Hogget met me and drove me into the city. He was a likeable young man. I found out afterwards that he had wangled the job of picking me up, displacing the commissioner's normal driver. As we approached the City, Ken said: "Commissioner, I don't know how much you know about the Queensland Police Force, but it's pretty corrupt." Not wishing to appear totally naive, I said something about having some idea of the problem.

"Well, it's pretty bad," Ken said.

8

In need of reform: Queensland

(1970–1976)

COLIN Dillon called to see me recently when he was passing through Adelaide. I had waited many years to meet him and to congratulate and thank him for his invaluable evidence at the Fitzgerald Inquiry into police corruption in Queensland. Colin was the only person who responded to Tony Fitzgerald's plea to members of the Queensland Police to come forward with information about corruption in the Force. Colin had been a sergeant in the now infamous Vice Squad and was in a good position to answer Fitzgerald's call. Nobody else did. Colin received commendation from Tony Fitzgerald, but since then he has not been promoted. When he went to the top to discover why all of his contemporaries had been promoted while he hadn't, all he got was a steely stare.

I told Colin that in the mid 1970s, because of certain events, I hadn't felt safe despite being the top policeman in the state. I had taken to locking my bedroom door at night and keeping a firearm with me. Colin said he had done the same thing after the Fitzgerald Inquiry.

Colin Dillon has been a very good officer and a fine role model for Aboriginal police. He told me how very disappointed his mother was with the stopping of his promotion, but how very proud she is of him. I told Colin that when Mike Ahern took over as premier, I immediately wrote to him asking that there could be some recognition of the great contribution made by those members of the

Queensland Police Force who had been prepared to publicly fight corruption in the force and who, as a consequence, had suffered much under the administration of my successor, Terry Lewis. I had mentioned Alec Jeppeson and Basil Hicks as two who had been grievously treated. I received a reply from Ahern saying that the matter would be considered. Nothing has ever eventuated. To this day, there are still many individuals in the Queensland system who are unequal to their responsibilities, who still seek revenge for others' refusals to be "yes men" or who wish to be seen as supporters of the old and now disgraced political machine. Colin and I talked of these matters for an hour. When he left he said: "I've always wanted to shake your hand." I said: "Let's keep in touch. I'm glad that you called." We hugged each other.

But all this was far in the future when Mavis and I moved to Brisbane in 1970. Mavis hunted out a lovely old home at St Lucia, close to the University of Queensland and to the Police Headquarters where I was to spend a great deal of my time over the next seven years. Again, we were establishing ourselves in a city in which we had no friends or relatives.

I soon became involved in a political struggle with the Police Union and with the premier, principally because I wanted to implement an existing police regulation. This stated that promotion would be by merit. My controversial administration of the force had repercussions for Mavis. We were subjected to a harassment campaign which entailed union-inspired media attacks on me personally. In the press I was said to be 'destroying the morale of the Force'. It was clear this piece of editorial opinion came from the journalists who report on police matters and rely on their contacts within the force; it was hardly surprising that they ran the union line. We received anonymous telephone calls and unrequested visits at all hours by medicos and taxis. The taxi companies soon got wise and took to ringing us to confirm any request for their services. But we still had to answer the phone at unearthly hours. The heart specialist who said he had been contacted by 'one of your sergeants' arrived on our doorstep at 3.00 a.m. expecting to find me incapacitated by a heart attack. I told him I was fine and he went away. Getting rid of the truckload of gravel that was dumped in our driveway was more difficult.

Much of Mavis's time was spent in supporting me socially and privately. She organised excellent dinner parties for influential guests, she joined me in visiting police cadets on their outings, she once provided a sick bay for a cadet whom we had found ill in the mountains. As well, Mavis soon had to contend with a family problem. The marriage of one of our son's had broken down and he had brought his son to Queensland. Mavis was asked to go to court to give evidence in the custody trial. Our grandson was placed in his father's custody and the two of them lived with us for some time, with Mavis providing out-of-school-hours supervision.

Mavis really propped me up at times when I felt beaten. I had few public supporters for my campaign to reduce corruption in the Queensland Police Force. It became increasingly clear that my code of strict honesty did not have general appeal to Queenslanders, and without a community base I could not win. I worked six days a week and on Sundays we drove to the coast and walked along the shore. I have always found the sea a soothing influence and that, coupled with Mavis's tranquility and wise counsel, would gradually restore my peace of mind. There were two occasions I remember well. When one of my few trusted senior officers, Val Barlow, retired in 1973, I felt lonely and vulnerable and thought of leaving. As we walked along the beach, Mavis gave me fresh hope and so I stayed. Later, when my ministerial protector was transferred by the premier, shutting off any opportunity to present my case to Cabinet, I again became dispirited. There seemed to be no point in continuing the struggle, but again Mavis inspired me to stay. This I did until the premier began overriding my operational control and, amidst some small public dismay, I left office. Later, the Fitzgerald Commission revealed some of the stress we had been subjected to.

When I decided to go to Queensland, I had just assumed that that state was simply another part of Australia, with similar values and customs. I had lived and worked in South Australia, New South Wales, Victoria and the ACT. And while there had been minor variations, I had felt at home in all of them. But Queenslanders are not like other Australians. Certainly, they drive on the left hand side of the road and pay federal taxes, but there are significant differences. There is no Upper House of review; Parliament meets on only a few days for short sessions; the struggle between the Irish mafia and its protestant equivalent is far more pervasive and intense than elsewhere; until quite recently, education had a very low priority; the squattocracy tradition persists; and local media are passive, perhaps as a result of the frequency of "stopper writs".

I gradually put together an assessment of the hurdles facing me. Most of these were new to me, and few people were keen to declare their allegiance to my cause. It soon became clear that there were three power bases on the sociopolitical scene: the Irish, the anti-Irish and the squattocracy. However, because of my philosophy that a police administrator should maintain strict neutrality, I was not prepared to seek the sponsorship of any of them. This was a position they did not understand, it was apparently a new concept in Queensland. Everyone accepted the slogan "If you are not for us, you are against us".

I found the Premier, Joh Bjelke-Petersen, to be a complex character. I had come to Queensland prepared to like him as I had immediately liked the Police Minister, Max Hodges, when Max had come to New Guinea. When I first met Joh, I think we both warmed to each other and elements of that warmth remained in an ambiguous fashion over the next seven years. I'd heard that Joh was a non-smoker, non-drinker, non-gambler and a Sunday School teacher and I thought I had some idea of what his values would be. I found him pleasant enough to talk to, but I was uneasy in his presence. Over the previous twenty years or so, I had spent a fair bit of time professionally and socially with Australian prime ministers and Cabinet ministers. I had got on well with them and was accepted by them as a friendly professional with my own area of expertise. Joh never gave me that professional recognition. He treated me as though I were another of his clerks, there to carry out his instructions while not impeding his plans. I kept trying to get through to him that I had a responsibility to maintain the law, that I had taken an oath to this effect and that I was responsible for my own actions as a constable. I said I would implement any legal instructions given to me by him or by my minister, but how I did this was my decision. Joh sensed, I think, that I would do no more, and perhaps that wasn't sufficient. Certainly his subsequent relationship with Terry Lewis was quite different.

I have never forgiven Joh for letting me walk blindfolded into the nest of ants that was the Queensland Police Force. Joh must have been well aware of the real state of the Force, but he never gave me any inkling. For example, I knew nothing of the Sir Thomas Hiley exposures until three years after I'd left Queensland. Joh must have known that Hiley had shown almost every police officer in Queensland to be participating in a giant scam, that they were accepting their immediate superiors' assertions that arresting illegal bookmakers was out of the question. Hiley had revealed that illegal bookmakers in every town in Queensland paid a substantial fee to the local police. The Fitzgerald Inquiry subsequently showed that there was an illegal bookmaker operating quite openly in Kingaroy, Joh's own town. If the police could be bribed on this scale to turn a blind eye to people committing one sort of offence, why not to other offences as well?

Looking back, Joh's reaction to me was much the same as my reaction to him. He was meeting a stranger: all he knew about my background was what Max Hodges had told him when putting me forward as a candidate, and his only experience with police commissioners had been with crooked ones. Perhaps he thought I was from the same mould. He did give me some advice at the time which I've always remembered, but I'm not sure how it should be interpreted. He said: "Ray, my two years as Police Minister taught me one thing about the Queensland Police Force. It's a big organisation, it's like a big bit of complicated machinery. If you lean on it too hard you'll put it out of kilter." I don't know what he meant by that. Did he mean that I was to go slow in introducing the recommendations of John McKinna, the South Australian commissioner who had recently written a report on the Queensland force?

If so, it was strange advice — I'd been given the implementation of the McKinna reforms as my main task.

I sometimes wonder what was covered in the Sunday School lessons Joh gave to the children in Kingaroy. I wonder if he ever brought up that biblical principle: you cannot serve both God and Mammon. The children's parents would have known of the SP bookmaker in Kingaroy, some of the children might have known themselves. Joh, it seems to me, has proved you can do something that the Bible says you can't do. Joh, in my opinion, has served both God and Mammon.

Luckily for me, Joh was not present at the gala picture night that I arranged soon after I arrived in Brisbane. I had discovered that, as commissioner of police, I was automatically the president of the Queensland Police Citizens Youth Welfare Association which ran about fifteen clubs throughout the state. Each club had a police constable as executive officer, but representatives of the community helped run the clubs and provided instructors. I found that the association was short of money and at our first council meeting we discussed ways of raising funds. I suggested that we hold a picture night. I had noticed a newspaper article about the famous actor, Leo McKern — usually known as Rumpole of the Bailey — who was back in Queensland on holiday. His new film, *Ryan's Daughter*, had just been released in Melbourne where the *Age*'s reviewer had found it to be very good. I suggested that the association should arrange an opening night at Brisbane's leading picture theatre.

We did this and the cinema proprietor agreed that all profits could go to the association. We publicised the event well and had Leo McKern arrive at the cinema in a limousine where he was met by an escort of mounted Police Troopers. There was a packed house. The first part of the program was completed without incident and then *Ryan's Daughter* was shown. It was an excellent and very interesting film, but it had a couple of bedroom scenes. These weren't all that revealing or suggestive by present day standards but, thirty years ago, they were far too advanced for Brisbane. They offended many of the parents with children present in the audience and I understood their concern. Unfortunately, I hadn't previewed the film; I had only read the review in the *Age*. The following day I received a number of angry calls from parents. There were complaints on talkback radio and letters to the editor of the *Courier-Mail*. I had to make a public apology for choosing the film and confess that I had been at fault in not viewing it beforehand. This was a very poor beginning for my stay in Queensland and I'm sure many people thought I was far too liberal. Joh is himself a strong family man and I'm glad he wasn't present.

I took to keeping out of Joh's way as much as possible. I was answerable to the police minister, not the premier. But Joh had once been the police minister himself and he retained much of his old interest in the job. This suited the executive of the Police Union, who routinely bypassed Max Hodges and myself, going straight to Joh. Joh believed he had God on his side. I always thought I had God on my side. But Joh also had a majority of influential Queenslanders supporting him. I had far fewer backers. I tried to gather support, but with very little success. I tried the Police Christian Federation, of which there was a strong branch in Queensland, but they were far more interested in personal salvation than in improving the ethical standards of the Police Force. The Police Scouters Branch of which I was a member wasn't interested in any political activity, and rightly so. The International Police Association, which I strongly supported and which gave me life membership when I left, never concerned itself with the ethical standards of the individual members of the Queensland Force. Mavis and I went to the evening services of a number of churches and spoke at random to members of the congregations, but most of them told us they were perfectly satisfied with the Police Force. They seemed to be unaware that there was so much corruption existing right under their noses. It was not clear to me whether they were simply ignorant or in a state of psychological denial.

I had a strong supporter in Zelman Cowan, the recently arrived Vice Chancellor of the University of Queensland. We were both Mexicans from south of the border and we were both subject to a lot of pressure. Zelman and I became good friends; he would offer me a shoulder to cry on briefly and I would offer him mine.

Zelman's methods of resolving problems were not confrontational. He felt that confrontation was not a very satisfactory way of resolving differences and he had other, perhaps more subtle, tactics. But I was launched on a confrontational encounter with the Police Union and there was no way I could back out of that without losing a great deal of respect. The union was implacably opposed to me. Every idea I produced, they immediately challenged. The union was very much under the control of its full-time civilian secretary, a man named Merv Callaghan who had once been an instructor at the Police Training College. I was told that he had entertained hopes that he might have succeeded Frank Bischof as commissioner. On my first day in office, Callaghan had rung me up full of bonhomie, calling me Ray and asking for my silent number, "in case of emergencies". I had remained fairly formal, telling him that perhaps the president of union might be given my number, but not the secretary. Callaghan soon began to spend much of his time attacking me through his membership, through the premier and through the media.

A very high percentage of the Queensland Police Force were members of the union and were spread right throughout the state. The titular head of the Police Union was Sergeant Ron Edington. He was a crafty, happy-go-lucky drinker with eleven children. He appeared to me more reasonable and less adamant in his views than Callaghan, so my minister and I went out of our way to establish cordial relations with him. I would invite him to my office for drinks late on Friday evenings. On various occasions I talked to him confidentially about such things as forthcoming promotions and transfers. I was very much aware that, with Queensland being so vast, there could often be family problems associated with a new posting. And since I was not acquainted with most of the members of my new Force, I was ignorant of many domestic details such as the stage of schooling of their children, the occupational demands of their spouses and the state of health of their parents. To minimise the potential adverse consequences of moving members of the force around the state, I used to consult Ron about problems that might arise from particular promotions or transfers. Ron was very helpful;

he knew many of the people involved and their family circumstances, so I was able to avoid causing some unnecessary hardship. I had told Ron that these were just confidential chats during which I sought his advice. After several of these meetings, however, I discovered that immediately after leaving me he would telephone the member of the Force whom we had been discussing and tell him that he, the president of the union, had been recommending that particular member's promotion to me and no doubt the member would be hearing shortly about his new status. When I challenged Ron about this breach of confidentiality, he said that he had his presidential responsibilities. I think he meant that he needed to gain extra kudos so that he could retain the presidency of the union at the next election. He eventually became a millionaire, having struck it lucky with some land purchases.

The Police Union executive was composed of sergeants of various classifications, all of whom had some Irish association; they were known colloquially as the Green Mafia. Outwardly they seemed to be a very cohesive bunch but, like any Irish body, the union was prey to internal friction. So I kept my ear to the ground and picked up a few leads as to who amongst the twelve executive members was on the outer at any one time. Very early on I found that Detective Sergeant John Huey was in poor favour. I checked his file and he had a good record as a detective. He had fallen foul of the union executive because he had married a policewoman while his first wife was dying of cancer. I found out that John Huey and Hilary, his new wife, were having a bad time in one way or another. Both of them had excellent work records. I asked them to see me in my office and suggested to them that they both be posted to a police station between Brisbane and the Gold Coast, in the new neighbourhood of Beenleigh, where a fair amount of crime was being reported. I said I'd transfer John as the detective sergeant and Hilary as his detective constable. I said that this would be an experiment, that as far as I knew the arrangement had never been tried anywhere else, and that I would watch the results with a great deal of interest. John and Hilary went to Beenleigh and did a first-class job. The idea of a husband and wife detective team attracted a lot of attention in the police world. The Australian Embassy in Bangkok even sent me a cutting from a Thai newspaper about John and Hilary. John lost his seat on the executive of the union so that he was no longer a voice for me at union meetings, if ever he was, but he and Hilary have produced a lot of useful work. I noticed that some years after I left Queensland, John Huey was assigned the task of investigating some of the suspect activities of Sir Joh Bjelke-Petersen. Hilary and John and I have remained friends: we correspond at Christmas and see each other whenever they come to Adelaide.

Another member of the union executive was Vince Murphy. He was not on the outer at this stage, but he seemed to me to have leadership qualities that would be very useful to me if I could involve him in the reform of the Queensland Police Force. Vince was a tall, well-built man, very capable, easy to get on with — a strong character in his own right. I asked him to come and see me. I told him I was going to form a small, independent unit consisting of a sergeant and eight hand-picked men. I told Vince that the state manager of a large department store had come to see me, complaining about the way his store in Fortitude Valley was losing customers because of disorderly conduct on the streets, drunken driving and the general air of lawlessness that was creeping into the Valley. The manager told me that he had spoken to the inspector of police in Fortitude Valley, who had said that he'd look into the problem. In the ensuing three months, nothing happened and the situation had simply become worse. I told Vince that I'd spoken to my senior officers, who confirmed that there had recently been a number of fatal road accidents involving drunken drivers in the Valley. There were some brothels and a growing number of clubs at which illegal gambling was thought to take place. I explained to Vince that my senior officers were of the opinion that little could be done because it was difficult to gain entry to the clubs whose doors had been reinforced with steel and because it was difficult to prosecute prostitutes and brothel keepers. Under Queensland law, such a prosecution would require hard evidence of sexual activity and the wives of investigating policemen would object to such evidence being obtained. I asked Vince if he could think of an indirect way of resolving the problem. At the time, I was unaware that the state Member for Fortitude Valley was Don "Shady" Lane, a former officer of the Queensland Special Branch. Lane was subsequently convicted and imprisoned. When I had spoken to my senior officers about problems in the Valley, they had seemed to be uninterested in my insistence that they get active. I hadn't realised then that they knew their inaction had the backing of the state member.

I told Vince to pick his eight men, to work independently of the Fortitude Valley divisional officers, to report directly to me and to take orders only from me. I told him to draw up his own rosters and to work his own hours. I said that, provided there was good reason, we would pay overtime. I stressed that I wanted to see real results. I asked Vince what he thought he would tackle first and he replied that cracking down on drunken driving would allow us to establish a strong police presence in the area, which might then result in a lower general crime rate. I told him to go ahead.

Vince picked his men and went to work in the Valley. When he reported to me it was clear that he and his team were making inroads into the drink-driving problem. This went on for some months and I began to suspect that we would soon be the recipients of a probe from people with vested interests and political clout, since we were in fact establishing a strong police presence in the Valley. It came — and this surprised me — through the Police Union. The secretary, Merv Callaghan, complained to me that his members were most upset at the way in which Vince Murphy's men were getting a large share of the overtime. Callaghan thought that the overtime should be spread more equitably.

I said: "Well, it's interesting that a member of your executive is doing something that your executive doesn't agree with."

Callaghan said it didn't matter that Vince Murphy was a member of the executive; all members of the Force were entitled to their share of the available overtime money.

I said: "Mr Secretary, I'd be very happy to pay overtime if it arises from your members' need to attend court to give evidence in the prosecution of drunken driving cases."

I heard no more from Callaghan, but I suspect Vince Murphy would have had to defend himself against criticism from the rest of the executive.

That year there was a reduction of about thirty per cent in the numbers of fatal road crashes in Fortitude Valley. The number of arrests for drunken driving had risen considerably. But then I received a direction from my minister. He told me that Cabinet had decided that the Fortitude Valley team had to confine itself to actions that were at least 50 metres away from licensed premises. Cabinet was not happy with the fact that the patrons of licensed premises were being questioned by Murphy's men the moment they entered their cars. It was bad for business and the licensees were complaining very strongly about it. I asked Max Hodges if this was an official directive from himself, the premier and Cabinet. He said it was and I indicated that I would instruct Vince Murphy to keep his men at least 50 metres away from pubs and clubs. I called Vince to my office and told him of the new policy.

He said: "Don't worry, Commissioner, it won't affect us."

I scanned the monthly returns and noticed that Murphy's men were still managing to operate with as much diligence as before. I sent for Vince and asked him how he was managing to be so efficient, was he sure he was operating outside the 50 metre mark? He assured me he was and mentioned that all his briefs gave the location of the intercept and that in all cases they were more than 50 metres from licensed premises. I congratulated him and said I'd pass this information to the minister, which I duly did.

I didn't hear any more about the matter for some time. Murphy's successes continued and in the second year there was another drop of about thirty per cent in the number of fatal crashes in the Valley and the number of arrests continued to grow. So one day I asked Vince how it was that he had not been handicapped by the Cabinet direction, which had clearly been designed to slow down his operations.

Vince said: "Well, Commissioner, I'll tell you what happens. My men come on duty at about five o'clock in the evening and they go to the car parks behind the clubs and they put a small sticker on the left headlights of the cars. Then when the patrons leave after drinking until nine or ten or eleven, they drive down the street and my men can pick every car that has come from a licensed premises. So we pull them over and give them a test. It doesn't matter how far away we are."

I said: "O.K., Vince. I can see nothing wrong with that."

I noticed that soon after I left Queensland, my successor, Terry Lewis, abolished Murphy's Marauders, as they'd come to be known. Naturally, Vince Murphy also lost his seat on the executive.

When we arrived in Brisbane, Mavis and I quickly found we had little in common with the Brisbane Baptist fellowship who were strictly fundamental in their religious outlook. The services were stuffy, but prior to the morning service there was a men's Bible class conducted by the Rev. Dr Athol Gill in a room at the back of the church. I had heard of Athol back in Canberra and I thought it would be interesting to attend his class, so I took to turning up at church an hour early. There were about a dozen other men of mixed backgrounds in the group. I found Athol Gill's approach to Christian living very refreshing. He was the deputy director of the Baptist Theological College and he had started a small Christian community house in an inner Brisbane suburb which he'd called the House of the Gentle Bunyip. He invited Mavis and I to visit the community, just to see what it was like.

We took up the invitation and one night Mavis and I knocked on the door of a comfortable, old-fashioned house. We were greeted by a bright young lady of about twenty years of age.

She said, "Come inside, Commissioner and Mrs Whitrod, I'm one of your piglets."

I said: "Piglet?"

She said, "Yes, my father is one of your sergeants."

She took us inside and we joined a group of about sixteen people of various ages in a large lounge. We all sat on cushions on the floor and ate a frugal supper while one of the young men related his day's experiences. I learnt that there were five people in residence at the house. Two were university students, two worked part-time and one young man was conducting leatherwork classes for unemployed youth at the back of the house. We were shown around and saw the single bedrooms. They were all sparsely furnished, but very clean. The kitchen was spotless. Both Mavis and I were impressed with the atmosphere and the environment in which these young people were working as a small Christian community. We left after about an hour, partly because my legs and back were aching from the unusual experience of sitting on a cushion on the floor. The young lady escorted us to the door and invited us to call again any time, saying she and her friends were delighted we'd come.

About four days later I received a telephone call from one of my sergeants, a man I'd never met. He said he understood that my wife and I had been to the House of the Gentle Bunyip. I told him we had. The sergeant said that he and his wife were very concerned because the young lady we had spoken to was their daughter. She was at university but she was living in the communal house. The sergeant said that he and his wife had grave reservations about the idea of young people of mixed sexes living together unsupervised. There was, he said, a bit of friction between their daughter and her parents because of this arrangement. I told him I understood his feelings. I said that we also had a daughter and that in general we would share his worries, but my wife and I had been delighted with the atmosphere of the house. I said we thought the place had the air more of a monastery than a young people's house — the place was quite spiritual.

I said: "I'm quite sure your daughter is a very capable, mature young lady of whom we can all be proud."

The sergeant said: "Well, you reassure me to some extent, Commissioner, but we're still worried."

I didn't revisit the House of the Gentle Bunyip, mainly because I soon became very busy. But we did hear soon afterwards that Athol Gill had not been reappointed to his job as deputy of the Theological College. He went to Melbourne where he was appointed principal of the Baptist University College at Melbourne University. Athol died a few years ago and I was very saddened to learn of his passing. He was an inspiring young man and I thought his approach to

Christian principles and practices was quite sound, although obviously too advanced for the conservative Baptists of Brisbane in the early 1970s.

As I've said, I quickly ran into trouble with my enforcement of the police regulation that promotion should be by merit. That this existing regulation should be enforced was one of the recommendations made by Brigadier McKinna in the report on the Queensland Police Force he submitted not long before my appointment. State Cabinet had charged me with the task of implementing all of McKinna's recommendations. When I began to examine the way in which promotion was determined by seniority alone, I asked what senior police officers actually did in their last year of service because most of them were promoted to inspector with only a little over a year to serve until retirement. It seemed unlikely that many reforms could be introduced in this short time. I was told by my assistant, Ken Hogget, that most inspectors picked a good clerk from the ranks of the younger officers. The clerk handled all of the inspector's paperwork at the inspector's desk, whether the inspector was there or not. But the inspector was often absent.

I said to Ken: "Perhaps he's inspecting his stations."

Ken said: "No, he's not doing that. He's just doing the rounds."

I said: "What do you mean, the rounds?"

"In the last year of an inspector's service," Ken said, "he goes around and calls on all of his old friends and reminds them that he will be leaving soon and that they will be invited to his public farewell."

"They need reminding?" I said.

"They need reminding that they will be expected to contribute to his going away present," Ken said. "At the farewell everyone comes along with little gifts and many of these gifts contain money. The inspectors get a fair bit of money that way."

I said, "Why would anybody pay a *departing* inspector a large sum of money?"

"Well, what they do," Ken said, "is they make sure the successor knows how much they are paying towards the retiring bloke's farewell. So then the new man knows that if he cooperates just as well as the last bloke he'll get the same when he retires. And since every constable expects to be an inspector before he retires, everybody knows that one day they'll get their turn. Many retiring inspectors have bought houses that way."

I said: "How much does it come to?"

Ken said: "Nobody knows. They don't disclose it because of tax, but I reckon the sums are large."

Allowing promotions to occur strictly according to seniority had one advantage: it neutralised sectarian rivalries. Trying to change this system at first put me offside with the premier, a Lutheran, when I promoted an Irishman on merit. Then, when I promoted a Protestant, I found myself facing strong Irish disfavour. I also fell foul of the squatters by politely declining a membership ticket to an exclusive racing club. My predecessor, Frank Bischof, had been a frequent patron of race meetings where he had been available in the Members' Enclosure to listen to requests for police action or for no police action. Frank had had an ulterior motive for his attendance. He used it to launder money he was unable to account for except as winning bets. He would bet on three likely horses in each race, as much as $500 on each. The bookie's clerk would initially record the bet as having been made by 'Mr B'. If a horse won, the name would be completed as 'Bischof'; if it lost, the bet had been made by a 'Mr Baystone'. Poor Mr Baystone: he never backed a winner in his life.

I'd first met Frank when I was running the Commonwealth Investigation Service and began attending the annual Australasian Police Commissioners' Conference. As I've mentioned previously, I first attended the conference in 1953 and managed to attend it every year except one until 1976. The conference was initially a big disappointment and nothing like the Chief Constables' Conference in England. By and large, the delegates to the conference were not very interested in the proceedings. The Queensland commissioner was usually the least interested of all. At first this was Paddy Glenn but he was soon replaced by Frank Bischof. Bischof was an imposing figure, well-dressed and big despite not carrying any excess weight.

He didn't speak much and his contributions to the conference were usually confined to saying 'yes' or 'no'. I had the distinct impression that he was just going through the motions of attending. So long as his own bailiwick wasn't under threat, he wasn't concerned. It was customary for weekends at the conference to be given over to socialising. The host commissioner would arrange an outing for the delegates and their wives, but Bischof never went on these trips. He would go instead to the horse races or the trots. At the time I had no idea that he was doing this to check on the progress of his money laundering scam back in Queensland.

Because he contributed so little to the conference, Frank gave me no opportunity to assess his intellectual capacity. It was only when I became the Queensland commissioner myself that I realised that he had been a very astute operator. Many years before, he had skilfully selected three of the very best of his cadet intake — Terry Lewis, Glen Hallahan and Tony Murphy — to be what the newspapers called his bagmen.

Just how Frank came by the money he bet at the track was discovered in 1964 by the then treasurer, Sir Thomas Hiley. As I've said, I was not told of Hiley's discoveries while I held office in Queensland and did not become aware of the information he revealed until some years after I had left when the *Courier-Mail* finally published his findings. Hiley had revealed the existence of a well-organised but surreptitious "levy" placed on all unlicensed bookmakers throughout the whole state. Payment of the levy guaranteed freedom from police action. According to Hiley, the "levy" was collected by local police officers on the understanding that it was a donation to the "slush funds" of a political party. No receipts were issued at any stage, so that nobody knew how much was retained at each step in the process. The balance from each town, calculated according to population, was forwarded to Brisbane where it disappeared — much of it at the racetrack. Hiley had only been made aware of this state of affairs when three disgruntled illegal bookmakers had complained to him that the levy was being raised to unreasonable heights. The bookmakers hadn't minded paying for protection from prosecution, they just didn't want to pay too much.

Hiley had called in the premier of the day and the solicitor general. The solicitor general had advised that there was little chance of prosecuting anybody unless the bookmakers themselves were prepared to give evidence. So all Hiley and the police minister did was call in Frank Bischof and tell him to stop the practice. At first Frank denied that it happened at all, but then Hiley had shown him the bookmakers' betting sheets which he had access to as treasurer. Where exactly were Mr Bischof and his alter ego, Mr Baystone, getting their betting money? Bischof had then agreed that perhaps the rules were being bent a little and he gave a verbal undertaking to put a stop to the levy. There was no question of him resigning from the Force for such a minor impropriety. When Bischof died, his estate was fairly small, so I've no real understanding of where all the money went. I could never get close to Frank Bischof. He was cold, not unfriendly but always very neutral as far as I was concerned. He seemed more preoccupied with personal matters than departmental ones.

Had I known of the "levy" raising practice — unapproved officially but condoned by those who benefited — I would not have accepted the invitation to become commissioner. Although I had guessed at the extent of the frequent social interaction between influential police officers and Cabinet ministers, I would have realised sooner that I had no chance of succeeding in reducing corruption. If the police controlled the inflow of "slush funds" to parliamentarians, they also strongly influenced voting in Cabinet.

Perhaps I had been misled by my own experience of a corruption-free state Cabinet in South Australia where committed Christian, Sir Thomas Playford, was state premier for twenty-seven years. "Honest Tom" came from a rural background, yet managed to make South Australia a large manufacturing region with happily settled, recent migrants from England. When he retired back to his orchard in the Adelaide Hills, his personal wealth had not increased. I had assumed that Playford's principles were the norm for Christian leaders but my Queensland years taught me otherwise. Queensland in my day was still permeated by a rural fundamentalism. Ownership of land was a goal for most men, and it was a male society. Even my own police talked about the time when they would "own a bit of soil". Rural cultures favour settling disputes informally and I came across a fair bit of this practice. I had to resign from a highly respected community service organisation because weekly lunch meetings were obligatory, and these were used by fellow members to approach me to cancel traffic tickets and other "trifles". I lost a few influential supporters this way, but at least I no longer had to put up with "Ah, Commissioner, good to see you. Can you fix this for me?"

My mail frequently contained similar requests from members of Parliament who were passing on pleading letters from their constituents. My minister, Max Hodges, supported my refusals. I was sometimes present in his office when he would receive a telephone call from another MP requesting special treatment. Max would reply by quoting the date and number of his own traffic violation and the receipt number of his own payment of the fine. We both lost supporters in this way.

When I first arrived, Max was riding high politically with a small majority of backers in Cabinet. At the time he was also Minister for Public Works and was able to approve some politically useful new schools and bridges. Joh Bjelke-Petersen was a new premier. He had not yet developed into the hillbilly dictator of his later years. But the potential had been recognised and was being developed by a couple of competent tutors, Sir Edmund Lyons and Sir Lesley Thiess.

Joh's progress in this direction was being hindered by the presence in Cabinet of one of Max's supporters, Gordon Chalk, the very able leader of the Liberals. Gordon Chalk and I were not soulmates, but we respected each other and he was always prepared to listen to our proposals. He often agreed with us and would support Max in Cabinet. Nevertheless, even Chalk was to some extent a politician in the Queensland mould. I sometimes wonder if I could have supported Max better by being more accommodating to Gordon Chalk and other influential people, by being less rigid in my moral standards. I received a telephone call from Chalk at a time when we were under attack by the Police Union and some powerful media critics. It was a time when Max needed all the help he could get in Cabinet. Chalk said on the phone that he needed a favour done. He said he knew that I was opposed to doing what he was about to ask of me, but he was in 'big trouble at home'. His wife had received a speeding ticket and she couldn't understand why her husband, one of the most powerful political figures in Queensland, couldn't have it nullified. Many of her friends had spoken of having tickets for traffic violations withdrawn in previous years.

Chalk said, "Can you help me?"

I thought about the request and then said, "Look, I'm sorry. I can't interfere with the traffic constable's decision. He's issued a ticket. Members of the Force know my policy not to interfere with any prosecution. So I'm awfully sorry."

Gordon Chalk was eventually eased out of Cabinet and, with his going, Max's political standing began to drop.

There was another decision of mine that put me offside with a number of my contemporaries — and not only in the Police Department but in other government departments as well. One of the perks of being a branch head or deputy was that you were provided with a car and a driver. Certainly there are times when a police commissioner needs a driver: for attending a ceremonial parade or similar formal occasion. But I was attempting to increase the output of the Police Department and it seemed to me that I would get better results if I drove myself about and allowed Slim, my driver, to get on with normal policing. Mavis also had her own car which we would use for personal shopping trips and the like, thus saving the taxpayer the cost of official transport. This ran afoul of the practices of other branch heads who exploited their official car and driver to the full. My predecessor would employ Slim to take his wife shopping in the afternoons. I know that some sergeants in suburban stations used to be driven home at lunchtime in the station car. It seemed to me that this was an extravagant practice that we could well do without. And then one day the minister said to me, with a note of triumph in his voice: "Ray, I've got your home phone switched over so that now the bill will be paid in full by the Department." This was also a bit of a problem for me because I didn't feel that the taxpayer should be responsible for meeting the cost of calls between the Whitrods and their interstate children. And so I kept the number of family calls to a minimum and other private calls I would not put through from the home phone at all. I suspected that there was a fair bit of Police Association business conducted long distance between the association's secretary in Brisbane and places like Cairns, Mt Isa and Thursday Island, all on departmental phones. I suspected that the department's phone bill could be cut as much as a quarter or a third if I could cut out private calls. But this is a very difficult thing to achieve. I thought about it for some time, but never really solved the problem. I did think at one time that I might ask the Postmaster General's Department for a list of the calls made on trunk lines from the Police Department, but it seemed to me that I had enough conflict on my plate as it was without inviting more by tackling this issue. At any rate, it appears that it was a general practice in the Queensland public service that people used official phones for private business, regarding this as part of their legitimate reward.

Once Gordon Chalk had been neutralised, Joh started to respond more openly to the approaches of the Police Union executive. Joh's political strength came not only from National Party ranks, but from the community as a whole. He regularly proclaimed the slogan of rural culture: that the place for women is in the three K's. These were kirk, kitchen and kinder (children). He was known as a committed Christian and in this way secured the allegiance of the various clergy and their flocks. Perhaps they shared his view of scripture: that possession of material wealth is evidence of God's approval of one's actions. In a rural culture, these "flocks" — and indeed the community at large — tend to be under educated. If government policies are difficult to understand, the leader can say reassuringly: "Just leave it to me. You don't have to worry your heads about that." Joh said that continuously. This reassured not only the people at large, but also Joh's "chooks". These were the full-time, supposedly hard-boiled, journalists assigned to the Queensland parliament. They, in turn, fed the newspapers, radio stations and television broadcasters with the premier's cheery assurances that everything was being looked after.

The media never referred to the fundamental contradiction of my position: that I was being criticised by the government for introducing the reforms the government itself had asked for. I endured adverse publicity in the media for the whole of my time in Queensland. The sole exception was the Australian Broadcasting Commission (ABC). The ABC provided me with an unbiased channel to the people of Queensland, mainly through sessions chaired by the late Andrew Olley. I would appear sometimes three times a week to explain my actions to the community as a whole and seek their support, but with little apparent result. Some years after I left, Andrew had the satisfaction of launching the move which led to the appointment of Tony Fitzgerald to inquire into corruption in the force.

There were other elements of the prevailing "rural culture" which affected my reforms. The literature suggests that these types of societies frequently have "squires" who prosper greatly in that environment, and Queensland had a large number of prosperous men who were so benefiting. They were quite satisfied with the status quo and they opposed attempts of any kind to alter the current arrangements. They were politically significant and shared the premier's views on most matters. Besides the well-to-do rural folk, there were urban businessmen who were exploiting legitimate opportunities for expansion under favorable government regulations. But as well as legitimate activities, there were questionable ones which involved the dubious transfer of money. As it was, the Queensland Police Force's detectives did not have the specialised skills necessary for bringing these white-collar criminals to court, even if they had chosen to investigate. To achieve results, Tony Fitzgerald needed a highly qualified team of accountants and lawyers as well as police investigators with special powers.

Rural cultures encourage a degree of supineness in their communities. After I left Queensland, I noted an absence of public comment about claims by my successor, Terry Lewis, that the crime clear-up rate had suddenly increased. Lewis was happy to make this claim despite having personally dispensed with the services of an independent auditor. There were able statisticians and social scientists in Queensland at the time, but they refrained from making any public observations. I have wondered why.

Soon after I started in Queensland, I noted the absence of an adequate filter to separate the knowledgeable from the ignorant members of the Force. In most police forces, this filter is provided by promotional examinations, but in Queensland the pass rate was a puzzling ninety per cent. I investigated this wonderful success rate and discovered that the exam papers were always sent out to police stations and kept there overnight before being presented to the candidates the next morning. McKinna had recommended changes to this system. I installed an independent examiners' panel, and introduced a different syllabus for each rank. I arranged for all papers to be delivered to central examination centres on the morning of the exam. The pass rate dropped to around fifty per cent.

I also noted that police briefs for prosecution showed a comparatively poor knowledge of English. I did a sample survey and found that most of the members of the Force, especially the older ones in the supervisory ranks, had left school with only a primary level education. Some had completed an extra year, leaving when they turned fourteen. Only a few members had managed to obtain an Intermediate level certificate. Modern police work requires a higher level of education than that, so I arranged with the Education Department to provide classes in literacy and basic arithmetic similar to the ones they gave to bricklayers' and carpenters' apprentices. I invited members of the Force to apply to attend these classes in departmental time. As a further inducement, I said I would grant them an extra week's leave for every subject they sat. For those who qualified there would be accelerated promotion. The Police Union executive objected. They bypassed both me and the Police Minister and took their complaint directly to the premier, who was pleased to grant them an interview. As a result, and without any consultation with myself or my minister, the premier made a public announcement that the Queensland people did not require their police to be Rhodes scholars. The media gave much coverage to Joh's rebuke. Again, there was a complete absence of comment by academics, lawyers, judges and teachers. The premier's avowed anti-intellectualism was rewarded some years later by an honorary doctorate conferred on him by the University of Queensland.

One other way I tried to raise educational standards in the force was by opening the field to women (who were usually better qualified than the men). In order to reduce Joh's hostility to any new plans I might have, I often camouflaged them by saying they were based on the approved McKinna recommendations. Most were; some were closely related; but it would have been difficult to establish the relationship with some of them. The truth is that the large-scale introduction of women into the Queensland force bore little relation to the South Australian model that McKinna had proposed. In South Australia, female police officers had very restricted roles. My program called for a tremendous change, both in terms of numbers and in the range of duties and responsibilities. I arranged that, in Queensland, female recruits completed the same introductory course at the academy as the men before being sworn in. They were then rostered for their twelve-month probationary period for a complete range of duties, both in suburban stations for general training and mobile patrols for street work. On completion of this training, they were posted to fill a whole range of police duties. They joined the Traffic Branch where they took on point duty at busy intersections. They worked in mobile units, including an all-woman traffic car. They participated in school liaison teams, controlled the desk in the operations room and performed beat duty on all shifts. Under the supervision of a male sergeant, we established a rape reporting centre run by female officers. Women officers became part of the mounted troop, cleaning out stables, exercising the horses and taking part in ceremonial displays. They became qualified searchers in the fingerprint department. They contributed as full members to the planning and research section. They became plainclothes officers in the drug and criminal investigation sections. They qualified as scene-of-crime officers. They joined the police pipe band. They became instructors at the academy. They joined the water police unit and the public order squad. They searched and escorted female prisoners and generally carried out all the duties of a constable of police. Most of these duties had not been undertaken by women in Australia's police forces before and accordingly, these female officers in Queensland aroused much interest. The results of these innovations varied, as might be expected, ranging from average to very good. At this time, Queensland did not have its own detective training school. Potential detectives were sent to Melbourne for training since the Victorian course was regarded as the best in Australia and was used by quite a few other states. When Hilary Huey went to Melbourne, she topped the course with the highest marks of any candidate.

During the six years when women were coming into full play in the force, there was only one charge laid against a civilian for assaulting a female officer. During the 1974 demonstrations in Brisbane, a plot was hatched to bring discredit on the police by causing male constables to use excessive force in ejecting female demonstrators from a government building. I sent in a squad of women police officers who very quickly resolved the situation. In the next day's *Courier-Mail*, the demonstrators claimed that I had been "unfair" in using female officers to remove female demonstrators.

One regret that I do have about my increased intake of women recruits is that I failed to attract Aboriginal women to the force. Despite strenuous attempts to recruit Aboriginal girls, only four applied and none of these survived the twelve-month training period. One of the four came from Thursday Island, another from Townsville and, being unused to big city life, they rapidly became lonely. One young woman left because she was offered a better job and the fourth was found to be pregnant a month before she was due to be sworn in. At that time there was no provision for retaining pregnant constables.

I have often wondered what happened to the women who joined the force in those days. In 1989 I received a letter from one of the first women cadets. She wrote:

> I have come to the realisation that what attracted me to policing was your vision. I shared that vision and believed that I could contribute towards it becoming a reality. Since you resigned there has been no visionary to replace you. As I look around for another employer I have actively sought out another leader with a vision. It seems possible that

I might have found another in the Director of Accident Prevention. I wish you well and thank you.

A. Lidgar

Although the increased numbers of women meant an increase in educational standards, the really major step I made in this direction was a cadet intake of very selected secondary school students. When I arrived in Brisbane, Max Hodges had told me that there had been some talk of establishing a Police Training College similar to the one McKinna had in Adelaide, but so far nothing much had come of it. I suggested that we needed to attract some young, intelligent people and that we needed to interest them in a police career. Max agreed and we built the academy where we offered cadetships to secondary school students, both boys and girls, who had successfully completed the Intermediate Certificate and were planning to proceed to the Matriculation Certificate. We offered them residential accommodation for the two years of schooling required, plus an allowance of $5000 a year. Those who wished to stay on after matriculation were offered a third year of specialised police training, so that when they entered the police force they would be well-educated and have a sound background in police matters. We attracted quite a number of applicants, mainly from high schools in country areas where there was less opportunity for completing the final years of secondary school while still living at home.

We selected twenty of the best applicants and got some really high quality recruits. They lived at the academy where we provided teachers who joined our staff from other high schools and colleges. We offered these teachers a small wage increase and were able to employ some very competent and experienced people. The academy was provided with laboratories, a library and other necessary equipment. For the position of principal, we were able to recruit Harry Alsopp, who had been the deputy head of a leading boys' college in Brisbane. I had met Harry through Baptist circles and thought that he could fill the position very well, which he did. I tried to develop an atmosphere at the academy which emphasised the independence of individual constables, so that the cadets realised they would not be like soldiers acting under orders, but would be required to use their own initiative and sense of responsibility when out in the front line, whether this was street duty or criminal investigation. Initially the cadets didn't attend parades or march around the academy in squads. I tried to emulate a university environment. However, after about four or five months the cadets themselves developed a liking for a more disciplined approach and they, of their own accord, developed some drill ceremonies which they executed with a great deal of pleasure and smartness.

The academy was very well-equipped and I impressed upon Harry that he needed to keep a faithful record of the contents. An audit was conducted about eight or nine months after the academy opened. It was discovered that a mattress in one of the spare bedrooms was missing. Harry organised an inquiry and subsequently rang me and said that the missing mattress had been found and that he would be forwarding a report. He said that, since it was the first case of its kind, he thought I might need to establish some policy guidelines. The report reached me and I discovered that the missing mattress had been found in the back of a station wagon that belonged to one of the leading cadets. Apparently he had converted the station wagon into what he called a passion wagon, for which he had found great use. The problem with this was that the young man was the son of one of my senior inspectors at headquarters, one of my few supporters. The inspector was well known in Brisbane and throughout the force and did his job with commendable efficiency. I had employed him on a number of occasions for special tasks. I knew that it had been a great joy for him and his wife when their son was accepted by the academy. Somehow a whisper reached me that word was going around that the lad would be let off with a light reprimand because of my friendship with his prominent father.

Mavis and I had been spending a lot of off-duty time in the evenings with the cadets at the academy. We had visited their camps in the bush. We had spent many after-dinner hours yarning with them and I had hoped that not only would we get to know the cadets this way, but that I'd be able to pass on to them my vision of what an ideal police officer was. I had stressed that one of the outstanding qualities for a police officer was integrity, that his honesty could be relied upon at all costs. If you couldn't trust a policeman to be honest, I said, the whole system broke down. So the missing mattress was a test case of some importance to me. I had to either confirm my position on the importance of honesty in a police officer's make up, or else be seen to offer concessions which would be attributed to my relationship with the cadet's father. It seemed to me that I had no choice in this matter. If I was to keep faith with the other cadets and with the philosophy I'd been preaching, I had to take some quite firm action. This I did. I suspended the lad and told him that if he found himself a job and if his record at the job was good enough, we would consider him for re-entry into the second intake. This was a bitter blow to him and to his parents. The lad's father came to see me and was most upset that I had imposed such a severe penalty for a mere peccadillo, for simply borrowing one of the academy's mattresses. I tried to explain that honesty was important to me, that I couldn't make allowances because of any personal preferences. The lad left the academy and soon got a job somewhere else. He never applied for readmission and I lost the very valuable support of the inspector. It was a hard decision, but it seemed to me that I had to demonstrate my belief in my own principles.

From time to time, I've had reports of the doings of the lads and girls I recruited into the Queensland force some twenty-five years ago. I was delighted to note that Tim Atherton, one of the first cadets accepted by the academy, has recently been appointed Assistant Commissioner of Police in Western Australia. That really puts the mark of approval on our selection and training procedures. For Tim Atherton to go from Queensland, which hasn't got an altogether clean record, to a high interstate position is a matter of some joy to those of us who started the academy. It is also a reflection on the government of Queensland which, in recent years, has tended not to choose people of the calibre of Atherton from its own ranks to fill the top positions, but has turned south to try to pick the eyes out of the Victorian Police Department.

9

A losing battle

(1970–1976)

NO doubt many of the uneducated in the Queensland community sympathised with Joh's jibe that the police force did not require Rhodes scholars, for surely he himself had shown that an ignorant country lad could amass a million dollars. And if Joh, as premier, didn't know what the doctrine of the separation of powers was, why should the man in the street care about such southern niceties? But not all Queenslanders were so ignorant. The Bar Council, the Law Society, the law professors and the more intelligent of the clergy might have been able to define the separation of powers if pushed — but from them came no comment in my defence. Were they just craven and scared of the consequences?

They had every right to be. My own experience confirmed this. After I left Queensland, I applied for an advertised vacancy for a researcher at the Australian Institute of Criminology in Canberra. The director, Bill Clifford, telephoned me. He said that with my Cambridge diploma and wide ranging career I was the outstanding applicant and the job was mine. He rang again the next day and said that, as a matter of courtesy and formality, he had notified the Commonwealth attorney-general of my selection. As a courtesy and a formality, the attorney-general had notified his state colleagues. Bill Clifford then had to inform me that I was not acceptable to Queensland and that other arrangements had to be made.

Yet it must be said that the "rural culture" of Queensland provided me with a most supportive minister, Max Hodges, and his able Departmental Head of Public Works, David Mercer. And in the Police Department I found a small core of loyal, intelligent and committed officers prepared to back my ethical standards. It took a little time for me as an outsider, but I somehow managed to reproduce a team in the Queensland Police Force that equalled the ASIO group I had had in Sydney. To do this I had to build upon foundations laid down by the corrupt Frank Bischof. Bischof had never employed a secretary or a typist. He never wrote anything himself; he never dictated anything. He had an outer office in which he housed his "legal section". This was staffed by some hand-picked, bright young men under the direction of an inspector. These men handled all correspondence, which Bischof merely signed. Bischof must have applied a different set of selection criteria when he picked his legal section from that which he used when picking his bagmen. It was from the legal secion that some of my strongest supporters came. One of these men was Sergeant Ken Hogget, whom I made my personal assistant. John Dautel and Greg Early also came to my team from the "legal section". These three, along with Val Barlow and Norm Gulbransen and my secretary, were in effect my kitchen cabinet. They not only embraced my policing philosophy of integrity and competence, but they built upon it with practical suggestions. They were insiders with a knowledge of how things had been done at the top. They had smelt a few rats in their time. Their knowledge of the force was far superior to mine, and their understanding of likely reactions by other members — in particular, those of the union executive — was invaluable. Hoggett and Dautel resigned not long after I did. Early stayed on under Terry Lewis and eventually became assistant commissioner.

Norm Gulbransen was a very popular man, a few years younger than myself and of medium build. He was a bright bloke, never moody, a pleasure to be with. He was always very courteous to me, even calling me "Commissioner" on social occasions, although I would have been quite happy with Ray. In some ways he, like the rest of my team, was an oddity: he had managed to rise through the ranks of the Queensland Police Force without becoming tainted.

Indeed, he had gained a reputation for honesty that impressed Max Hodges so that, when we were forming the Criminal Intelligence Unit, he was Max's immediate candidate for leader. I suppose it is one of the ironies of promotion by seniority alone that such a system cannot deny promotion to non-corrupt officers. Norm was very fit. He was a marathon runner and an enthusiastic cricketer, a better bowler than batsman. For a number of years, Norm captained and chaperoned a team of students at the academy. I'm sure that his approach to cricket in particular and life in general must have had a good influence on the students.

Ken Hogget was also a likable young man. As I have said, he had wangled the job of picking me up at the airport when I first arrived in Brisbane, and was the first to warn me of the true state of policing in Queensland. I thought he was very brave to tackle a new appointee with such news. In the coming years, he proved to be a very loyal, thoughtful personal assistant. If I wasn't at my desk and Ken answered the phone, he would give nothing away, even to the minister, merely insisting that I would ring the caller back when I was free to do so. He wrote shorthand, which was unusual. Somehow we just seemed to click. He had a young family of boys and taught Sunday School at a Baptist church. If I thought up a new scheme, Ken would immediately start adapting it to Queensland conditions — he had an encyclopedic knowledge of the state's geography, both physical and political. After he had been my assistant for about four years, I pointed out to him that in the interests of his own career he had better have a bit more on his CV than having worked in my office. So Ken set up a schools' liaison committee and soon had a working relationship with many of Brisbane's high school principals. It was in this capacity that Ken cracked a housebreaking crime ring that had been eluding police for some time. The houses were always broken into at lunchtime and the thieves always picked empty houses, although they did not employ the usual method of determining whether anyone was at home: knocking on the door, pretending to be collecting for a charity or some similar ploy. Ken discovered that the thieves were school boys who, before wagging school for a bit of lunchtime thievery, first checked the school canteen to see whose mother was working there that day, leaving her home unattended. A few years before I left Queensland, I encouraged Ken and a few others to undertake part-time degrees. It was becoming obvious to some of us that a close connection with me could well become a liability under a new regime. Ken completed his degree just before I was forced to resign. He soon resigned himself and obtained a position with the Brisbane Harbours Trust, the chairman of which was my former minister, Max Hodges. Ken eventually became CEO of the trust.

John Dautel was another invaluable member of my team, although I got off on the wrong foot with him. He had been a sergeant in the legal section but had recently been promoted to senior sergeant. Within a week or two of my arrival, there was an appeal against his promotion by another sergeant who had seniority. I was called by the appeal committee to give evidence about the role of my office staff. The only objective bit of evidence of superior skills that John Dautel could muster was his ability to write fast shorthand. The committee asked me only one question: did I think that the ability to write shorthand was an essential qualification? I said that since I was now employing trained secretaries, there was little need for sworn police officers in my office to have this skill. The promotion was given to the sergeant who had appealed. I soon discovered that this was a great pity because Dautel was easily the superior candidate. I told John that, had I known this at the time, I might have indicated that I regarded shorthand to be a very valuable asset. John Dautel, like Ken Hogget, was of great use to me in placing things in a Queensland context. Like Ken, he completed a part-time degree and, also like Ken, he resigned not long after Terry Lewis took over as commissioner. He and his wife opened a successful high-class restaurant in Maryborough.

Perhaps it would have been a good thing if Tony Fitzgerald had included in his investigation an attempt to determine why these particular men were prepared to openly join my attempts to identify their corrupt workmates. It was a courageous thing to do because they would have known better than me that our chances of success were slim. In any case, they would be — and did become — outcasts in Queensland for the rest of their lives. I still wonder why this small group of men was different.

Instead Fitzgerald chose the time-honoured method of trying to introduce change in individuals by imposing further departmental procedures and reorganisations from the top down. I remember well the wise response of Nigel Powell, Queensland whistle-blower of the century and former member of the notorious Licensing Branch during the Bischof era, who resigned when he found out what was going on and told the press all he knew. "Lasting change can never be imposed or even legislated for," Powell said. "Lasting change will occur only if we as individuals decide we want to change."

My choice of a personal staff team was not perfect. Unwittingly, and on good recommendations, I included an opportunist who benefited personally in subsequent years. But one error in a dozen choices, with my starting from scratch, was unfortunate but acceptable. The others have suffered rough treatment to varying degrees. Some have developed psychological problems. As I told Colin Dillon, I wrote to Joh's successor on their behalf but the unfazed "rural culture" denied them recognition for their and their families' sacrifices.

There was one idea of mine that won Joh's immediate support. I had heard from army contacts that there were some serviceable aircraft about to be sold off. The army wasn't expecting to raise much at auction for these planes as they only had three seats. I checked our files and found that we had three qualified pilots who were serving policemen. I went to Joh and suggested that it was about time we developed an air wing. Joh is himself a qualified pilot and fond of flying, so he soon saw the merit of my suggestion that we could save time and money by using small planes to transport prisoners to district courts, transport police witnesses to hearings, take inspectors to their outlying police stations and alleviate the necessity of chartering planes every time we needed them in an emergency. We purchased one of these planes, the department paid for the three pilots to upgrade their licences and we started our Air Wing. I must acknowledge that the idea came from South Australia.

John McKinna already had an air wing, but the pilots were not themselves policemen and the planes were chartered. We found our planes most useful. When they were not in use for other business, I encouraged my inspectors to use them for visiting remote police stations. I discovered that some stations in the far west of the state had never previously been visited by a superior officer. I arranged that Mavis and I would pay these stations a flying visit, so that I could talk to the police and the local shire people and Mavis could talk to the police wives about their housing conditions.

One of the police stations we visited was in Birdsville. It was my second visit, but Mavis's first. We only stayed two days, but I managed to pay a visit to the school house. It was not the same building that my mother had attended. It was light, well-ventilated, clean and well cared for with many posters, charts and diagrams on the walls, but it was simply a single room with a porch entrance. Inside there was a class of about twenty children, all dark skinned except for one boy with red hair. All the primary grades were represented. It was only a one-teacher school, but that teacher must have been very committed to his job. I met him and I was impressed: he clearly meant to make his stay in Birdsville worthwhile for the children in his care, but he only planned to stay one year. I found that that was the rule: teachers only ever stayed one year in Birdsville, so the children experienced an ever-changing parade of teachers. The teacher told me that no child from Birdsville, as far as he could determine, had ever gone on to secondary school. I asked about the red headed boy and was told that he was the policeman's son. I paid for a couple of years' subscription to the *National Geographic* for the children and told them that my mother had greatly benefited from her time in the school. I asked the policeman, Senior Constable Kern, about his boy and his progress at the school. He said that most of the children at the school found European education difficult and that he felt that his own boy was being handicapped by being brought up in such a remote spot. He hoped that his boy would proceed to secondary school, but this would mean that the lad would have to board somewhere else.

While I was there, I checked around amongst the station managers, the hotel licensee and others and they all gave me good reports about Senior Constable Kern. They said he was very community minded and on public holidays would often organise a barbecue in the police station grounds. People would come from miles around to grill steak from their own cattle and drink beer. Senior Constable Kern would play his banjo. I was told that the policeman really livened up existence in Birdsville.

When I returned to Brisbane, I still kept thinking about the disastrous film night and what it had done to my reputation amongst the good families of Brisbane. I talked about this with my little team at headquarters and wondered if there was something I could do to lift my public image. Ken Hogget said that Clem Jones, the Lord Mayor of Brisbane (which included a lot of the surrounding countryside), maintained his reputation from year to year by appearing once a fortnight on a talkback radio program on a local commercial radio station. Ken said that Jones usually managed to answer listeners' queries on air and he gave the impression of being a caring Lord Mayor. So the next Tuesday, at about eleven o'clock, Ken and I listened to Clem Jones's program. I was impressed. He started by giving a quick rundown of recent council development programs and then invited listeners to phone him with their problems. The queries came in thick and fast and Lord Mayor Jones handled them with aplomb. I asked Ken how Jones was able to answer detailed questions about obscure suburban roadworks, about paving, about when the sewerage would be laid on, about overflowing creeks and the like. Ken said he'd make some inquiries. A few days later, he had the answer. Ken told me that Clem Jones had a very nice little system for dealing with on-air enquiries. Ken said that when a listener rang the station with a question there was a 90 second delay before the caller was put through to Jones, who was probably on air answering another question. In that 90 seconds, the caller had to give the station receptionist a brief outline of what he or she was calling about. Unbeknownst to the general public, Clem Jones was accompanied by the city engineer and the city treasurer, who were equipped with suitable reference material. During the 90 second delay, these two would consult their records and quickly jot down the details. When Clem Jones took a call about the potholes in a particular street, he would be able to tell the caller that he thought he could remember the street in question.

He'd ask the caller: "Doesn't it run off the main highway and isn't the bit you are worried about near the intersection with Cardinal Street?"

The caller would confirm these details and Jones would say, "Well, I think we last paved that section ten years ago."

The caller would then say: "Yes, it was ten years ago and it's about time you did it again."

Clem would then say that that particular bit of street had been discussed at council a couple of meetings previously and that an allocation of $5000 had been made in the budget for the work to be done next year. Without fail.

The caller would then thank the Lord Mayor, clearly reassured by the close and informed interest he was taking in her little street.

Ken suggested we emulate Clem Jones. I gave him the go ahead and he contacted the radio station, which was delighted and offered us the spot immediately following the Lord Mayor's. So on the next Tuesday, Ken Hogget, John Dautel and myself went down to the station armed with some books. I talked briefly about how the crime rate was falling in Brisbane and about our mobile patrols and our system for phoning incident reports to headquarters. Then I invited calls. These didn't come in very fast at first, which gave us time to break in our little team, but they soon picked up. People rang in about traffic intersections, about highway patrols, about the strength of police at various stations and such like. No one called to report the operation of an SP bookmaker in their suburb. I tried to get through to the listeners that I was a family man and a grandfather, with a care and concern for the well-being of Queenslanders. I somehow worked into replies to traffic problems personal details indicating that I lived an ordinary life and wasn't an advocate of free love and wild parties. The radio station management congratulated us after the program and invited us back. I appeared on the fortnightly show for some months, silently assisted by Ken and John, but eventually pressure of work meant that we had to give up the program, much to the management's disappointment.

I introduced the concept of management by objectives, using quantifiable data, as a way of assessing our annual outcomes. Once a year the executive heads of the force's branches would meet to check their performance against goals which had been set twelve months previously. If, for example, it was found that the target of decreasing housebreaking by five per cent had not been met, reasons would be sought and remedies proposed. There was a set procedure for communicating these decisions and initiating debate down the line. The branch heads would talk to their inspectors who would talk to their district sergeants who would talk to the rank and file members of the force. I provided a detailed breakdown of this procedure in my annual reports.

After some years I was able to report that all of the McKinna recommendations had been introduced and were being implemented, with the exception of the principle of promotion by merit. I had given the McKinna material my prime attention as Cabinet had requested, but there were other departmental activities that caused me concern. Soon after my arrival I had spent some hours inspecting the Special Branch office and files. Most of the files I examined contained information that was unclassified as to validity, reliability and degree of relevance. I found references which appeared to be purely anecdotal, hearsay or at best third-party reports. The range of people investigated seemed unjustifiably large and selection appeared to be based on the personal judgments of investigators rather than a systematic analysis of any threats.

Obviously the branch had simply grown from small beginnings and was staffed by men who had received little if any training in intelligence duties. Perhaps their calibre can be gauged by the fact that Mr Don ("Shady") Lane, the now-disgraced ex-MP, had once been a long-time member of it. The staff operated almost autonomously and had frequent access to the premier. It was clear to me that if the premier was receiving the type of information I had found in the files, he could be basing his decisions on unreliable reports.

There seemed to be no system of accountability in operation, and no overall supervision by a senior police officer, yet in theory I was responsible for the branch's operations. But since the Special Branch officers were on good terms with the premier, and since any attempt to improve its operation was likely to be a long, drawn-out struggle, I postponed taking action until I had cleared my more immediate objectives.

There were other almost autonomous units: the Pipe Band, the Mounted Cadre and the Water Police. Each had built up a considerable body of public support and any attempt by me to produce a cost–benefit analysis was likely to be met with strenuous opposition from both the Police Union and the media. Yet I had come across disturbing features in each of these bodies and my immediate reaction was to consider the possibility of a community advisory committee which would provide expert advice and propose operational guidelines for them. But again, I could foresee organised resistance from vested interests. Some of these "interests" were in high places. On one of my rare inspections of the Water Police vessels, I came across a very large freezer in the stern of their largest boat. I was curious and was told that this was needed to hold the catch when "X" was out with them. This fishing was a regular duty. "X" wanted the fish for official dinners since his entertainment allowance was pretty thin. When later my wife and I were dinner guests of "X", we were served fresh fish! He made his point. I postponed my review of the Water Police operations.

When the number of women recruited as police officers had reached about one hundred, I called them together and addressed them in confidence. I was the only male present. I explained that their recruitment had been controversial and that any mistakes they made were likely to be given magnified public coverage. I asked them to be prudent in their behaviour at all times because at the moment they were in the public eye. I told them that they were sworn officers with the same powers and responsibilities as their male colleagues, and that every position in the Force was open to them until it was established that females could not do those particular duties. I told them I planned to have an all-female rape squad and a female traffic car to begin with, perhaps introducing more units like these if the scheme worked satisfactorily.

I explained that the union executive was not in favour of my moves because a male of any rank was traditionally considered senior to any female, regardless of her rank. I suggested that the female police officers might consider attending branch meetings of the union with a view to influencing the union's views. I told them that this talk was just between them and me. Within two hours the police union secretary rang me and was able to describe the details of that confidential meeting with the police women. But generally my policy of recruiting women to up to twelve per cent of the total force strength proved successful.

The 1970s were a time of much student agitation over a number of issues. At the University of Queensland, Zelman Cowan was also having a rough ride. The students invaded his office and refused to leave. He appealed to me and I had police forcibly remove the trespassers. This got me off to a bad start with the students. They began a strike during which they occupied the central quadrangle for several days and disrupted lectures. Zelman again appealed to me and I went to the university and spoke to the ringleaders. The outcome was their challenging me to a public debate, which I accepted. It was held the next evening in a large university hall overflowing with heckling students. It was known that the debate was being televised live by the ABC.

My opponent, a third-year student, an articulate and presentable young woman, outlined the students' side, and then I responded. I remember I startled them by saying that my objective was not only to get them to agree to go back to studies but also to agree to my setting up a permanent police station on their campus. They were all aware that in Melbourne a similar situation had been resolved by the police agreeing that the campus was a "no go" area for them and that they would not enter without getting permission to do so. I told the students that, quite recently, I had been a student myself. I knew their problems. At the ANU I'd attended classes while I was Commissioner of Police and had young radicals sitting beside me, lighting up marijuana cigarettes, just to egg me on. I cannot recall all the details of the debate, which was rowdy and full of interjections, and so the exact outcome is only vaguely remembered, but the strike finished at that time. With the consent of the vice-chancellor and the students, I set up a small one-man police office in the university. The officer appointed to this task was already a part-time student at the university.

I instructed him to go out of his way to be helpful to students who wanted to report accidents, renew licences, report lost property, arrange driving tests and the like, but otherwise to keep a low profile. The arrangement worked satisfactorily for all concerned until it was discarded by my successor, Terry Lewis, some years later. I was pleased with an invitation to be the patron of the Engineering Students' Society and flattered when they repeated this offer the following year. I was proud of that invitation. I was asked to speak after dinner to the residential colleges and relationships between police and students were good. However, at the time of the Springbok confrontations they rapidly deteriorated.

The South African rugby team had already been the subject of violent confrontations between anti-Apartheid protesters and the police in Adelaide, Melbourne and Sydney. In Brisbane, we managed to provide a secure playing field, but the protesters gathered outside the Tower Mill Hotel where the Springboks were staying. On the second night of the protest, I took charge myself. There must have been about a thousand demonstrators facing six hundred police outside the hotel. Things started to hot up at about a quarter to seven, just as the main television news broadcasts were about to begin. I received a call from the matron of the next-door hospital. She was worried about some surgical operations then in progress. The noise was making the surgeons edgy — would it be possible to quieten things down a bit? I went to the leader of the protesters, a theological student, and explained the problem. I pointed out that the Springboks would still be here on the following night. Couldn't the proceedings be adjourned for twenty-four hours?

"I believe you, Commissioner," he said. "But my mob won't."

I suggested he go into the hospital to talk to the matron himself.

He did this and on his return addressed the crowd through a megaphone. The situation in the hospital was serious, he said. Come back tomorrow and we'll have another go. Everyone went home.

By the next night I had brought in a large number of country police to reinforce the metropolitan members of the Force. Country police are not used to being tolerant of political protest, especially when it is couched in the terms that some of the protesters were then using in their taunts. We were Nazis and fascists and we ought to go back to Germany. I divided my men into three shifts and rotated them every quarter of an hour. During the half-hour they had away from the front line, the hotel supplied them with sandwiches and tea. As the seven o'clock news approached and things were getting rowdy, I was standing in a room on the first floor of the hotel surveying the scene with a loudspeaker in my hand. A brick was thrown through the window, landing at my feet. I realised that the time for passively absorbing the provocation was past. I spoke to the crowd through the loudspeaker, telling them we were going to clear the street in three minutes and asking them to disperse. Everyone waited for three minutes. The police charged. Some protesters were knocked over; most ran away. The police clearly took the action very seriously. I got the impression that many of the demonstrators were treating the proceedings as a game. As the demonstrators and the pursuing police disappeared down the hill, I used the loudspeaker to recall my men. They didn't hear me.

The next morning I received a visit from Zelman Cowan. He said that the university had had senior academics in the crowd to monitor police behaviour. The general feeling was that I had over-reacted in ordering the street cleared. I put my side of the story to him and I think he half-accepted that I couldn't have stood passively by while the hotel's windows were being broken.

I received a bitter note from some postgraduate (and therefore presumably more mature) students, charging me with betrayal of our joint understanding that police were not to be used to repress dissent but only to maintain civil order. Then it became known that the police union had passed a motion of no confidence in me because of my policy of using as little violence as possible — called "gentleness" — in dealing with demonstrators. It also became public knowledge that the premier had signalled which side he was supporting by granting the police extra leave without any application for this from me. The postgraduates then sent a note of apology for their earlier letter. As it was, the Tower Mill Hotel was blacklisted by the trade unions. It went rapidly downhill and the owners had considerable difficulty selling it.

It was another student demonstration that played a major role in my final showdown with the premier. Joh had decreed that there were to be no street demonstrations without permits from the police. He had instructed me to issue no permits. The students had decided to march from the university to the city. I talked to the leaders and told them I couldn't issue a permit and advised them that if they were going to march, it would be best to do it on the footpath. Of course, they didn't keep to the footpath. Their route took them under a bridge, which provided a useful vantage point for the television cameras. It was just before this bridge that the inspector in charge of the Motor Traffic Branch used his men to stop the demonstrators. A slight, seventeen-year-old girl with a placard on a stick directly confronted the inspector. The inspector grabbed the stick. The girl held on. The inspector hit her over the head with his baton. The cameras on the bridge captured all the action and I, like most Queenslanders, saw it on the TV news that night.

Zelman Cowan and the president of the Student Union came to see me. I told them I would inquire into the matter. On their way out of Police Headquarters, the student leader said to the waiting press: "The Commissioner is going to investigate this." It was a tactical error, although obviously unintentional. All I had told him was that I was going to "inquire". This meant getting a report on the incident, which I could do as a routine internal procedure. But when the fact that I was going to investigate the incident was published in the midday press, Joh immediately issued a decree that I was not to conduct an investigation. If I was to investigate anything, he said, I was to investigate what the students were doing on the road without a permit. I still thought it was my right to inquire into the conduct of one of my own officers and that the premier's pronouncement breached the doctrine of the separation of powers. But to conduct an inquiry I would have needed the cooperation of the members of the Motor Traffic Branch. Now that the premier had issued his decree, I doubted that I would be able to obtain this cooperation. If I couldn't obtain it, the way would then be open for charges that my men had revolted, mutinied. I couldn't afford to run the risk of this happening. I backed down and there was no inquiry. This did my reputation with the students no good.

The raid on the Cedar Bay commune was a different matter. Here I could go against the dictates of the premier because I could use officers whom I trusted. The Cedar Bay raid had been carried out by local police on a hippie commune in the far north of the state. About a hundred people had been involved in the raid, which included the use of a naval patrol boat. It appeared to have been an extreme over-reaction — the hippies were alleged to have been growing marijuana. In the raid, property had been destroyed and vegetable patches trampled, but no charges were laid. People from the commune complained to me and again I said I would arrange for an inquiry. When the premier heard of this he decreed that I was not to send any officers north of Cairns to investigate. Cedar Bay is north of Cairns. I called in Norm Gulbransen and a junior officer whom I knew I could trust. I told them that I was issuing a direct order to them in contravention of the premier's directive to me: they were to go to Cedar Bay and investigate. They indicated that this was good enough for them and proceeded to Cedar Bay. Their report was critical of the local police's actions.

When later I announced I would be leaving the Queensland Police Force, the president of the Students' Union at the University of Queensland sent me a card endorsed with the words: "We are very sorry that you are leaving. You gave us hope." It was the nicest thing that happened to me.

Nigel Powell has made a strong plea not to take police problems out of their social context. Police come from, marry into, survive and retire in a social milieu. In this regard, Jill Bolen quoted a number of social commentators who described the culture of

Queensland society during my time in office as "populist, conservative, anti-intellectual, and authoritarian". I found Queenslanders to be cheerful, self-reliant, family- and community-orientated and industrious, but overall my experiences in that state did nothing to disprove the commentators' descriptions.

These characteristics explained the public support for the policies of the hillbilly dictator, Sir Joh, and his continuing endorsement of the long reign of Commissioner Lewis. Lewis was more a true son of this culture than I ever could be. At best I was an adopted son from a different, and therefore inferior, culture — a "Mexican" from south of the border. I did not condone a black — albeit prosperous — economy supported by the delivery of large sums of money in brown paper bags.

In my foreword to Jill Bolen's book, *Reform in Policing: Lessons from the Whitrod Era*, I suggest that the material in it may justify the upgrading of the folk saying, "A community gets the type of police force it deserves" into an accepted social principle. And this is true in a general sense. But it was my predecessor, Frank Bischof, who bequeathed the particular network of corruption and resistance to change that ultimately drove me to resign. As I have said, I came to the conclusion that Bischof, in his own way, was an astute operator. His selection of Tony Murphy, Glen Hallahan and Terry Lewis as his personal team showed considerable managerial acumen. What the exact relationship had been between these three and the commissioner I never knew. But I discovered that Detective Hallahan had enjoyed the freedom of travelling interstate whenever he chose. I had come across some references to him when I was Commonwealth commissioner, which had placed him in a western country town when some counterfeit notes were being unloaded. And later, on Shirley Brifman's information, I learnt that Hallahan was mixed up with eastern states colleagues in the distribution of counterfeit notes.

Soon after I had arrived in Brisbane, I was called upon by a young barrister. He told me he had been given the task of defending a man who had been charged with breaking and entering a warehouse and stealing a large stock of goods. The barrister said that Hallahan had given evidence that he had found the man in possession of the stolen goods and consequently the man, who had a criminal record, was convicted and sentenced to four years' gaol. The barrister told me that the criminal had complained that he actually had nothing to do with this particular break and enter; it was a set-up by Glen Hallahan. The criminal said that Hallahan had loaded him with a portion of the goods, having disposed of the rest for his own profit. I said I'd make inquiries. I sent for Inspector Bill Simpson, who was then head of the CIB. I thought Bill Simpson was a friend of mine because I knew him from the course that McKinna and I had run some years earlier in Canberra and we'd got on well together. I told him I'd received a complaint about Glen Hallahan, that he'd loaded up a criminal with goods he didn't steal.

I said: "Bill, what sort of chap is Hallahan? Can you give me any assessment about him?"

Simpson said: "Yes, Commissioner, he's a first-class detective. It's common practice for criminals to make these allegations. Don't believe a word this bloke says. I'll vouch for Hallahan's honesty."

Now I knew that Hallahan was a doubtful character, so it seemed to me that Simpson was saying: "Is this what you want me to say for the official record?" But he didn't wink or give any indication that this was so. Or he was saying: "If you don't know, Commissioner, you're a dope and I'm not going to tell you."

I said: "Thanks, Bill. That's helped me a lot," and he left.

All this meant, of course, that I was going to have difficulty getting through to the detective branch my vision of what I thought police work was all about.

But while Bischof had been very astute in his selection of these three young men, I think that in any circumstances they would have risen to the top just through hard work and their abilities as detectives, if they'd chosen to do it that way. Of the three, I formed the opinion that Murphy clearly was the controller. There was mention by one of the Fitzgerald witnesses that Murphy was known as "The Boss". In comparison, Glen Hallahan was a very bright, good-looking, active young man and a very capable operator. Murphy and Hallahan were, in my view, superior to Lewis. Terry

Lewis had something about him that worried me. I never knew what it was, but I thought that he was not as robust as the other two. As the years have gone by and Lewis has maintained his innocence during his seven years of imprisonment, he has surprised me. According to newspaper reports, he has shown no remorse for the crimes for which he was convicted. I think that this supports Bischof's judgment of him.

Murphy was an all-round figure of authority. He was a member of the Police Union executive and he would tackle me most aggressively any time I was invited to address the executive. He treated me with some degree of superciliousness — he clearly thought he knew a great deal more about the Queensland Police Force and the associated justice system than I did. He was able to work the system very much to his own advantage. As an example, after he retired as assistant commissioner — a position he reached despite the premier knowing his background — he was able to secure a TAB contract for himself on Stradbroke Island following a recommendation by Sir Edward Lyons, then chairman of the TAB.

I discussed with my little team at headquarters what we might do to minimise the Lewis, Murphy, Hallahan influence. We set up the Crime Intelligence Unit (CIU), as we called the small group designed to investigate police corruption, with a few very brave souls, especially Basil Hicks who really did get rough treatment later on. Just before he took up his appointment with the CIU, Basil tells about being taken to the roof of Police Headquarters by Tony Murphy, who said: "There's no need for us to be always fighting. Why don't you join us? There's nine of us — Terry, Glen and I are the main three and there's the other six. If you join us, you will be one of the main ones — there will be me, you, Terry and Glen."

Hicks said: "What about Whitrod?"

Murphy said: "We'll surround him."

According to Basil Hicks, he made a vague arrangement with Murphy to meet again and left to report the conversation to Norm Gulbransen. Tony Murphy has always denied that there was any improper discussion between himself and Basil Hicks.

Two days before I left the Queensland Police Force, Basil came to me and said that he had acquired a lot of information from outside informants about the rat pack. He said that he'd given the informants his word that their identities would never be revealed to the rat pack. With me leaving, Basil was worried that he would no longer be able to shield his sources. He asked me what I thought he should do with his files.

I said: "Burn them. I'll give you written instructions to burn them."

He took the files home and burnt them. He had a hard time in the Queensland Police Force after I left.

We were alarmed when suddenly Shirley Brifman died so mysteriously a few days before she was due to give evidence against Murphy on four counts of perjury relating to the National Hotel Royal Commission case some years previously. Shirley Brifman was a prosecution witness. It had taken some time to find Brifman and convince her to come to Brisbane to give evidence. She had been promised police protection. Then she died very suddenly from what was found to be an overdose of drugs. She left no suicide note and questions have been asked as to whether her death was actually a suicide. The Fitzgerald Inquiry found there was no evidence to suggest Murphy was involved in any way in Brifman's death, her death being a fatal occurrence which had since been associated with a number of other informers who had been drug users. Because of Brifman's untimely death it meant that Murphy's guilt or innocence on the perjury charges was never resolved, although he is of course entitled to the presumption of innocence.

I had arranged for Murphy and Lewis to be posted to far western police stations at Longreach and Charleville in the hope that this might minimise their influence. I think that at least one newspaper has claimed that by being posted out in the far west they were able to gain closer contact with Sir Joh Bjelke-Petersen and the National Party and to convince Joh that I was an ardent ALP supporter.

Whoever thought up the move to get Lewis appointed assistant commissioner was a very shrewd man. With Joh's pronouncement that Lewis would be appointed to the position, my opponents put themselves in a win–win situation. If Lewis was appointed my assistant and I remained commissioner then there would be a direct channel that would allow Bjelke-Petersen to get things done in the way that he wanted, by simply bypassing me. I now had no avenue through which to complain. My minister, Max Hodges, had been downgraded and I had no supporter left in Parliament. On the other hand, if I decided to retire because of the appointment of Lewis — which is what I did — it meant that Lewis could be appointed commissioner at a very young age with many years in the position before him. As I say, it was a very shrewd move, made, I think, with some knowledge of the way I was likely to react. I could have stayed on and been a thorn in their side, but if I felt my name was being used to give legitimacy to activities that I did not agree with, then obviously I would eventually resign. I wondered how Joh obtained that correct assessment of my likely moves. It seems to me that the impetus or information must have come from somebody who'd known me for a long time. There is only one person I can think of who fits that description, an old drinking mate of Lewis and Murphy.

As for Joh, I have very mixed feelings about that man — very mixed. I'm sure Joh takes his problems to the Lord in prayer, but I wonder if he waits for any answer. Or, if there is an answer, perhaps the reception is very bad. I make this comment because there were times during my seven years when the little team in my office felt up against it. We would retreat to the coffee table in the corner and Ken and Linda, my secretary, and I would sit quietly for a little while and meditate, thinking about the next task, hoping we might get some inspiration about what the next step should be. We must have been getting a different set of celestial signals from Joh, because he would often veto our ideas. As I've said, I didn't see much of Joh during my seven years and on the few occasions I did meet him, we had pleasant conversations. But, from a distance, it seems to me that he treated me rudely, arrogantly and ignorantly. I was the state's police authority, chosen by his government. In practice, I was probably the most experienced and best qualified police commissioner Queensland had ever had. Yet Joh dismissed many of my suggestions out of hand. It was treatment I had never experienced before. In my other appointments, the minister, if he wanted to discuss a matter I was proposing, would ask me to visit him or give him a paper setting out the pros and cons. Such a paper would then be discussed and the minister would let me put my side of the story; he would explain his stance, and I always I felt I had received a fair hearing. As a matter of fact, in the seventeen years I had been in charge of a police force, none of my recommendations had ever been turned down. But in Queensland, while I had a most sympathetic minister in the person of Max Hodges, it was the premier who often made the decisions. And Joh never gave me a chance to explain my reasons for introducing certain changes. Often the first news I had of a reversal of one of my policies was in the pages of the daily newspaper. He merely said: "Mr Whitrod will not be doing that." Joh never extended me the courtesy of talking about it.

Bjelke-Petersen's own knowledge of police principles and practices was largely confined to stories he would have been told by his police drivers. As for his knowledge of democratic theory, the Fitzgerald Inquiry exposed that as being nil. Joh had never heard of the basic principle of the separation of powers. Yet while he was prepared to dismiss my recommendations out of hand, it is obvious from the evidence of the Fitzgerald Inquiry that he listened — probably open-mouthed — to the lies that Lewis was telling him about me. For instance, Lewis told Joh that I was a staunch member of the ALP. I have never been a member of the ALP nor associated with it. After I had been replaced by Lewis, two of the trustworthy members of the Criminal Intelligence Unit went to Joh with complaints about Lewis. Joh merely listened to them and then transferred the information to Lewis himself.

In 1976 I had spent some time in a Brisbane hospital, partly because of the stress and partly because of a recurrence of malaria. Mavis had suffered another bout as well.

I had a final showdown with the premier over the forced appointment of Lewis as my deputy, and voluntarily left the force. There was a fair bit of media coverage, with some members of the public raising a petition for me to stay. I didn't have another job to go to but Mavis supported my decision. My superannuation was in a mess because I found that my previous credits were not transferable to the Queensland fund, and I lost considerably over the conversion. This affected our lifestyle in retirement but Mavis never complained about my actions. She truly was a two-cow wife.

On the day I left the Queensland Police Force, the editor of the *Courier-Mail*, wrote in a front-page article entitled "The Last of the Honest Cops" that my minister and I had done our best but we had been naive. At the time, I thought that this was an unfair comment, but as I now look back I recognise the justice of the statement. We really had no chance of bringing reforms to the Queensland Police Force.

In selecting me — an outsider — to be the state's new commissioner, Max had chosen someone who did not have the backing of either the Masons or the Irish, the two dominant social groups. He had chosen someone to occupy a position of authority in a conservative society who was tolerant of Aborigines and other minority groups, who encouraged female participation, someone who was over-educated by local standards and therefore automatically academic in judgment, a male who each day went home for lunch instead of socialising in his club, who was barely of minimum police height and who was a former soccer player in a state which worshiped the big men of Rugby League, who preferred walking along a beach to horse racing or trotting, who had to operate in a society criss-crossed by a network of obligations and prearranged mutual benefits, who thought rationally about police policies and practices instead of parochially, who was not ill at ease and inarticulate when being televised, who had a wife who did not attend fashion shows and fraternise and, perhaps worst of all, who did not blindly accept government directions but examined them for their legal validity and community benefit — all of this in a community largely content with its existing standards of ethical conduct.

If I had given more weight to the failure of Orlando Wilson to reform the Chicago Police Department, of Patrick Murphy to reform the New York Police Department, of Sir Robert Mark to reform New Scotland Yard, I might not have been so confident of being able to achieve a worthwhile outcome with the Queensland Police Department.

As it was, I recruited numerous enthusiastic and idealistic young men and women, many of whom suffered much frustration and severe disappointment in subsequent years. One of my recruits, Jill Bolen, is now a doctoral candidate in New South Wales. She joined the Queensland Police Force in 1973 and served for twenty years, working her way up to the position of chief superintendent of a region on the Gold Coast. This was an admirable feat, since the regime in which she worked was far from sympathetic to the cause of female police officers. In her published Masters thesis, Jill Bolen analyses my years in Queensland and she notes that when I was on leave in 1973 — that is, halfway through my term — Acting Commissioner Barlow highlighted the changes made under my stewardship. These included:

> the circulation of a newsletter, the construction of the Academy, reorganisation of the Information Bureau, the rebuilding and restructuring of the police operations centre, the introduction of lunch time conferences at Headquarters, setting a syllabus for police qualifying examinations, the appointment of a panel of markers to permit early notification of results, various aspects of reorganisation, enhanced numbers of women police, changes to uniforms, the formation of the Crime Intelligence Unit, enhanced education and training programs and many others. (Commissioner's Newsletter No 84, 11 July 1973 — cited in Bolen, 1997 p. 67)

Jill Bolen notes that many of the extended roles undertaken by women police officers in the Queensland Police Force were "firsts either in Australia or internationally and Whitrod took great pride in trumpeting the achievements to quell criticism of the strategy and to explain local administrative policies in relation to women" (Bolen, 1997 p. 66).

While I was in hospital for a short while in 1975, Norm Gulbransen, as acting commissioner, listed in the newsletter "just some of the real benefits gained by all police from Mr Whitrod's administration during the past five years". He wrote:

> Those which spring quickly to mind are: Increased salaries and allow-

> ances (Mr Whitrod gave evidence in support of the Police Union case!); Increase of seven days' recreation leave per year; Granting of seven days' study leave per subject for Police Arts and Sciences studies; Two opportunities per year to sit for police examinations; Provision of an examinations syllabus; Opportunity to gain Senior Constable grade at seven years' service; Extended In-Service Training courses; The Study Assistance Scheme with reimbursement of fees to members who successfully undertake approved courses; Supply of a departmental motor vehicle to each station; Provision of more comfortable and suitable uniforms. (Commissioner's Newsletter No.167, 14 Feb 1975)

With hindsight, it is still difficult for me to identify where I went wrong — if, indeed, I did go wrong. Bjelke-Petersen's public farewell comment was that I had done nothing wrong, I had just tried to do too much too quickly. I had had ten years — from age fifty-five to sixty-five — to introduce all the McKinna recommendations, recommendations that had been endorsed by Cabinet. I lasted seven years. The only recommendation that I hadn't managed to introduce was promotion by merit, and I had tried long and hard to bring it into practice. But promotion by seniority was ingrained in the whole public service system. This made it doubly hard to introduce it in a single department. There were lots of reasons why members of Queensland's police force would hang on to the notion of seniority. It had many advantages for them. It meant that almost everybody would retire as an inspector or superintendent, and promotion to these ranks would have come in the last twelve to eighteen months of service. The officer could leave the force with some glory and a superannuation payout commensurate with his recently gained rank. I do not know what other strategies or tactics I could have adopted. Perhaps we could have accepted the Police Union's suggestion that we introduce promotion by merit, but with a "grandfather clause" which meant that all serving members would be exempt from the new rules. In practice, this would have divided the force; it would have meant that the force would have had two types of members: those who were winning their promotion by virtue of their skill and dedication, and those who were having it given to them by virtue of their age. But since the older group would be slowly working their way through the higher ranks, these would have been denied the younger group for many years, regardless of their ability.

I have been back to Queensland twice: once to give evidence at the Fitzgerald Inquiry and once to give a paper at a public seminar on the Inquiry. On the first visit, I discovered that fieldwork for the Inquiry was being conducted by an Inspector James Patrick O'Sullivan. He was unknown to me when I was commissioner a few years earlier. He had never come forward to join our little group of corruption fighters, he had never volunteered any information about corruption, but presumably Fitzgerald had good reasons for selecting him. He was later appointed commissioner, probably on the strength of his work for Fitzgerald. I asked some of my former colleagues at the Inquiry if they knew Inspector O'Sullivan — he must have had twenty years' or more experience in the Force. No one knew him at all; he was an unknown quantity. How Fitzgerald had discovered him, I don't know.

It was something of a physical effort to get to Queensland. My health has not been good these last few years and I'm normally confined to home and a walking frame, but I got to Brisbane and was pleased to be able to give evidence. I followed the daily newspaper reports of the Inquiry and was delighted with both the scope and the depth of Fitzgerald's approach. Clearly the Inquiry would not have happened if Joh had not been absent from the state when the decision was taken to hold it. I was grateful to Fitzgerald for pursuing his objectives as faithfully as he did. The acting premier who instituted the Inquiry, Bill Gunn, deserves a lot of thanks for his perseverance in ensuring that Fitzgerald received all the help he needed.

I have been flattered by the suggestion that perhaps I was Australia's first modern police commissioner, but any impact I may have made on Australian policing was only possible because I was standing on the shoulders of Brigadier McKinna. He showed how even a competent and honest force like the South Australian Police could be much improved simply by utilising managerial techniques already operating elsewhere, by creating innovative programs, and by outstanding leadership. I owe much to him. He was always available when I needed to discuss plans or problems and was most generous in offering me well-considered options and practical aid. He set a personal example in commitment, innovation and integrity, not only to his own members but also to his fellow commissioners as well. Unfortunately, too few of his colleagues interstate recognised or wanted to emulate his strategies. It was his integrity in carrying out his responsibilities that subsequently brought about his too-early retirement. He certainly impressed Max Hodges when Max inspected the South Australian Police Academy at Fort Largs leaving an impression that later resulted in my appointment as commissioner of the Queensland force. McKinna was the first modern Australian police commissioner — I was merely his protégé.

10

Retracing our steps

(1976–1993)

I had no fresh appointment to go to when I decided to leave the Queensland Police Force, but within two days I had been offered academic posts at La Trobe and at the Australian National University. We decided upon Canberra because we had a married daughter living there, and many old friends. Mavis quickly sold our nice old home at St Lucia to a friend of ours who had admired it for some time. We arranged with a well-known firm of removalists for our furniture to be transported to Canberra — this included my filing cabinets and all the documents inside them. When the removalists' van was a week overdue in Canberra I began to phone the company asking about our furniture. After three weeks, I was told that everything had been burnt. On its way to Canberra, the truck had hit the side of a bridge and burst into flames. This was distressing enough, but I had strong doubts that the fire was accidental. I thought of having the matter investigated, but this would have involved using the Queensland police, now under the control of Commissioner Terry Lewis. I hadn't the heart to even try.

In Canberra I taught criminology to law students and lectured on deviant behaviour to sociology students in George Zubrzycki's department. I remember my first academic staff meeting. Various lecturers wandered into the room and plonked themselves down at the table. When George came in last, I stood up. Everyone looked at me in surprise, as if I were about to say something. So I said: "Don't you clots stand up when the boss comes in?" There was a certain amount of laughter and someone said: "We don't do things like that here, Ray." But George seemed to appreciate the gesture, so I repeated it at subsequent staff meetings, usually to good-natured laughter. I got on very well with most of my students, but one or two went to George and complained that I wasn't teaching them enough theory, that I kept talking about the way things actually happened when new laws were introduced or new enforcement procedures adopted. George told them they were lucky to have someone who could talk about these things from first-hand experience. He said that if what I was telling the students appeared to contradict some theoretical point, they should change their theories. About four years after I left Canberra, I received a letter from one of the students saying how much he now appreciated my frankness in talking about what life was really like when one was trying to enforce unpopular laws.

While I was teaching at the ANU, I was given an MA student to supervise. The girl was from Bangkok where her father was a major-general in the Police Special Branch. I had never met the man, but I knew of him. His daughter's Master's work involved measuring crime rates in Bangkok from a sociological rather than a statistical prospective. I asked her where she was going to get her data from — it could hardly be from existing literature, as there wasn't any about Bangkok crime rates. I told the girl that if she could gather reliable data in this area she would be doing something really significant, but I was dubious about her ability to do so. She said that she had already been to all eighteen district police headquarters in Bangkok and obtained access to their records. I asked her how she had managed this and she said: "Oh, my father arranged it." I told her that if the material she'd collected was valid, it was solid gold, as no one else had ever been granted access to these records. I gave her some hints as to how one goes about verifying police records — matching arrests against reports and so forth — and she set to work. She produced a colour-coded map of Bangkok that showed, amongst other things, that the Christain enclave had a lower crime rate than anywhere else.

"Don't Christians commit crimes?" I asked her.

She was quite dismissive. "Not serious ones," she said.

A few weeks later, George Zubrzycki came to me and said that the student had petitioned the department to have her MA candidature upgraded to PhD level, citing my claims about the significance of her research. The Department had agreed. In some ways, this was a disappointment to me: the girl now needed a more qualified supervisor and I lost the opportunity to gain privileged insight into the workings of an Asian police department.

We lived in a university flat and Mavis quickly made friends with our new academic neighbours, who were mostly from overseas and strangers to Canberra. She was able to help them adjust to their new locality. She was also able to spend some time with our Canberra family and got to know our grandchildren. She recommenced her tertiary study and in February 1979, then aged seventy-four, qualified for election as a member of the Australian Institute of Horticulture. But it was becoming clear to us that we could not live in Canberra for ever.

The principal reason for our return to Adelaide was family responsibility. I had completed two years as a Visiting Fellow at the ANU and was asked to continue, but short visits back to Adelaide had made me feel guilty about leaving my widowed mother, then living independently, as the sole responsibility of my younger brother. In addition, we had a married son, Ian, whom we had not seen much of since he left home and he had a growing family. Mavis agreed that we would return to the city we had both grown up in. We purchased a house near the beach and resumed the life we had left in 1949. We even rejoined our old church.

While in Canberra, I received a grant from the Australian Institute of Criminology for a project designed to produce a way of measuring a community's fear of crime and I continued this research in Adelaide. Most studies up to that time had relied on subjective accounts of people's feelings. I looked for objective indicators of a person's level of concern about the potential threat of crime and found three factors that looked interesting. One was the number of dogs that people kept for protection. Another was the number of people who had had safety door locks installed in the last twelve months. The third was the percentage of people who went out to post letters at night. I picked three suburbs in Adelaide and door-knocked all the houses in two randomly selected streets in each suburb. Six months later I returned to conduct a follow-up survey. I found that in those six months: (a) two of the local councils had raised the dog licensing fee from fifty cents to ten dollars with a resultant fall in official dog-ownership numbers; (b) one of the councils had advertised the services of a handyman for elderly people living alone and one of his main tasks had been the fitting of new and improved door locks; and (c) the time of the last postal collection had changed from nine o'clock to six o'clock. As research projects go, this one was not a great success.

Very shortly after my return to Adelaide, I became involved in forming a new voluntary organisation to help victims of crime. I had been to a meeting where an old aquaintaince of mine, Ray Kidney, had talked about the rehabilitation of ex-prisoners. In the discussion that had followed Ray's talk, a woman who sounded as if she was a retired school principal and probably was, said: "Mr Kidney, it is all very interesting to hear about what you are doing for criminals, but what are you doing for their victims?" Ray had said that it was unfortunate, but nothing was being done — it wasn't within the charter of his organisation to spend money on anything other than the rehabilitation of offenders. Not being one to sit back quietly, I stood up and pointed out that convicted criminals had money spent on them because people like Ray Kidney had created an organisation. I said the victims of crime were an almost randomly selected cohort of isolated individuals; they had no organisation so it was hardly surprising that no money was spent on them. My comments were reported in the *Advertiser* the next day. A couple of nights later, I was rung up out of the blue by a woman who said that her name was Ann-Marie Myketa and that one of her daughters had been murdered. She had been talking to another mother in a similar situation and they had decided that an orgainisation was in order. They'd been impressed by what I was reported to have said at the meeting and they understood that I'd spent my life organising things — would I like to found an organisation to represent the victims of crime? I said: "Not me, I'm going fishing." But Ann-Marie had a powerful personality and she wasn't accepting this sort of cop-out. I finally agreed to host a small meeting at our place. Ann-Marie, Judy Barnes and some other parents of murdered children, as well as some people who had themselves been badly beaten up or raped — about a dozen in all — met in our lounge room on the following Sunday afternoon. Mavis provided hot scones and tea and immediately expressed her support for the notion that those present establish the Victims of Crime Service (VOCS). I became the unpaid executive officer and, after securing an unwanted city office, our home telephone became the out-of-hours contact point.

I worked long hours talking to victims, delivering speeches to service clubs, seeking sponsorship and writing regular newsletters. By the end of twelve months, we had 1800 members. We had made contact with the Attorney-General Chris Sumner, and then with his replacement, Trevor Griffin, who promised us a small grant. We also helped initiate a government investigation into the needs of the victims of crime — the first of its kind in the world. As a result, the government established a fund, using money raised by a levy on court-imposed fines, to compensate the victims of crime. As far as I know, South Australia is still the only state in Australia to have such a scheme. Members of VOCS formed a Court Companion Scheme, of which Mavis was the first member. Victims frequently sought our help on weekends and holidays, and often it was Mavis who responded. She helped in our volunteer office and, with a small team, folded and posted thousands of newsletters.

I became an Australian spokesman for the World Society of Victimology and was elected to a small international executive of academics which met in Europe each year. I was the only frontline worker on this executive. I thought it important that victims have a direct voice in policy issues and so determined that for the six years of my appointment I would attend the annual executive meetings. Since VOCS had no funds, Mavis agreed that I could use the money we had put aside for our own holidays in order to attend.

The cheapest airfares required a three-week stay, so each year Mavis spent a lonely three weeks in Adelaide while I worked in Europe. But the executive did achieve good results. It was primarily responsible for a United Nations Declaration of the Rights of Crime Victims, although getting this accepted by the UN took some doing, and this party justified my absence from home.

The executive had drawn up a draft of the declaration and sent it to all member states of the UN seeking a sponsor. Every country, including Australia, refused. The only government prepared to back the declaration was that of South Australia, hardly a UN member in its own right. Chris Sumner was back in office as attorney-general and was keen to do what he could. In the interim, the executive of the World Society of Victimology had discovered that it was possible for declarations such as ours to be proposed at the UN by certain non-government organisations, although these organisations had no vote. The executive arranged for the declaration to be sponsored by an NGO and the process was put in train. But before the declaration could go to the full body of the UN, it had to be considered by a sub-committee meeting in Milan. I went at my own expense and Chris Sumner led a small government delegation. I booked into a cheap hotel within walking distance of the UN meeting place and was mildly astonished when I went down for breakfast on the first day to see Sumner and his delegation walk into the dining room. I said: "Are you blokes slumming or something, come to have breakfast with me?" I knew perfectly well that they had all been booked into a four star hotel. Chris said: "Yeah, we checked in last night, but I looked at the prices and decided it was all too much for the taxpayer. So we've moved down here."

Our draft declaration came up on the UN agenda and a proposer was called for. The non-government organisation that had arranged for its inclusion had no vote and perforce remained silent. For a second or two, it looked as if no one was prepared to propose the declaration. Then Chris stood up and declared that Australia was backing the declaration. To the best of my knowledge, he had no authority to do this whatsoever — he was only the representative of a state government and the Australian federal government had already indicated that it was not prepared to support the declaration. But no one questioned Chris's status, Argentina indicated that they would second the declaration and it went to the committee stage. We then had a week during which we lobbied every national delegation we could get access to, talking long and hard. We had to redraft the declaration to satisfy an Israeli desire to include victims of oppressive power but, at the end of the week when the declaration was voted on, it was passed unanimously. We had turned almost universal indifference into universal support. It really was a magnificent result.

During these years, however, Mavis and I never had a family holiday together except for one year when Mavis came with me to a biennial symposium on crime victims in Tokyo. This lasted a week after which we spent another week visiting the ancient Japanese capital, Kyoto.

Les Radcliff's nine-year-old daughter vanished from the Adelaide Oval a few years before we started VOCS. She and another girl had been at a sporting event with Les. The girls had gone to the toilet. Les waited and waited for them to return, but they never came back. Judy Barnes brought Les to our first VOCS meeting. I liked Les a lot, but he had one overwhelming obsession: he thought he would be able to recognise the man who had kidnapped his daughter. I questioned him about this and in reality he only had a very vague idea of the features of the man he suspected. Indeed, I was not sure that Les had any valid recollection on which to base his conviction.

Les felt the loss of his daughter very deeply and I suspected that he was experiencing guilt over her disappearance, that he felt he should have looked after the girls better at the oval. The disappearance totally dominated the Radcliff family for years after the event. Les used to take his son to Rundle Street and wait outside the picture theatres, watching the patrons emerge after a film because he felt sure that if the man appeared he would recognise him. He did this for years, going anywhere there was a large crowd. It really was a complete obsession.

Les and I became friends, although I didn't see as much of him as I'd have liked. I was fairly busy with other victims and Les felt he had this duty to find his daughter's kidnapper. The case was a complete mystery and remains so to this day. Some years ago, Les's wife rang me and said that Les had not been well for some time. He had cancer and only had a few days to live. I went out to their home and knocked on the door with some trepidation. I wasn't sure in my own mind what I could say to Les. I had never faced such a situation. Their son came to the door and welcomed me and led me into the lounge where Les's wife told me Les was in bed and expecting me. I went through into the bedroom and found Les in a nicely made-up bed, propped up with pillows.

Les said: "Come in Ray, sit down."

I said: "Les, I've just come to see if there is anything I can do to help you."

He said: "No, it's all arranged. I've drawn up a list of pall bearers. I've been through the service with the minister. It's all organised, Ray, you needn't worry. Now, what about you? It seems to me you haven't spent all that much time on yourself these last few years. What would you have liked to do?"

I said: "I'd have liked to have gone fishing. I'm no sailor, I'd have had to fish off the wharves."

He said: "Ray, you're one of us. I really enjoyed the time I spent fishing down at Port Adelaide." He turned to his son and said, "Go and get the street directory."

The lad got the street directory and Les opened it at the map that showed the Port Adelaide wharves.

"When the tide's high," Les said, "you fish here, at this spot, I'll mark it with an X. But if the wind's blowing from the north you have to transfer over to the other side and fish there. Now, there's a seasonal change you have to take into account, but my son knows all about that. So when you next want to go fishing, ring him up and he'll take you down to the wharves."

Then Les asked his son to bring him his supply of hooks and the lad fetched a glass jar of fishing hooks. Les went through the collection, placing some aside in a smaller, vaseline jar. He said: "Now, Ray, these are special hooks. The best I've got. I'll give you two samples of each. My son will show you how to rig up the line, and which hooks to use and which sinkers to use. And I hope you have many happy years of fishing."

I suppose I must have spent an hour with Les, fifty-five minutes of which involved Les seeing how he could help me get fun out of fishing. When I left Les and his wife and son, I left in a much happier frame of mind than I'd been in when I arrived. Les died two days later. I couldn't get to the service because I had to visit another VOCS member who urgently needed to see me. But Les's complete disregard of his own situation when he knew he was dying touched me deeply and has stayed with me ever since. I've not yet been able to take up his offer of having his son show me where to fish, but I still have those hooks in a glass jar. They occupy a special place in my study.

By 1993, VOCS had become recognised by the state government and was in receipt of a substantial annual grant which enabled it to employ a full-time professional staff of seven people. Mavis and I were given a public dinner in recognition of our contribution to the founding and developing of VOCS. Over two hundred people attended, including the state attorney-general, judges, barristers and many crime victims.

11

But presently …

THE South Australian government appointed me to the Prisons Advisory Committee for a three-year term. Once a month, the committee visited a prison and reported on conditions and made recommendations for improvement. On one occasion, we were visiting the medium security prison near Murray Bridge. I was already experiencing difficulties with my hips and was not looking forward to the brisk walking that our visit would involve. I suggested to the other five members that they undertake the full inspection while I just pottered around on my own. I went out into the grounds and discovered a prisoner digging with difficulty a garden out of very hard-packed earth. He was using four heavy sleepers to establish a border to his patch. I fell into conversation with him and he told me his name was Big Jim Smith. He was indeed big, a fit bloke, pleasant to talk to. He didn't appear to be an experienced gardener, but he said he was determined to grow something in the dirt. I suggested that he try to get hold of some manure or fertiliser. Later I sent him a copy of *Yates' Garden Guide*. I asked a few questions and discovered that Big Jim Smith was in the last two years of a life sentence imposed because he had drowned his wife and two children in a bath.

The next time the committee visited the prison, the plot was looking quite respectable. Jim told me he was doing well, he'd read *Yates' Garden Guide* and had high hopes for his little patch. He reckoned that by the time his two years were up he'd be able to leave behind a well-established garden. But on the next visit, the garden was gone. It might never have existed. There had been a break-out from the prison and the escapees had used the timber sleepers from Big Jim's plot to get themselves over the wall. The prison guards were of the opinion that Jim had only pretended to be interested in gardening to get his sleepers into position. Jim protested and managed to get himself transferred to Cadel, an open farm prison near Renmark.

In Cadel he was put in charge of the chooks. There were two types: egg-layers and meat chooks. When the committee later visited Cadel, I asked Jim how he was doing. He was full of enthusiasm, saying "Come and look at this, Ray" and showing me his chook sheds. "Of course," he said, "these screws are numbers mad."

I said: "What do you mean?"

He said: "We have a roll call in the morning and a roll call at night, and if the numbers are right, things are fine. But if we're a bloke short, there's all hell to pay. The guy might be on the toilet or at the doctor's or something, but the screws go bananas. The screws are just mad about numbers. They're even making things difficult with the chooks."

"How come?" I said.

"Last week," he said, "I had a batch of eating hens to go to Eudunda."

I said, "Why do they have to go to Eudunda?"

Jim said: "That's the central dressing place. It's fully-automated. You put your chooks in live one end and they come out packaged in plastic at the other. I had to take down a hundred and the screw came to me and said: 'You got a hundred ready to go, Jim?' and I said: 'Yeah,' but the bloke went and counted them all and said, 'There's only ninety-nine.' The guy was carrying on, reckoned I'd eaten the last chook. So he did another count and there was still only ninety-nine. So then the screw said the truck couldn't leave, not until there's a hundred on board. So when the screw wasn't looking I grabbed one of the little laying hens and stuck it in with the meat chooks. Then I said, 'Let's do one last count', and whaddayou know, there's a hundred in there."

Jim and the warder had left for Eudunda in the truck. At the chicken processing plant it was necessary for the growers to place their chooks on the conveyor line, hanging them upside down by their feet. The first stage in the line was automatic beheading by a machine set at the right height for meat hens. After that the bodies were plucked, disemboweled, dismembered and packaged. The trouble was, the single laying hen was shorter than the others. The blade missed its neck.

"You can guess what happened," Jim said. He thought it was a huge joke.

In the meantime, Big Jim had fallen in love. He had been exchanging letters with a social worker in the United States, one thing had led to another and they had agreed to get married. The young woman left the United States, much to the dismay of her parents, arrived in Adelaide, married Jim in gaol and found work in the Government Insurance Office. She rented a house and set up a home in anticipation of Big Jim's release. One day Jim rang me up and said that he was in Renmark hospital after a hernia operation. "It's a pity I can't get my wife up here," he said, "just for the day. Because I can scrounge an extra day in hospital by saying I'm not fully recovered. We haven't been together since we were married. The doctors are very sympathetic."

I told Jim I'd see what I could do. I rang his wife and suggested that Mavis and I drive her up to Renmark hospital. This we did. We met Jim wandering around the wards and I told him that Mavis and I would go and have lunch down by the river. We had to leave at about three o'clock in the afternoon, but this would give the newlyweds a few hours together. Jim said that this was excellent; the hospital had given him a private room. We left them to it.

Jim was very grateful. He wrote me a letter saying how much he appreciated what we'd done for him and his wife, and what great friends Mavis and I were to them. Eventually his time was up and he was released. He moved in with his wife and not long after he rang and invited Mavis and me to be the first guests they entertained in their home. We went out to their house; it was a warm and friendly place. Jim's wife had gone to great lengths to make it a real home, putting photographs of family and friends on the walls. We had a very nice meal. Jim and his wife were both beaming. Jim thought he would be able to get a job in a few days' time. Mavis and I left, full of hope for them.

About three days later I read in the *Advertiser* that Jim Smith had been arrested and charged with rape. He had picked up a hitch-hiker on the road and raped her in the back of his wife's car. When he let her go, she went straight to the police with his description and that of the car. From a police point of view, it was a very easy case to solve — they arrested Jim almost immediately. He was sentenced to five years in gaol. His wife went back to America and sued for divorce.

One can only speculate, but my feeling is that Jim wanted to go back inside. I think he had already spent so long in prison that he had become institutionalised. He wanted to go back to where he knew the ropes and the meaning of things. The tasks of living permanently with a woman and functioning in the world of gainful employment or unemployment were just too much. He still sends me the odd Christmas card. Shortly afterwards, the *Advertiser* published a photograph of Mavis and I celebrating our diamond wedding anniversary and I received an attractive little postcard from Big Jim Smith. The message read:

> Dear Ray and Mavis,
> What a wonderful photo of you both that appeared in the *Advertiser* one day last week. Reading the story of you both and to see the love that sparkled out of your eyes for each other really made my day. It is so very rare in this day and age to read warm stories in our papers as the story on you both was depicted. I hope that you both have many more happy years together and I wish you both all the best.
>
> Regards
> Jim B-Smith

Interesting comments from a man who was convicted of murdering his wife and two children and of a recent rape.

In 1993, I began research for a PhD in psychology. I initially planned to investigate the plight of very elderly victims of crime who were required to give evidence in court. Did they need special consideration of the sort that is routinely given to very young witnesses and victims? But a short spell in hospital with bladder problems changed my mind. There was a two-day wait between the operation and the results of the biopsy being known. It was a tense, uncomfortable time. There was blood in my urine and the possibility of cancer was never far from my mind. I was sharing a ward with three other men and the bloke in the next bed was in the same boat as I was — and he just *knew* that the results of his biopsy were going to be malignant. On the morning of the third day in hospital, my urologist arrived in the ward and said to me rather brusquely: "Oh, Ray, yours is negative" and walked on quickly to the next man. My initial reaction was one of total dismay: *negative* means failure, I've got cancer. My spirits sunk. I knew little about cancer, but I was well aware that people died from it. Then I became dimly aware that the urologist was speaking very gravely to the man in the next bed: "I'm awfully sorry," he was saying, "but your biopsy is positive. I really am very sorry." I realised with a feeling of total relief that *negative* meant I was clear — I didn't have cancer, I was not dead yet. It was an entirely selfish feeling, but no less heart-felt for that. But then I realised the bloke next to me just had all his worst fears confirmed. I listened as the urologist said again before leaving the ward how very sorry he was. My companion looked devastated. I did my best to talk to him. I'd studied psychology, I knew about counselling and how to help people. But I did not know what to do in this circumstance. I got out of bed, went over to him and put my hand on his shoulder and said how sorry I was. I said we'd talk about it some more later. But I felt incapable. I'd been in distressing situations hundreds of times in my police work, but for some reason this was a very personal thing — partly, I suppose, because I felt guilty for feeling so relieved that it wasn't me who had cancer.

I was released from hospital that afternoon and went straight to the Adelaide University library and checked the holdings on prostate cancer, which were next to those on breast cancer. I found a whole shelf full of books on breast cancer, but I found next to nothing on prostate cancer. I eventually hunted out some figures that showed there were as many men dying from prostate cancer as there were women dying from breast cancer. I went to my PhD supervisor and suggested I change my research topic from elderly witnesses to the ways men deal with prostate cancer.

The outcome of this was the formation of a number of successive small groups of men with prostate cancer who met at our home for several years. Mavis always made these men feel welcome and always offered refreshments, never reproaching me for the time I spent with them rather than with her or on household chores. Some of my subjects are now dead. One, Peter Schade, died recently in the Wagga Wagga hospital after surviving just over four years with stage 4 cancer. Peter had been the first to telephone me when I spoke about my proposed research on the ABC. One Sunday I had happened to ask a fellow church goer if he knew anyone with prostate cancer because I wanted some subjects for research. He said that he did not know anyone, but asked why I didn't appeal over the radio. He offered to mention it to Philip Satchell. On the next day, Monday, I received a call from Satchell saying he had a vacancy on that day's program which I could use. I would have to go into the studio immediately. I hurriedly shaved, made my way to the studio and, without any preparation and gave my little talk appealing for volunteers. Peter was a goldbuyer in his car on the way from the east coast to Coober Pedy opal fields when he tuned into the Philip Satchell program. He told me later that he always listened to the commercial stations but he happened just then to be in a remote region where only the ABC could be picked up.

As well as Peter, another dozen men called in to volunteer to form a small support group meeting at my home fortnightly with me as an observer–participant. Peter was a great help. He came to Adelaide and stayed for two weeks to get the project off the ground. He had benefited from being a member of Alcoholics Anonymous (AA) and so we initially used that as a model, calling ourselves Prostates Anonymous. Peter was also suffering some added stress. His partner of some years had just died from breast cancer and he was himself already at stage 4 with his prostate cancer. He had become accustomed to sharing his woes and victories with fellow sufferers in AA and looked for something similar for prostate cancer victims.

Our group found that meeting together and sharing difficulties and knowledge did benefit them. Peter left to return to the east coast where he spent the next three years forming similar small support teams in Queensland, Victoria and New South Wales. When he occasionally visited me in Adelaide, he would encourage the local teams. He did this at our own expense until he was able to gain a worthwhile sponsorship which enabled him to begin producing and circulating a very professional journal at regular intervals. With his continual appeals on all media channels and at public meetings, and my occasional academic input, we managed to raise the level of public interest in prostate cancer, and there is now a well-organised effort by the established cancer foundations to provide better support and knowledge.

I doubt if there will be any obituary or other public notice describing Peter's courageous lifestyle for the four years he coped with an advanced form of cancer, or the great contribution he made in Australia by helping fellow sufferers face the trauma of a cancer diagnosis. As far as I know, he battled on without a great deal of personal support. He and I shared our problems and hopes but we met all too infrequently.

I pursued my research for four years. The life span for most men with stage 4 cancer — when the disease has spread beyond the prostate and is attacking other organs — is two years and three months, give or take a few weeks. This remains true regardless of the form of treatment they undergo, be it surgery, chemotherapy or nothing at all. But between ten and twelve per cent of men in stage 4 last for ten or twenty years. I became intrigued by the question of why this group was so spectacularly different from the vast majority of sufferers. My research seemed to indicate that the vital factor was not diet, genes, lifestyle or drugs, but long-term marital support. There was something about the relationship that the long term survivours had with their wives that was arresting the progression of the disease. But this was a very tentative finding, which I'm afraid I must leave it to others to follow up. For, alas, my time and resources are strictly limited — I am down to about one hour each day and this is insufficient to maintain a research program and I never know when I will be needed by Mavis.

Ayton Avenue is an even quieter street than Murrays Lane and our house is different in every other respect. It faces a wide road surface that is well-maintained and kept clean, not by patient council horses and drays, but by mechanical sweepers that come by in the early hours of the morning. Ours is a long street of individually architectured houses — those near us are imposing and double-storeyed. They are not owned by recent migrants but by earlier ones, for our suburb was once market-gardens. On one side we have a retired Greek couple, caring and kindly, but not intrusive, and opposite there lives their married daughter who has two school-age daughters and who frequently brings across a hot dish on weekends when Meals on Wheels does not operate. We have ample food, but I miss the hot roast lamb at midday on Saturday and the apple sponge that accompanied it. We don't share confidences over the side fence, and I don't sit out on the door step to watch the passing parade.

Unlike 1 Murrays Lane, we do have occasional visits from politicians such as Chris Sumner and his wife, from priests such as our Baptist minister, Graham Pitt and his wife, and from my old detective office team-mate, former Assistant Commissioner Ted Calder. A young mate of mine, David Air, a recent graduate of Adelaide, sometimes cooks us a splendid meal and we drink some wonderful wines — but not of course Mavis, who stays with fruit juice. We assess the world situation and consider the remedies for its shortcomings. Another difference is that the local council is our most frequent caller and provider of assistance. Each morning and evening a helper arrives to aid my wife to shower, get dressed, get breakfast and wash up. The same happens in the evening. As well, a shopper comes weekly, and a housecleaner twice weekly. A chiropodist calls every twelve weeks — all for the sum of twenty-six dollars per week for each of us. A district nurse is on tap for emergencies and our GP visits on call. The oil fire burns in the lounge all the winter, and we have ample lighting.

On Sundays, instead of hearing the Salvos play outside the Angel Inn in Gouger Street, I watch *Songs of Praise* on the ABC with Mavis and then in the afternoon I send by e-mail my Situation Report to the children in Brisbane, Canberra, the Cook Islands and Kiev, and check for their replies. This is a great time and cost saver, yet I miss the physical touch of a loving hand. Mavis reads and rereads the news from the children, and we once again share a common bond. But, despite all of this support, I have to confess that on rare occasions I find myself in tears — although not for long. The Bluedog, who is now middle-aged, senses my mood, looks up at me and comes slowly across wagging his tail. I pat his head and both of us return to normal. I only hope I can last out here until Blue has moved on to the place where all dogs and humans go.

Unfortunately Mavis, at ninety-one years of age, has two progressive illnesses and I am myself handicapped in a couple of ways. Mavis spends much of her time in our sunroom looking out over the lovely back garden she has largely created. Although she is exceedingly frail, she cannot resist the temptation, on a fine day, to do what she has spent a long lifetime doing — some garden maintenance. She still maintains her family birthdays procedure. As I went to bed last night, I said to her: "I am sorry that I growled at you today. I was worried that you might fall over and if one of us got sick people might use the opportunity to move us into a nursing home, and I want us to stay here." She replied firmly: "We will stay." But she doesn't realise that we are no longer in complete control of our destiny — if ever we were. With my horizons closing in fast and hers probably faster, it becomes hard at times to practise that scout law which says "A Scout smiles and whistles under all difficulties". So I think it possible that by the time you are reading this final paragraph I may have moved on from obsolescence to decadence. If you feel like writing to me, our new address may be The Bleak House Nursing Home. I suggest that you affix a return of undelivered mail address, just in case we have completed the cycle.

When one is very old and not very well, when sleep is fitful, empathetic visitors rare and one's lifelong partner is also not well, one's mind starts to play tricks — at least mine does. For some unknown reason, my mind keeps turning to Birdsville — neither to my mother's schooling, nor to the kindly police sergeant, but to the lonely, isolated Chinese gardener struggling to survive on the bank of the billabong. I keep wondering how he came to be there near the centre of arid Australia in the 1890s — perhaps he was a disappointed goldseeker, but why Birdsville? Cut off from any possible contact with another Cantonese speaker, visited only by white customers seeking to buy his vegetables, what did he do in the evenings? Dream perhaps of his family back home, wonder how he could arrange for his bones to be shipped back to rest with his ancestors. Maybe he found peace in an opium pipe. I now understand better why the Chinese in Australia patronised opium dens, but these were in the big cities, not outback Queensland. How could he have got opium? Did he grow his own poppies? My mother never mentioned flowers but she would not have understood the significance of poppies when she visited the garden. Did he experience or understand that every four years the Diamantina would flood and carry away his shelter and his seeds? Did he die and is his grave in the small Birdsville cemetery? I didn't bother to look when I had the opportunity to do so. Perhaps in the not too distant future I will be able to ask him these questions myself when we meet in Heaven.

12

The new millennium: Obsolescence approaches

As it is, I wouldn't mind if we didn't see out the full distance, for we have moved since I last wrote. Moved from our much loved home of twenty years in the Fulham neighborhood, and are now residents of "Bleak House" at Norwood. This is also known in some quarters as "Melancholy Manor". Despite the nickname, it is a cheery, friendly home for the aged, run with love and care by a dedicated staff. However, since everyone here has been assessed as having one or more serious medical conditions which cannot be treated at home, there is an underlying stratum of sadness.

Our move signalled the end of three years of independent careing for Mavis. For all of this time we had been under constant pressure from the family and our GP to transfer to a nursing home. Mavis was assessed as qualifying for high care when she was diagnosed with dementia and Parkinson's disease. My own bone surgeon believed my hip problems qualified me for low care assistance. We were forced to seek institutional care when Mavis first developed blindness in one eye after the removal of a tumour, and then also lost sight in the other eye. When the malignant tumour was removed from behind her left eye, and subsequently an artificial eye inserted, the right eyelid also refused to open. For years Mavis had insisted on her independence, but because of her blindness had suffered several nasty falls. When she fell, I was unable to help her get up from the floor. But she had discovered that, by lying on her back and dragging herself along the floor on her elbows, she could — with considerable difficulty — reach our bedroom. There she was able to pull herself upright with a little help from me and support from the bed. A district nurse called frequently at our house to bandage the skin-tears on Mavis's arms. Each of these took time to heal because of her fragility but she never complained. Every time it was a big struggle for her, aged ninety and more, and I was quickly exhausted from my small input. The falls became more frequent, yet she was determined to get to the toilet when this became necessary.

At Bleak House we are accommodated separately. Mavis shares a bedroom with another woman in the Nursing Home while I have a comfortable larger room with all facilities in the hostel area. Mavis cannot understand why we have this nightly separation and why we cannot sleep in a double bed as always. The home was designed and built many years before common sense recognised this need and overcame prudish prejudice. That commonsense opinion is now buttressed by numerous scientific investigations, which conclude that conjugal support is the most important form of social support for the elderly and is a major factor in preventing institutionalisation of the aged. The overall importance of this support towards achieving life satisfaction for both spouses is sufficient to justify any additional administrative inconvenience associated with providing double beds. The research suggests that any measures taken towards assisting couples to maintain their intimate relationship is worth serious consideration.

Otherwise, the accommodation is excellent. There are no odours and the meals are adequate and tasty. The staff are competent and caring. Surprisingly, there is an abundance of fresh flowers whose perfume and colours would gladden my horticulturist wife if only she could smell or see them. Mavis is spoon-fed, showered, dressed, and each morning put on a barouche with a soft sheepskin rug. She is then moved to a large lounge where most of the other residents of the nursing home spend their daytime hours watching television. There is a program for the sighted. Bingo is a popular pastime and there are "quizzes" on general knowledge for which small prizes are given. She is the only blind patient and is unable to participate in such group activities. There is a religious service on Sunday for those who wish to attend but this is optional. A minority of residents attend these services, but no pressure is exerted on those who don't. Fish is invariably served on Fridays to ensure no one is offended.

Because of her short-term memory loss, Mavis had difficulty remembering the new daily procedures, and her most frequent question to me is "What should I do?" Some carers never present her with choices so that she is becoming automatically submissive — a state of dependence that she would never have accepted in her normal existence. Our granddaughter, Becky, wrote to her not so long ago saying that Mavis had been a model for her in regard to women's rights and responsibilities. There are one or two of the staff who have not kept pace with the changing relationship between resident and carer, and who obviously regard seeking an opinion or consent from those in their care a waste of time. This attitude is understandable because some of the residents are almost robots, but not all of them are. These staff are easy to identify because they do not bother to discriminate. But we are lucky to be here. It is rightly regarded as one of the better places.

Early each evening, Mavis is returned to her bed. She is unable to use her watch and does not know whether it is day or night. When she wakes she is unsure whether she should try to go to sleep again or whether she will soon be dressed by a nurse. She has not been encouraged to continue walking with a frame and has deteriorated further as a result. Maybe this would have occurred even if we had remained at home. She frequently reminds me that she has no easy way of getting in touch with me. She cannot now read, write or use the telephone and has difficulty locating the staff call button. Her situation is both helpless and hopeless, but she is kept warm and her other physical needs are well looked after. She is no longer able to turn on her side, and so lies flat on her back. She has no bed sores, an indication of good nursing, for she sometimes developed one when at home under my care.

Towards late afternoon her rational moments, when we can have a shared conversation, become less frequent. At this time of day, she becomes concerned about preparing an evening meal for the family as she has done for over sixty years. This makes her agitated and confused, and I find these periods stressful. Because I need to be there when she is rational, I stay with her for an hour or so each morning and three hours each afternoon. Sometimes I am unable to continue.

Today, for example, she said to me: "Ian will be coming soon to take us home." Later on she said: "I know Ian will not be long now." Then: "He should be here by now." I try to explain that we are both in wheelchairs, and cannot go home until we are better. I do not have the courage to tell her that our house is up for sale, that Ian has already disposed of some of our furniture and fittings at a garage sale and that we no longer have a home. When it becomes obvious that Ian will not be coming she asks me to help her get to her feet. It seems that she wants to go looking for him because, she says "I know he would come." When I explain that I cannot lift her, she calls out in a loud voice: "Please someone come and help us." I tell her that she cannot walk now. She says: "I can try." She makes futile efforts to lift herself. From a prone position in a barouche, this is difficult. I go to Sister Heather's office for help. She sends a nurse to look after Mavis, gauges my condition and spontaneously gives me a hug. One evening before I had been allocated a hostel room, this nurse noticed me on the footpath waiting for a taxi. I was upset at our predicament and she came out to give me some comfort.

On the other hand, in my nearly seventy years of close association with Mavis, she has never uttered a negative word about another person or about a situation. She always says that she is all right, but I have suspected that for her things are not "all right" for her here at Bleak House. Today I got an indication. Dave Hunt, former South Australian Police Commissioner, paid us a short visit. When he asked her how she was, Mavis replied: "I'm having a rough time."

I do not know what she does in her bed to occupy her mind between tea at 4.30 p.m. and the time when she goes to sleep. All external doors to the nursing home section are locked at 5.30 p.m. Because of this, I have a feeling that I would inconvenience the evening staff if I were to pay her a visit. Yet there must be something that I can do to relieve the mental torment she must endure in these lonely, sightless hours. Chris, our helpful activities officer, suggests that a radio with a programmed on and off switch may fill the gap. I will discuss this with the family. I am concerned because I am the one, the only one, who six decades ago promised that I would love and cherish Mavis ... until we were parted by death. She promised the same for me. Nobody, but nobody else, has the same responsibility. Our three children and their spouses take a fair share of the load whenever they can, and we talk on the phone and by e-mail, but they have their own families to be concerned about. The middle-aged clean linen lady at the home who passes Mavis and me several times daily has obviously noticed that I am always holding Mavis's hand. On two occasions, she has loudly commented (and I think admiringly, judging by her smile): "Such devotion." The first time I replied by just saying, "She's my wife." Now I only smile back, but I suspect that she notices the watering of my eyes.

The great mystics of the past, such as St. John of the Cross and St. Teresa of Avila, speak of a "Black Night of the Soul". Carl Jung writes of people feeling hopeless and lost, often because they find no meaning in either human or divine relationships. He believes that in depressions like this there is an "abscess of the soul" that leaves an aching, consuming void. He develops this belief further by stating that the trouble can begin with physical suffering or frequently the death of a loved one. My physical suffering may not be all that great, but every day for months I have faced my wife who has "died" a little more each time I see her. I now know what these mystics are referring to because that is where I am.

I have had two bad periods earlier in my life — the first was when I was carrying my swag as a teenager and hopelessly in love with a schoolteacher. The second was when I returned to our home after four years' absence. I had completed two tours of operational flying, was stressed out, bad tempered and disillusioned. In each of these cases, Mavis had been the one to lift me out of my depression, but not now. I no longer have the companionship of a knowledgeable, loving wife; the family is scattered over three states; I am no longer the owner of a family home; I miss my faithful Bluedog; I am surrounded by strange faces and unfamiliar routines; I am confined to a wheelchair and experiencing chronic pain. With diminishing faculties, I am unable to write up my research. My soul is indeed experiencing a Black Night.

I get help from a ninety-six-year-old Baptist minister who lives in the hostel section. He also has a wife in the nursing home. He detects my depressed mood and sometimes just rests his hand on my shoulder for a few moments, and says: "It's a heavy burden you are carrying." I know that he understands. I know he is sincere. But I squirm and feel guilty for there comes immediately to mind that famous drawing of the urchin teenager struggling up a hill. He is carrying a younger boy in his arms and stoutly declaring to the world: "He is not heavy. He is my brother." I empathise with that lad. Mavis is my wife, and I shouldn't feel her weight, but I do. Heaven must know this if it is awake. Perhaps one has to first bang a loud gong, as in a Japanese temple, to attract the attention of the sleeping gods. When I am more composed I will talk to this minister about a God who doesn't appear to intervene even when people are at breaking point. And perhaps there are reasons why God should not intervene. But then, why do we sing hymns that claim God "to be a shelter from the stormy blasts". I want to talk to the minister about a God who has somehow botched our style of departure. I would like his explanation of the unfairness of a system that permits a completely selfless, gentle person like Mavis to undergo so much agony.

Perhaps God did hear my plea for support, for I have received quite unexpectedly a letter posted in Rarotonga from Ron Crocombe. I met Ron when I went to Port Moresby as the commissioner of the Royal Papuan and New Guinea constabulary. He was then a member of the Australian National University Research Unit in Port Moresby. I went to him for information about local problems and grew to respect his opinions. We became friends. He left Papua New Guinea about the same time as I did, but he went on to the Cook Islands and married a Cook Islander. We have not been in touch since then, which is some thirty years ago now. In his letter he wrote: "Your contribution to PNG was superb." Not knowing that I was preparing these memoirs, he recommended that I write a book about my experiences.

I should have been prepared for the possibility of Mavis having to endure a very troubled terminal stage. I was aware of that Principle of Life that proclaims that good deeds do not guarantee a good ending. Two of my early heroes were Baden Powell and Winston Churchill. The first of these enthused the youth of the world to achieve higher moral standards; the other mobilised the English-speaking peoples of the world to defend those standards. Both suffered similar fates. Yes, there are many aspects of faith I would like to discuss with the minister, for he remains untroubled despite ten years' joint residency with his wife at Bleak House. Meanwhile, I assess my own faith as fifty-one per cent. Perhaps he would agree with my thought that each of us at birth should be given a "use-by" date, say seventy years (in Biblical terms three score years and ten). After that date, we should ourselves choose to live or die.

Somehow a few sunbeams have penetrated through this Stygian darkness, and I have made overmuch of them as a result. John Murray, a police friend from way back, made a point of visiting me a few days ago. He has just been appointed the new chief federal police officer of the ACT. I told him that I was delighted with his new appointment, for John and I are on similar wavelengths in many respects. He told me that he had been on a three-month consultancy with the Hong Kong police. While there, he had noticed that my 1976 Sir John Barry Memorial Lecture at Melbourne University was still required reading for promotional examinations. He went on to say that I was still the only police officer invited to deliver this prestigious address. John also made the point that I had been the first to break the Australian tradition that academia and the police only provided quite separate careers. I had done this when I became a Visiting Fellow at the Australian National University — John himself had just surrendered an Associate Professorship at Charles Sturt University to take up his Canberra appointment. After John had left, I thought to myself that it would have been nice if he had mentioned a few other firsts. For example, being the only Australian Police Commissioner so far to head a territorial, state and Commonwealth force; the only Australian policeman to be awarded the Queen's Gold Medal, and the Gold Medal of the Australian Institute of Public Administration, the only Commissioner made a Companion of the Order of Australia. Then I realised that never before had I felt the need to trumpet my achievements. It must have been a symptom of my depressed state — normally I have always found enough challenges ahead to fully occupy my thoughts, but this time the future looked gloomy indeed.

Luckily, John Myrtle, the principal librarian at the Australian Institute of Criminology in Canberra, e-mailed me to say that he was pleased that my memoirs were about to be published. He stated that he would circularise his fellow librarians around the world recommending they purchase the book. He added that he had shown a draft to Professor Terry Birtles who told John that it was my going to Cambridge that had encouraged Terry to follow in my footsteps.

There were a few other "sunbeams" breaking through. The other day, a staff member of Bleak House approached me with a document requiring my signature. She explained that Mavis was unable to sign so she needed my signature to authorise a treatment. It turned out that she was employed at Bleak House as an aromatherapist, and she proposed "treating" Mavis. I asked what she did and she replied that she helped patients become calmer by meditating while incense candles were burnt. I explained that Mavis had long ago lost her sense of smell, so she then suggested she could massage Mavis's lower legs where the circulation is poor. As well, another staff member asked me to sign an authorisation form so that side rails could be put around Mavis's bed. I was puzzled at this and she explained that side rails were a form of restraint and therefore needed approval by the patient's guardian.

Why I regarded these two small matters as sufficiently significant to temporarily change "the Blackness" to a mere "Dark Grayness" stems from an earlier encounter with the administration of Bleak House, who were apparently ignoring my responsibilities under the South Australian *Guardianship Act*. This required me, as Mavis's guardian, to approve or disapprove all forms of medical, dental or surgical treatment. If I abused or neglected these responsibilities, I was liable to criminal prosecution. I was told that the requirements were widely ignored because they were impractical. However, I persisted, pointing out that it was the law in this state and that for forty years I had been enforcing the law. We finally reached agreement and I now certify as "approved" all new forms of Mavis's treatment. Incidentally, when I approached the relevant authority for support for my stand, I was told that I was legally correct but that "in exceptional circumstances unofficial arrangements are acceptable". No wonder that the requirements are widely ignored!

Then an interesting letter came from Ron Edington in Brisbane. He had been the Queensland Police Union president during my time as Commissioner, and therefore the titular head of the Green Mafia that opposed my reforms so bitterly. They had supported my replacement, Terry Lewis who is now about to be discharged from custody. Ron informed me that "most, if not all, of your proposed changes are now in place" and that "most people of any intelligence always respected you".

These small triumphs from a past era have been especially welcomed by me for they have come at a time of personal crisis. I leave each session with Mavis emotionally exhausted. In Papuan pidgin terms, "I am all buggered up". I sit alongside her, holding her hand while she strives, with diminishing brain power but a still indomitable will, to remember the correct words she needs to convey her concerns. The Parkinson's effect has been to make her throat muscles less amenable to control and thus her ability to speak clearly — a relic of her teacher training — is fading. I turn my less deaf ear towards her, but usually it takes two or three repetitions before I grasp what she is trying to say. I have to concentrate all the time because there is often background noise from the television set, or from the voices of passers by. I offer her some weak reason why she cannot try to stand up, or go home, or prepare the evening meal, or why Ian hasn't yet come to drive us home to Fulham. Her severe short-term memory loss means that this conversation is repeated many times during the afternoon. There is another "Mavis" who also sits in the lounge and is sometimes called by the nurses.

My "Mavis" picks up the name and hopefully responds, thinking that it might mean a change in her miserable situation. Yet if a passer by inquires, she always politely replies: "I am all right. Thank you." I cry inwardly, for this was my wonderful wife, loving, caring, articulate and perfect.

In this regard, the need for control over one's environment has long been viewed by psychologists such as Rodin as a basic human motivation. It has been found to have profound effects on the elderly's well-being. Presumably, in Mavis's situation, absence of control may well have a detrimental effect on her well-being, but this may be masked by the presumption that it is a symptom of her Parkinson's disease. I want to share her distress in the hope that this will lessen its impact on her, but it is difficult to communicate orally. I am usually restricted to just holding her hand. On good days she seems to enjoy being given small chocolates or spoonfuls of yogurt.

After I leave her, promising to return, I have a quick meal in the hostel dining room and go to my room where I take two tablets to dull the pain in my hips. I try to have a short nap to get myself back to what passes for normal these days. I wonder how it is that the staff in the nursing home remain cheerful, so I ask Margi, the clinical sister in charge, how she manages the daily stresses of her job. (Margi always finds time to have a reassuring but jocular exchange with me three or four times a day.) Margi replies that she gets strong family support at home. I ask Sister Heather how she avoids burnout or becoming case-hardened. She says that she is happy in her job and that she has a husband who listens. I observe a smiling younger carer giving help to people in the closed Dementia Unit. Her answer is simply: "They are not my parents."

I thought about these coping responses and decided that none of them applied in my situation. I review in my mind the choices and options available to men in the final stages of prostate cancer. I decided that we had different agendas — they were desperate to live; I have no great desire to survive without Mavis. Perhaps I should make time to meditate more. It could reduce the tensions under which I exist. I am concerned that I should use these last moments of rational exchange with Mavis to implant an idea that will survive her memory loss. I hoped for an idea that would offer the reassurance that we will be together again some time, somewhere, in happier circumstances, perhaps with Bluedog.

I am a little concerned about Bluedog, our fourth Australian terrier. He was with us for twelve years and, especially during the past four, he became my shadow. Slowly following me from room to room, he gave my feet a friendly lick when I felt distressed. I believe — and there is increasing biological evidence to support this belief — that animals do have feelings. When we were finally leaving our home, I lacked any ability to convey to Bluedog that he and I were parting forever. I hoped he would realise that I would always remember him. I tried to explain that he was going to Canberra to live with Ruth, who would look after him because she was now better able to do this. I understood he would find it difficult to exist with another bigger dog whose territory he would be invading. I was grateful that Ruth was taking him for she would be sensitive to his predicament and give him much love. I think of him often. His photo hangs on my bedroom wall just above my desk. His birthday is in two weeks' time and I will not be there this year to celebrate it with him. Buddhists, Hindus and Moslems have a better understanding of the spiritual place of non-human animals in the universe God created for all and of which we are but one species.

I have often wondered why there are so few "doggy" people amongst Baptist pastors. Perhaps their migratory lifestyle is a handicap, although one Baptist minister who stayed in his Canberra manse for twenty-one years never had a dog and he was a country-bred boy. Bleak House is a Baptist institution, and perhaps that is the reason why residents must somehow dispose of their animal friends before taking up occupancy. This enforced separation comes at a time when the new residents are suffering from the deprivation of most or all their other possessions. I suppose that instead we can cherish the pets that are provided — two small cages, each containing a solitary budgie. Budgies in their natural state are flock birds. They have been so for many hundreds of thousands of years before Baptists emerged for a short time as progressive Protestants. It might be rewarding to subject serving Baptist pastors to a personality questionnaire just to see if there is any factor that explains this assumption that they do not share the Australian community's fondness for dogs. I wonder how many of them watch *Harry's Practice* or *Animal Hospital* on television, or devote a few moments to viewing the fascinating sheepdog trials at the local agricultural show. The impact of the animal-loving Saint Francis of Assisi seems to have dimmed over the ages. As far as I know, Baptist clergy have never become involved with the Royal Society for the Protection of Animals or Animal Liberation organisations — perhaps due to their lack of time. However, some manage to join Rotary.

To a psychologist, entry as a participant–observer into this closed culture of the elderly sick ought to be a stimulating opportunity — although, it is obviously, one that is tempered by the psychologist's own level of fitness. Up until now I have been so obsessed with my responsibilities to my wife that I have not looked professionally at my milieu. The few thoughts that I have had so far are doubts gathered from a little reading, observations at Bleak House and personal experience. These relate to the claim that there is an inevitability about social and emotional disengagement by elderly folk. In the past, public interest in the lifestyles of the very elderly was limited and consequently comparatively fewer resources were allocated to researching this area. Now, however, the Australian population is becoming an aged one and this change has many social ramifications.

Research into the lifestyles of elderly individuals is beginning to attract the attention of scholars in the same way that the behaviour of infants and juveniles has done in the past. And there is some scholarly interest in elderly individuals confined to institutions, just as there is interest in the lives of convicts. Not so long ago, a Flinders University professor received a substantial grant to study how sick children feel about the possibility of early death. I suspect many of the residents at Bleak House are concerned about dying, but there doesn't seem to be much research data available. We are all facing a fate, not far off now, which we are powerless to change.

However, I have found some interesting data. One survey considers a group of elderly Americans who responded to a 1995 questionnaire that asked: "If there is one thing in your life you could change, what would it be?" The most frequent response expressed their wish for "the return of their dead spouse". The next obvious question (which was not asked) was, "if your spouse cannot join you, have you thought about joining your spouse?" Truthful replies, if these could be obtained, might help provide some understanding on a number of important social phenomena. These could include single and joint suicides, murder-suicides and deaths from a "broken-heart". Other replies in the same questionnaire showed that the majority of widowed elderly felt that their former spouse was not replaceable. I noted, with some ambivalence, one result from the same survey that suggested the more someone believes in God, the happier he or she is.

Meanwhile, I am not getting any better. The advent of the electric wheelchair coincided with my decision to reduce walking to an absolute minimum for not only was it painful but I kept remembering my bone man's prognosis. He said that if I kept using the damaged hips they would shortly become quite useless. Mavis picked up that I was now more mobile because of the electric wheelchair and she asked me questions about its battery and range. She spoke somewhat wistfully, I thought, for she said it must be wonderful not having to rely upon someone else to move you around. She remains the stoic as always. She has not been outside in the fresh air for two months, and she was a person who loved gardening in all of its forms. Today she was lucid all day despite being confined to her bedroom for the morning because the lounge floor was being cleaned. The bedroom is a depressing place, lacking any form of stimulus. It is isolated, and it is a place in which she must spend long hours alone. I told Mavis that it was the first of September and the Royal Show had opened. We talked about jonquils and daffodils, and how our church was filled with daffodils when we were married sixty two years ago next week. We mentioned her two bridesmaids, Gert and Jean, two lifelong friends now both dead, although neither of us referred to that. Jean, who was Mavis's younger sister, was a much-loved Brown Owl. After she retired she spent seven years bedridden at Bleak House as the result of a stroke. After her retirement, Gert, a friend from secondary school and teachers' college, spent nearly as long being shunted around various nursing homes. She suffered from dementia. It seems that humanity is paying a substantial price for assuming that a longer life means a happier life. My own research showed that individuals — at least men with prostate cancer — preferred "quality of life" to "quantity of life". Perhaps the time has come when some of the resources now being used to increase life expectancy should be used to improve the quality of the added years. As I know from my own although this is difficult to do. Margi has advised me that soon Mavis will have to be fed through a tube. If Mavis becomes aware of this seeming indignity, I know she will be mortified. Our family made much of having enjoyable meals together. She was the best cook of lambs' fry and bacon; she produced the tastiest cornish pasties, and the weekend roast with fresh mint sauce stimulated the weakest of appetites. Our meals were happy family occasions. If she is able to remember these and think about her present situation she will be in despair. I am frustrated that I will be unable to change anything.

It requires effort to remain in contact with old friends. I have not yet made it across the road to the home opposite Bleak House where one of my friends, Dr Donald Beard, lives. Nor have I ventured just up George Street where a school and RAAF friend, Dr Dennis Shortridge, has his home. I did make it to The Parade once but found it a fairly stressful experience. The choice to go or not is mine, but Mavis cannot take the initiative. She must wait for people to visit her. A few do, and the knowledgeable ones, like Claire Withers, bring fresh fruit and yogurt, which Mavis enjoys. My regular visitors include Gordon Barrett, an Adelaide barrister, who arrives on Friday evenings with a supper of fish and chips and the latest issue of *The Adelaide Review*, Max Dawson, a scouting colleague for seventy years with homemade biscuits, and Rory Barnes, with two or more stubbies of Coopers' Light Ale. Rory is one of my former Canberra scout patrol leaders, vintage 1960s, a professional writer now living in Adelaide. If these memoirs ever get published it will be because of his skill in knocking my raw material into readable shape. I remember our last combined scout and guide campfire on the Murrumbidgee at which Mavis and Rory were present. It had been a happy week in the bush and we would be leaving in the morning. We would have finished the evening by all singing together that well-known campfire song which in part goes:

Adieu, adieu good friends. Adieu adieu,
I can no longer stay with you, stay with you,
I'll hang my harp on a weeping willow tree,
and may the world go well with thee, well with thee.

And the Guides would have sung their version of "Taps", that traditional bugle call played at nightfall in all Army barracks, which goes:

Day is done, gone the sun, from the sea, from the hills, from the sky, All is well, safely rest, God is nigh.

The campfire embers burn low, the warm cocoa is all gone, and now is the time to retire, TO SLEEP. Good readers, I'll also say, "Adieu, adieu."

Later on you might have an opportunity to sing the second verse which goes like this:

Dig a grave both wide and deep, wide and deep,
Put headstones at its head and feet, head and feet,
Inscribe on it a turtle dove, turtle dove,
And say he died of love, died of love.

Diary entry: Sunday, 25 March 2001

Mavis had a rough night according to the night sister who gave her morphine.

At 10.10 a.m., Mavis left Ruthie and I to go to "heaven". When she arrives there I expect her to start a Residents' Committee and personally organise some overdue consumers' input. Over the years she has always respected and where necessary fought for the recognition of everybody's inalienable rights. She firmly believed that these are based on the universal principles of democracy and not on those emanating from a celestial theocracy. For far too long the

Triumvirate have been impervious to repeated criticism from intelligent humans that their creation had been imperfectly planned. The outcome of that production is that in this world Happiness is at least matched by Misery. In many cases the Misery is quite undeserved. Mavis is a good example. All of her life she has given first consideration to the needs of others. During the many years we were "best friends" to each other, I never knew her to be other than the Perfect Girl Guide — trusty, loyal and helpful, sisterly, courteous, kind, obedient (to God's laws), smiling, thrifty, pure as the rustling wind. As proof, our loving and responsible children reflect that credo.

Her ageing years deserved, in Australian terms, "a fair go". Yet one consequence of the imperfect planning has been that for nearly four years she had been aware that parts of her brain were wasting away. It is true that from time to time odd flashes of her former clear-thinking mind broke through, but her once happy face was eventually replaced by a heart-breaking grimace. It was the very best that her damaged mind and weakened muscles could produce. It became obvious to me as I held her hand that she was struggling to get messages through to me. Twice I was able to make sense of them. She was asking me: "How are you?" To the very end she was more concerned about my well-being. In these last few days she could not drink or eat. She became emaciated and the nursing staff asked if the family wanted her to be force-fed. I thought that this was an indignity that she would not want to suffer, and the family agreed with me. I spent my last hours with Mavis reminding her of our happier times. I felt sure she could hear what I was saying for occasionally she would twitch her eyelid. It was ironic that we were communicating in this way. Ironic because for the past year her eyes have given her very poor service. With one completely artificial eye, only ten per cent vision in the other and an inability in recent months to sit up, her sensory deprivation was considerable. This must have caused her much frustration. But she hung on — a remarkably resilient lady who gave out Happiness to others all of her lifetime and was then rewarded with such Misery.

Wherever you are, Mavis, please understand that not only I, but also your family and all of your many friends, were greatly saddened by your illness. Yet I know we are inspired by your courageous example of how to face unjustified adversity. May we be as strong as you to withstand the blows of this imperfect world and, like you, continue to strive for the betterment of our fellow beings. Please, please, do not completely leave us. In my memory I can see you in a thousand happy situations: swimming with me at Henley Beach, dancing with me in the Scout Hall at Black Forest, standing alongside me at Flinders Street Church when we undertook to be with each other for the rest of our lives, my visiting you at the Memorial Hospital with our three babies, Andrew, then Ian, and later Ruth. I recall your encouragement to me at the Adelaide Railway Station when I left you and the boys for four long years. I remember clearly at a later time how you stood, for a further seven long years, shoulder to shoulder with me in Queensland when, under media and other attacks, we were ignored by most of our church fellowship and abandoned by a goodly number of fair-weather friends.

I only wish I had your confident hope that we will meet again, somewhere, somehow, some time, and that once more, we will hold hands and be together again to face the future, whatever it may be. Your face smiles down upon me from the photographs on my bedroom wall. I shall sleep better tonight knowing that you have at least been freed of all your suffering. Tomorrow will bring its usual challenges and I promise that I will do my best to face them in the way you would expect of me. I will always be forever grateful for the happiness you first brought me when I was seventeen. A happiness that only gained in intensity in the next sixty-nine years. Shalom, my dear wife.